CAMBRIDGE COMPUTING

The First 75 Years

HALL OF FAME COMPANIES

1960-1989

Media Dynamics Ltd.
Shape Data Ltd.
Micro Focus
Orbis Ltd.
Acorn Computer Ltd.
GST Technologies Ltd.
Camdata
APM Ltd.
First DBS Ltd.
Global Software Publishing
PC Communications Ltd.
Qudos Technology Ltd.
SRI Cambridge
Olivetti Research Ltd.
Perihelion Software
Three-Space Ltd.
Xi Software Ltd.
Equisys
Sophos plc

1990-1999

Cunning Running Software Ltd.
NextBase Ltd.
Questionmark
Software Integrators
JMEC Ltd.
Leading Technology Inc.
Rubicon Software Group plc.
Software Solutions
Yudkin Consulting AG

2000-

Cambridge Broadband Ltd.
Filonet Korea Incorporated
FiloSafe Corporation
Metanate Ltd.
Tenison Technology EDA Ltd.
Xandera
Zoonami
Blue technologies
break-step productions
Business Web Software
Datanomic Ltd.
Governor Technology Ltd.
Grex Games Ltd.
Interactive Digital Television Ltd.
Ionsquare
Jagex Ltd.
Jawasoft
Lemur Consulting
Linguamatics
Linguit GmbH
Micropraxis Ltd.
Paradigm Design Systems Ltd.
Azuro
Bid Management Ltd.
CacheLogic Ltd.
Level 5 Networks
Cotares Ltd.
eCosCentric Ltd.
Fraser Research Inc.
Great East London S
Invest Solutions Ltd
Masabi
Ndiyo
RealVNC Ltd
Saviso Group
Tideway
UK Broad

CAMBRIDGE COMPUTING

The First 75 Years

Haroon Ahmed

THIRD MILLENNIUM
PUBLISHING, LONDON

© 2013 Cambridge Computer Laboratory and
Third Millennium Publishing Ltd

First published in 2013 by Third Millennium Publishing Limited,
a subsidiary of Third Millennium Information Limited

2–5 Benjamin Street
London
UK
EC1M 5QL
www.tmiltd.com

ISBN 978 1 906507 83 1

All rights reserved. No part of this publication may be reproduced or
transmitted in any form or by any means, electronic or mechanical,
including photocopying, recording, or any storage or retrieval system,
without permission in writing from the publisher.

British Library Cataloguing in Publication Data: A CIP catalogue
record for this book is available from the British Library.

Written by Haroon Ahmed
Photography by Alan Davidson
Managing Editor, Susan Millership
Editorial assistance by Neil Burkey
Designed by Matthew Wilson
Production by Bonnie Murray
Reprographics by Studio Fasoli, Italy
Printed by Gorenjski Tisk, Slovenia

Contents

	Preface	6
	Foreword	8
1	Babbage's 'Magical Machines'	10
2	The Genesis of the Computer Laboratory	20
3	Maurice Wilkes: Computer Pioneer	34
4	Maurice Wilkes and the EDSACS	44
5	Maurice Wilkes: New Directions of Research and the End of an Era	66
6	Computing for All: Networking the University from EDSAC Users to Desktops and Laptops – *David Hartley*	84
7	Spreading the Word: Teaching Computer Science and Technology – *Peter Robinson*	94
8	The Computer Laboratory, 1980–2012: The 'Needham Years' and the Modern Era	104
9	Entrepreneurs, Spinning Out, Making Money and Linking with Industry	122
10	The Computer Laboratory on its 75th Birthday: A Centre of Research Excellence	142
	Bibliography	162
	List of Subscribers	166
	Index	170
	Acknowledgements and Picture Credits	176

Preface

Cambridge Computing is an illustrated history celebrating the 75th anniversary of the foundation of the Computer Laboratory on 14 May 1937 and marks the 100th anniversary of the birth of Professor Sir Maurice Wilkes on 26 June 1913.

Remarkably, the history of the Laboratory began almost a decade before the first modern electronic computer was built. Professor Sir Lennard-Jones, founder and first Director of the Mathematical Laboratory (now Computer Laboratory) had the foresight to recognise that numerical methods would become increasingly important in all branches of science, but the central figure of this commemorative book is Professor Sir Maurice Wilkes, who reigned over the Laboratory for three and a half decades.

In his obituary by the BBC, Wilkes was nominated the 'Father of British Computing', a perfect accolade for a true computer pioneer, and three chapters here describe his early career, his work in the era of mainframe computers and his last 15 years of research before retirement. At the heart of the book is an account of the seminal achievement of the Laboratory, the construction and commissioning of EDSAC, the first stored-program digital computer to come into regular service.

Although this book is primarily about the Computer Laboratory it does not ignore two great giants of computing, Charles Babbage and Alan Turing, who were both Cambridge men. Babbage conceived mechanical digital computers with almost all the features of a modern stored-program computer nearly 100 years before electronics made it feasible to build practical computers; while Alan Turing is, undoubtedly, the most famous computer scientist of all time and a national hero in the UK. Short accounts of the life and work of these two great men are included in the book.

Preface

The early remit set by the University for the Computer Laboratory was to provide a computing service to the University, and its history is outlined by David Hartley, the first Director of the Computing Service. Undergraduate teaching is an essential activity in any university and from its earliest days the Computer Laboratory took this commitment to heart. Peter Robinson describes the evolution of Computer Science teaching in chapter seven.

By 1980 computers had become ubiquitous and the Computer Laboratory had to expand and modernise its research to keep up with the extraordinary advances taking place in computer science and technology. Its third Director, Professor Roger Needham, led the Laboratory for 16 years into the modern era, and towards the end of his tenure he helped the University to secure a benefaction from the William Gates Foundation for a splendid new building to house the Laboratory. Since then the Laboratory's research has gone from strength to strength and the last chapter of the book demonstrates the great range and depth of the current research programmes.

Although teaching and research are the main activities in the Computer Laboratory it also prides itself on the culture of entrepreneurship it instils into many of those who graduate with a degree in Computer Science. A chapter is devoted to the Laboratory's formal and informal links with industry and to the spectacularly successful business ventures of some of its alumni.

Throughout the writing of the book it has been necessary to balance the historical content against technological details. The choices have been difficult to make but in a book of 176 pages with a large number of illustrations it was necessary to restrict technical details to the essentials.

This book could not have been written without the support and cooperation of members of the Laboratory past and present, and they are acknowledged at the end of the book. Documentary sources and the oral evidence from interviews are included in a bibliography.

On a personal note, it was necessary to keep to strict deadlines to ensure that the book could be published on the 100th anniversary of the birth of Maurice Wilkes. Writing hours were long and interrupted only when Keir Nizam, aged three, came to visit and demanded to play with his grandfather, bringing a welcome respite. And finally, my wife Anne read all my first drafts and improved them immeasurably with her comments and corrections.

Haroon Ahmed
January 2013

Professor Ahmed is Visiting Professor at the Computer Laboratory.

Foreword

Cambridge Computing is more than just the story of computing in Cambridge. Professor Haroon Ahmed sets his history in the broader framework of how calculators and computers evolved worldwide. He also describes how computer technology has been commercialised, using 12 successful companies that have spun out of the Cambridge Computer Laboratory as examples, and provides an update on what is happening in computer research by describing current research in the Computer Laboratory.

The first electronic computers were built to improve our ability to calculate, to outperform mechanical calculating machines. It was clear from the start that electronic switches, initially using radio valves, would be faster than mechanical mechanisms and that they could be used to build faster calculators, but no-one predicted that through the use of semiconductor integrated circuits these calculators would become so powerful that they would impact upon almost every aspect of human life: the way we communicate, travel, entertain ourselves, grow food, design buildings, improve our health, and so on. There is little that computers have left untouched, and it seems amazing that they did not exist 76 years ago. How to build the first machines, however, was anything but clear. It was a daunting task, highly complex and filled with unknowns.

Haroon Ahmed tells the story from the beginning, starting with mechanical calculating machines, and then describing how Cambridge's first stored-progam electronic machine, EDSAC, was built by Maurice Wilkes and his team. He tells how others were making excellent progress in the UK in Manchester, and that in the USA they were operating on a much larger scale, but Wilkes's small team kept up with the pace and was the first to use their computer in a routine manner to help scientists and engineers in their research.

Lord Broers was Vice-Chancellor of Cambridge University, 1996–2003.

The William Gates Building is the home of the Cambridge University Computer Laboratory.

Ahmed's explanations of how these early machines were built are clear and readily understood by non-experts. Occasionally he goes into a depth that may be difficult for the layman but only when it is necessary to explain the sequence of events, and even in these cases it doesn't interrupt the narrative. In the beginning the pioneers concentrated on building machines. Their attention then shifted to the way the machines were used, and to educating those who could benefit from them. The next step was to link machines together in rings and networks thereby connecting scientists and engineers, firstly in different laboratories in Cambridge, then around the UK and finally around the world. These 'networks' eventually led to the Internet.

In the late 1960s it became apparent that there was no point in universities continuing to build their own computers. The resources required to remain competitive became too great for universities, and users around the world wanted to exchange their data and their programs and this required uniform standards. By then the computer industry was able to provide the resources and the standardisation and Cambridge along with other leading universities purchased rather than built their computers. Similar situations have been reached in other science-based technologies and when this occurs future success depends on universities and industry working closely together. Cambridge excelled in its collaborations with industry and has therefore remained among the world leaders in computer research.

Professor Ahmed carefully and completely describes the evolution of computers going back and forth in time as he alternates between describing technical progress and talking about those who made it happen. He has produced a volume that is a good read for anyone who wants to learn how things work in the 21st century, a must read for those who are working on the advancement of computers, and a valuable reference book for historians of science and technology.

Alec Broers
December 2012

CHAPTER ONE

Babbage's 'Magical Machines'

SOIRÉES IN 19TH-CENTURY LONDON

Charles Babbage, Cambridge graduate and arguably the 'Father of the Computer', invented mechanical 'computing' machines. His Difference Engine No 1, Difference Engine No 2 and Analytical Engine were all invented almost 100 years before computers, using electronic devices, were built at the end of the Second World War. Sadly, not one of these three remarkable digital computers could be built in his lifetime. Only a very small fraction of Difference Engine No 1, occasionally referred to as the 'magical calculating machine', was constructed and it operated primarily as a mechanical calculator. Despite Babbage's disappointment at the failure of his grand design, he used the small unit to good effect. He was a wealthy man who had become something of a celebrity and he held soirées at his home to which notables of the day were invited to view demonstrations of the machine as part of the evening's attractions.

Following one of Babbage's soirées (circa 1837), Sir David Brewster wrote 'that of all the machines which have been constructed in modern times, the calculating machine is doubtless the most extraordinary'. Brewster had watched a demonstration of the model Difference Engine in which the machine had calculated the numbers that arose as the value of x was increased from zero to 44 in the expression x^2+x+41. Babbage fed the values of x into the machine while a colleague noted down the answers which appeared on dials at the machine's output. The assembled company was amazed that the numbers were all correct! The speed of the calculating machine was also impressive. The human 'printer' was quite unable to keep up with the machine when the numbers reached five figures. In the Victorian era Babbage was considered more a magician than a scientist.

At one of these soirées, guests included the 17-year-old Augusta Ada Byron, only legitimate daughter of the notorious Lord Byron. Unusually for that period, Ada had been well schooled in elementary mathematics and had sufficient understanding of algebra to grasp the capabilities of the machine. She was enchanted by the animated demonstration while Babbage was both surprised and delighted by the knowledge of mathematics displayed by this charming young lady. Thus began an ambivalent friendship lasting 20 years until Ada's premature death at the age of 37.

Part of Charles Babbage's Difference Engine No 1 – a fine example of Victorian mechanical engineering. This small part was used by Babbage for demonstrations. The Engine was not completed because of manufacturing difficulties and disagreements between Babbage and his engineer, Joseph Clement.

Chapter One: Babbage's 'Magical Machines'

Tables of numbers were important in Babbage's time and much used despite doubts about their accuracy. Babbage's ambition was to produce tables free of all errors by using calculating machines instead of 'computers'.

Ada married well and became Countess Lovelace in the fullness of time. The relationship that developed between her and Babbage was not without its problems but there is no doubt that at least some of Babbage's fame in his lifetime, and subsequently, rests on her efforts on his behalf. She described and publicised the capabilities of Babbage's machines in remarkably lucid prose and in so doing gained a unique place for herself in the world of computing. She was not a great mathematician herself but through her association with Babbage, his constant guidance and her own perseverance and imaginative interpretations of his work, she staked a claim to being the very first computer programmer.

Tables of Numbers

Tables of numbers mattered in the age of Queen Victoria when the British Empire encircled the globe. Industry and commerce were booming and maritime adventures were taking British sailors across the oceans. Numerical data were essential for enterprises to be successful and huge tomes with tables of numbers were available for all sorts of purposes. There were tables of multiplication and division, more advanced tables of logarithms and trigonometric functions, financial tables for accountants, businessmen and bankers, actuarial tables for insurance companies, astronomical tables for travellers and navigators and tables for construction engineers. The problem of the age was that these tables were not totally accurate and had to be used with caution. They were generated by mathematicians working with human 'computers'. The work was tedious and inherently subject to human fallibility and serious errors could arise from miscalculations, during the transcription of results and in the typesetting for printing.

The compilers were perfectly well aware that the number of errors could be reduced greatly by using teams of 'computers' but this added to the expense of producing the tables and there was even then no guarantee that errors would be eliminated entirely. It was not just Babbage who was aware of the problem; the government of the day was also concerned. It was common knowledge that inaccuracies in tables could lead to harmful consequences. Babbage had convinced himself that errors could not be eliminated altogether as long as humans were involved in the preparation of the tables. He is said to have declared publicly that only when a machine, or more dramatically 'steam', could be used, not only to perform calculations but also to print the numbers, would all errors be eliminated. His purpose in building the difference engine was partly to ensure the printing of accurate tables but he believed also that the engine would be able to solve hitherto intractable mathematical problems. The scale of his enterprise was immense but he was determined to tackle it. The French government had paid a fortune for the production of tables of logarithms printed in 17 large folios. It had used teams of 'computers' whose work was constantly cross-checked to minimise errors and the tables produced were believed to be the best available. The British government wished to buy an abridged version of these tables in 1837 and offered the French £5,000 to participate in a collaborative project.

Difference Engine No 1, the Calculating Machine

Early in his life Babbage had come to the conclusion that the method of differences, the well-known mathematical technique used to produce the tables by hand, could be

CHARLES BABBAGE (1791–1871)

Victorian Polymath and 'Father of the Computer'

Charles Babbage was admitted to Trinity College in 1810 to read Mathematics, but moved to Peterhouse before graduating. Increasingly dissatisfied with the low standard of Mathematics teaching, he and some of his friends urged the authorities to make improvements, and later established the Analytical Society for serious scholars of mathematics.

Babbage married Georgina Whitmore in 1814 and settled in London, where he became prominent as a scientist and gave lectures at the Royal Institution. He was elected a Fellow of the Royal Society in 1816 and became a founding member of the Royal Astronomical Society in 1820. He was also one of the founders of the British Association for the Advancement of Science, and in the course of his life published a number of books and papers, including his remarkable work *On the Economy of Machinery and Manufactures*. In 1828 Babbage was appointed Lucasian Professor of Mathematics at Cambridge University, a post he held until 1839. This renowned Chair had previously been held by Isaac Newton, and Babbage was flattered by his own appointment. The duties of the post were light and Babbage was not required to live in Cambridge or to give any lectures.

In the course of his life Babbage became known as something of an eccentric because he took up unusual causes such as the suppression of street music and the banning of 'calling shouts' by street vendors. He also invented the ophthalmoscope, although it was not taken up in his time, and both devised and broke cryptographic codes. Today he is recognised as a polymath who among his many and varied interests created computers a century before they were constructed using electronics.

Babbage died a sad and disillusioned man with his genius unrecognised and his computing machines incomplete. Posterity arguably sees him as the 'Father of the Computer', so far ahead of his time that it would take almost a century before others could reach where he had already been. Today there are numerous memorials to his name scattered across the world. In London the Science Museum is the repository of a great deal of material on Babbage and there are excellent exhibits of his inventions.

implemented with machines. He had also realised that the results could be transferred directly to another machine that could print tables without any human intervention and he argued that the outcome from a mechanical calculator or 'computer' would be entirely free of errors. He proposed therefore to build a 'difference engine' which would carry out all complex calculations using only addition. To demonstrate the viability of his proposal he constructed a

Engraving of Babbage at the age of about 40, when he was in the prime of his life and actively pursuing the construction of Difference Engine No 1.

Chapter One: Babbage's 'Magical Machines'

Babbage graduated from Peterhouse, the oldest college in Cambridge, founded 1284.

small portion of the Difference Engine and described its operation to the Royal Astronomical Society in 1822 in a paper entitled 'Note on the Application of Machinery to the Computation of Astronomical and Mathematical Tables'. Babbage demonstrated that the machine could be used to calculate the members of a sequence of numbers but at this stage of the machine's development its capacity was limited and the numbers had to be noted down by hand.

Babbage argued that a larger and more elaborate version of his demonstration machine could not only prepare tables free of all errors more quickly than human computers, but also be very much cheaper to make and use than the cost of employing teams of 'computers'.

The Royal Astronomical Society was impressed and not only awarded Babbage a Gold Medal in recognition of his achievement but also commended his ideas to the government of the day. The Royal Society was also persuaded to support him. Having gained the support of the scientific establishment, Babbage's proposal to build a large difference engine was presented to the government and gained the approval of the then Chancellor of the Exchequer. Public funds amounting to approximately £1,500 (over £150,000 today) were made available for the project which Babbage undertook to complete in just three years. Unfortunately both the cost and the timescale were grossly underestimated.

AUGUSTA ADA BYRON, COUNTESS LOVELACE (1815–52)

An Enigma in the History of Computing

In one of his letters to her, Babbage referred to his friend and protégé, Ada, Countess Lovelace, as 'The Enchantress of Numbers'. Their relationship is one of the more intriguing features of Babbage's intellectual life and his claim to fame as the pioneer of modern computing. She became deeply involved with him from the moment of their first meeting when she was just 17.

When Ada was 19 she married William King, who later became the Earl of Lovelace. There followed the birth of three children, but when she was in her mid-20s, she returned to her interest in mathematics and particularly to her passion for Babbage's engines. Throughout her years of marriage she had kept up a correspondence with Babbage and was very aware that he had moved on in his thinking, from the Difference Engine to designing the Analytical Engine.

She studied carefully the concepts of the Analytical Engine, which had been explained to her in some detail by Babbage, and developed a clear understanding of the working of the machine as one that could be instructed or 'programmed' to carry out problem-solving tasks without any intervention from the operator other than inputting initial instructions.

In 1843 she received an article on the Analytical Engine written by Luigi Menabrea, an Italian military engineer, based on a presentation by Babbage in Italy. Ada translated the article from French into English and wrote extensive appendices to the article. These notes included a program in the form of instructions to the Analytical Engine in a logical set of steps by which a solution to a problem could be obtained.

She likened the programmability of the machine to the way in which a weaver made patterns in a loom, thus demonstrating clearly that she understood the need to follow a sequence of steps in strict order when instructing the machine. In her notes she included several programs including one designed to calculate the sequence of Bernoulli numbers. She also speculated on the idea that the machine might be useful for tasks other than the numerical work that had so preoccupied Babbage. She wrote that the engine might be able to compose music and that symbols used in the machine might have a more general meaning than just numerical; today composers of modern music use computers extensively. Because Ada included examples of 'problem-solving

Ada Lovelace publicised Babbage's work and with her writings earned for herself the title of the 'First Computer Programmer'.

instructions' in her appendices to Menabrea's paper she is frequently nominated the 'First Computer Programmer'.

There is no doubt that she wrote the appendices to the translation of the paper by Menabrea and her name is the only one attached to it. Moreover in her work she speculated that computers would be able to do much more than Babbage had envisaged. In her contributions to the paper by Menabrea, this gifted and passionate woman predicted applications that computers would only be able to achieve a century and a half after her death.

Babbage realised that the manufactured quality of some of the parts he needed for the Difference Engine exceeded state-of-the-art mechanical engineering in the 19th century, and he therefore needed an outstanding engineer who could make technological advances in metal fabrication before designing and building some critical parts. Following a recommendation from his friend and great Victorian engineer, Isambard Kingdom Brunel, he decided to employ Joseph Clement, who was not only a highly skilled toolmaker but also a draftsman with the skills necessary to translate Babbage's ideas into working drawings. Clement had a nationwide reputation for producing high-precision work but his quality came at a high price. He expected to be paid well for producing such excellence. Those who had employed Clement before Babbage knew that it was a case of caveat emptor if a firm price was not agreed before he started work.

As work progressed, Babbage and Clement were faced with three problems for which Victorian engineering did not have ready answers. The first was the extremely high precision Babbage, perhaps unnecessarily, demanded for the parts. The second was the large numbers of identical parts needed for the engine in an age when mass production methods were not commonplace. Thirdly unusual shapes were required compared with the parts conventionally manufactured for Victorian machines. These problems could only be addressed by first making advances in machine tools, machining techniques and mass production methods. Clement had been given a considerable challenge by Babbage!

Just as the work was gaining momentum it was delayed by the unexpected and untimely deaths of Babbage's wife, his father, and two of his children. These were personal tragedies on such a scale that Babbage found it impossible to work on his project for 18 months. Unfortunately, when Babbage was able to resume work serious disagreements arose between him and Clement on a number of issues. They were eventually resolved but work on the engine was halted for a year while negotiations took place; Babbage realised that he needed more money and better premises for Clement if he were to complete his grand design. Perhaps only about half the requisite number of parts had been fabricated after many years of effort and his funds from the government were exhausted. Although he had a very considerable private fortune he did not feel justified in using it to meet his costs. After all he was working for the public good and receiving no personal benefit. He made an application for increased funding which was supported by the Royal Society and was granted considerable funds towards acquiring new premises for Clement as well as for the increased cost of building the engine. Babbage believed, perhaps now quite realistically, that he needed just another three years to complete the task. Regrettably a disagreement with Clement arose over the move of his workshop to the site acquired by Babbage. The relationship between Babbage and Clement completely collapsed. Clement fired his men and stopped all work and the project to build Difference Engine No 1 was terminated. Babbage had spent a great part of his life and as much as £17,000 of public money, an enormous sum in 1840, on an enterprise that had come to nothing. He was left with only a small working part of Difference Engine No 1 together with a feeling of immense frustration that a great opportunity had been lost. For three decades he had dreamed of printing error-free tables and he now faced the bleak prospect of never being able to realise his vision.

Computer Pioneer

Babbage is widely recognised as the first computer pioneer, not so much for his work on the Difference Engine but because of his work on his Analytical Engine, although it too was never built. His claim rests on theoretical work, notes, drawings and designs which have gradually come to light over the years, and on a very small fraction of the machine which was completed just before his death. These documents and objects have established his primacy in conceiving, in the middle of the 19th century, many features that are incorporated in the 21st-century general-purpose computer built with electronic devices.

His concepts and designs were so far ahead of the contemporary developments that they were forgotten – or perhaps more to the point, they were not understood. His work was neither used nor referenced when computers based on electronic devices were developed at the end of the Second World War. The gap in time between the concept of the Analytical Engine and the modern computer was a discontinuity of 100 years, and in this lapse of time all records could well have been lost. Fortunately almost all his

JOSEPH CLEMENT (1779–1844)

A Forgotten Victorian Engineer

Joseph Clement was one of the outstanding mechanical engineers of the Victorian era. He was a craftsman who could produce work of exceptional quality and a designer and draughtsman who could translate the ideas of his customers into accurate and comprehensive working drawings.

Clement was the son of a weaver and received only elementary schooling. His father taught him the rudiments of mechanical engineering and he acquired various other skills in the course of his many different employments as a young man.

He moved to London and gained employment as a works manager and later as a draughtsman. Having saved a little money and gained in both skills and confidence he set up his own works which specialised in high-quality mechanical engineering and draughtsmanship. Some of the great Victorian engineers used his services, and among them was Brunel. Clement won the gold medal of the Society for the Encouragement of Arts for his tools, which included a very high-precision lathe with a self-adjusting chuck. He also made a planing machine which was unique in the range of mechanical tasks it could carry out. He pioneered the ideas of standardisation in mechanical parts such as screw threads. After falling out with Babbage, Clement continued working and made a good living until he retired to take up his old hobby of making musical instruments. He died leaving a considerable estate.

Lathe designed and constructed for Babbage by his engineer, Joseph Clement.

work was preserved by his family for posterity to re-examine and reassess. Professor Sir Maurice Wilkes, Director of the Mathematical Laboratory in Cambridge and one of the most prominent figures in the history of computing, studied Babbage's work in 1949 and again in 1971 and recognised the range and originality of Babbage's thinking.

The question remains as to whether or not the Analytical Engine conceived by Babbage would have worked as a general-purpose computer. There is a move to build an Analytical Engine as conceived, and if the outcome is a working computer, any residual doubt that Babbage has a claim to be recognised as one of the great computer scientists of all time will be entirely removed.

The Analytical Engine was conceived to have programmability via punched card inputs, a store for numbers generated at intermediate stages of a computation and a separate processing unit, the mill, where the numerical work of adding, subtracting, multiplying and dividing could be performed. The machine's features included conditional branching, looping, micro-programming, parallel processing, iteration, latching, polling and even pulse shaping. Babbage did not ignore the output stage and proposed many different forms of output. The analytical engine was planned to have a printed output, a punched card output, a graphical output and a stereotype output. He had separated the store, which is essentially the memory, from the mill, which is essentially the processing unit. With extraordinary prescience he had included almost every feature that is to be found in a modern computer!

Chapter One: Babbage's 'Magical Machines'

The Analytical Engine's concept is that of a user-controlled, multi-purpose machine, or in today's terms a programmable computer. Babbage started working on the Analytical Engine mainly because of his frustration with the failure to complete the Difference Engine, and moved far into the future when he conceived and designed the Analytical Engine, although he had neither the technology nor the funding to construct it. Manual operation of the Analytical Engine would not have been possible because of the enormous forces necessary to drive the machine by rotating its numerous cogs and wheels. Here though we must leave the story of the Analytical Engine, as did Babbage.

Difference Engine No 2

Babbage at the age of 50 was at the height of his powers but frustrated because Difference Engine No 1 had not been built and the Analytical Engine was too complex and too costly to construct. He turned his attention back to difference engines and designed Difference Engine No 2, essentially an improved model of Difference Engine

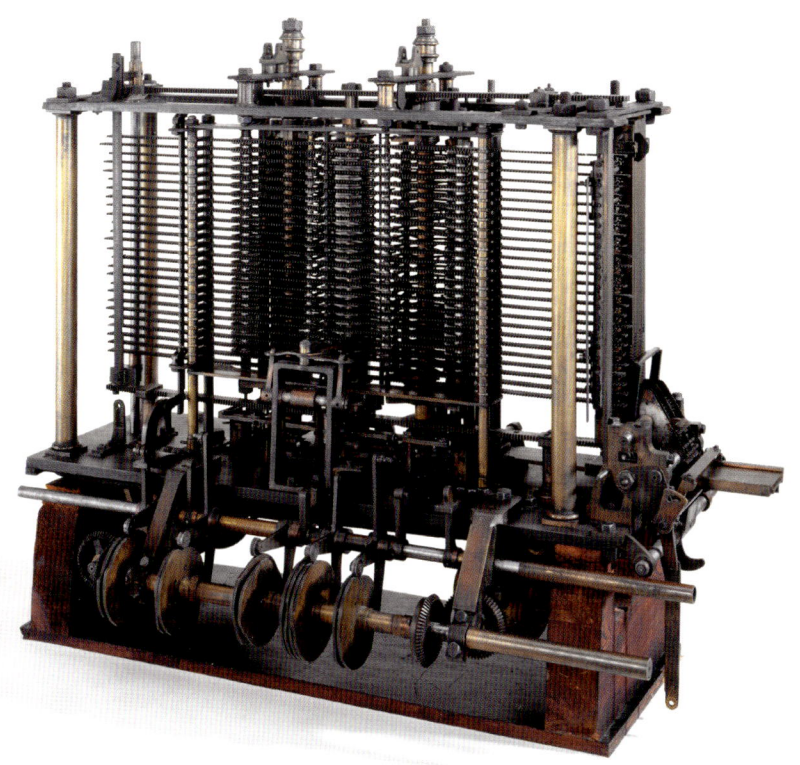

Above: Part of the 'mill' (processing unit) of the Analytical Engine. Only a few fragments of this programmable mechanical computer were built in Babbage's lifetime.

Right: Babbage's design of the Analytical Engine c.1840. The 'mill' or processor and the 'store' or memory are shown.

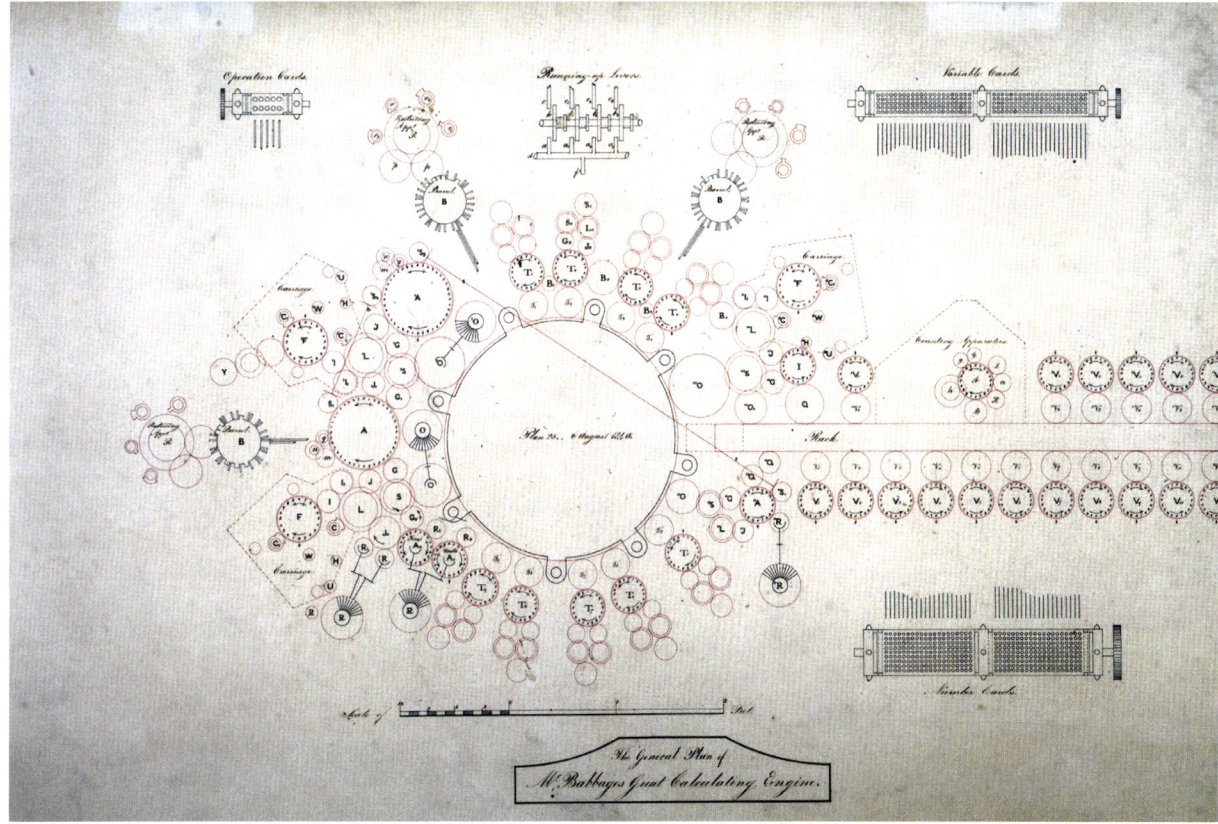

17

Cambridge Computing: The First 75 Years

Difference Engine No 2 was designed by Babbage but built more than a century after his death by Doron Swade along with his colleagues at the Science Museum, London.

No 1, and produced a complete set of drawings for it. He made the new design much simpler. Although he retained the principle of a difference engine the number of parts required for the new machine was reduced to just 8,000 including the printer section, a small fraction of the number required for Difference Engine No 1.

He noted that Difference Engine No 2 was much more efficient to operate than Difference Engine No 1 and much easier to manufacture. He offered the design to the nation using the then President of the Royal Society as an intermediary but he was rebuffed and retired from the fray.

Fortunately he retained the drawings and they survived the passage of time. The story might well have ended with the drawings gathering dust in some gloomy archive of the Science Museum but there was 'a modern sequel'. More than 100 years after Babbage had produced his drawings, Doron Swade, newly appointed Curator of Computing, together with his colleagues at the Science Museum in London, took up the challenge to construct Difference Engine No 2 using Babbage's drawings but employing modern manufacturing techniques. To their delight and gratification Difference Engine No 2 worked perfectly

Chapter One: Babbage's 'Magical Machines'

Babbage is remembered in Cambridge with a Charles Babbage Road in West Cambridge, where he joins other great Cambridge scientists, J J Thomson, discoverer of the electron, and Clerk Maxwell, whose famous equations laid the foundations of electromagnetic theory.

when it was completed. Babbage's place in the history of computing had been enhanced and the tremendous effort made by Doron Swade and his co-workers well rewarded. Today any computer enthusiast making a visit to the computing history gallery in the Science Museum will spend a very interesting and informative afternoon.

Wilkes, Babbage and Cambridge

Maurice Wilkes's interest in Babbage was first aroused in 1946. The mathematician Douglas Hartree had told him that Babbage had suggested that a computer could exercise judgment before deciding to carry out certain types of calculation. In May 1949 Wilkes was given access to the Babbage papers deposited in the Science Museum by one of Babbage's sons and had begun work on the papers, but just four days later the EDSAC computer that he had himself been commissioning in Cambridge came to life. Wilkes was understandably distracted and did not return to his interest in Babbage for two decades. His enthusiasm was revived when he was invited to speak of Babbage as a computer pioneer, on the occasion of the 100th anniversary of the inventor's birth. His research into Babbage's notebooks unearthed a treasure trove of material describing Babbage's pioneering contributions to computer science and technology. Among the discoveries, he found that Babbage had devised a mechanical version of microprogramming which was, of course, one of Wilkes's own major contributions to computer science. Wilkes had the advantage of reading Babbage's work long after computers constructed with electronics had become well established. As a consequence he immediately recognised that Babbage had invented almost everything necessary to make a stored-program computer but had used different terminology from the established nomenclature of the 1970s. For example he used the word 'hoarding' when he meant 'storage' in modern usage. One outcome of Wilkes's research into Babbage's papers was that Wilkes himself became a historian of computing and his fascination with Babbage became so great that he even wrote a play based on Babbage's life.

19

CHAPTER TWO

The Genesis of the Computer Laboratory

In the 1930s, when the Computer Laboratory was founded in Cambridge as the 'Mathematical Laboratory', the word 'computer' had a very different connotation to the one we understand today when referring to the machines that sit on our desks. A 'computer' was then a person employed to carry out tedious numerical calculations by hand. As late as 1945 and after the Second World War had ended, 'computers' were girls leaving school with a Higher School Certificate. Some of these young women had exceptional skill and ability in mathematics but no prospect of gainful employment in which such knowledge could be used. In a report to a University Committee Maurice Wilkes, the Director of the Mathematical Laboratory in 1945, bemoaned the fact that he was having difficulties recruiting girls for whom he had vacancies as 'computers'. The university had allocated him a total of six 'computers' for the Laboratory but he had been able to recruit only three. Wartime opportunities for women had obviously helped to create new and better employment prospects in peacetime for clever girls. Some could now avoid the mind-dulling task of carrying out repetitive calculations all day long.

In the 1930s there were far fewer lecture theatres, laboratories and libraries in the University than there are today, and the buildings were heavily concentrated in the heart of the city. There were 20 colleges reserved exclusively for men and just two colleges for women, who had been somewhat reluctantly accorded the privilege of attending lectures and taking University examinations but were not eligible for degrees. Instead they were awarded the title to a degree, Titular BA. The emphasis in the University was on the teaching of undergraduates. There were no graduate colleges and the PhD degree by research had been available for only a few years.

Most of the science-based departments, including the Cavendish Laboratory and the Chemical Laboratory, were clustered in the New Museums Site, just off Free School Lane. For organisational purposes the science-based disciplines came under the jurisdiction of the School of Physical Sciences. The dominant feature of University life was the collegiate structure which enabled academics working in disparate areas of research to meet each other within their colleges, where they were able to exchange ideas and discuss matters of mutual interest. Cambridge academics were also fortunate in that they were made aware of research activities through open lectures and seminars that were provided within departments. The Cambridge Philosophical Society, founded in 1830 for the propagation of knowledge of natural philosophy throughout the University and across interdisciplinary

A typical accounting office in a large commercial organisation showing women 'computers' at work using mechanical or electrical machines as calculators.

Chapter Two: The Genesis of the Computer Laboratory

The New Court of Corpus Christi College, Cambridge, where Lennard-Jones had rooms, and in which the founding of a computer laboratory in Cambridge University was planned.

boundaries, was also very active in enhancing academic exchanges. This society was the earliest to be founded for such a purpose and is still prominent in Cambridge today. A lecture at one of the society's meetings given by the distinguished mathematician Professor Douglas Hartree in 1937 played an important part in the founding of the Computer Laboratory in Cambridge.

A University Computing Laboratory

In 1932 John Lennard-Jones, Professor of Theoretical Physics at Bristol University, was appointed to the John Humphrey Plummer Chair of Theoretical Chemistry at Cambridge University, which had become available thanks to a munificent bequest to the University of £200,000. In his new position Lennard-Jones continued the research he had started at Bristol University on the application of quantum mechanics to problems associated with chemistry. He and his students identified a number of problems that gave rise to complex equations which could only be solved by numerical methods. He was aware that some of his colleagues working in other subjects were facing similar problems and he became the prime mover in forming a Committee of Science Professors, an embryonic pressure group which met to discuss interdisciplinary topics. Meetings were usually held in Lennard-Jones's rooms in Corpus Christi College, close to the science laboratories on Free School Lane. Notable members included *inter alia* the physicists Lord Rutherford and Sir William Bragg, both Nobel Laureates, and two successive heads of the Engineering Department, Sir Charles Inglis and Sir John Baker.

Mindful of the possibility that the need for computing crossed interdisciplinary boundaries, Lennard-Jones approached the Mathematics Faculty to take forward his ideas for founding a computer laboratory for the University as a whole rather than creating a computing section within his department. In 1936, a report was sent to the General Board of the University (the University's governing body) by the University's School of Physical

21

Cambridge Computing: The First 75 Years

SIR JOHN EDWARD LENNARD-JONES (1894–1954)

Early Life and Career

John Edward Jones was born in Leigh, Lancashire, and educated locally. He went to Manchester University to study Mathematics and graduated with a first-class honours degree just at the outbreak of the First World War. He served in France initially as a Flying Officer in the Royal Flying Corps flying a Sopwith Camel, the renowned fighter aircraft. He was transferred to serve as an Experimental Officer in the Armaments Experimental Station at Orford Ness and later to an aerodynamics laboratory of Boulton Paul. After the war he returned to Manchester University as a Lecturer in Mathematics, studying at the same time for a DSc in Mathematics, which was awarded in 1922.

He gave up his teaching post in Manchester when he obtained the Senior 1851 Exhibition scholarship from Trinity College, Cambridge, to study for a PhD. His research extended his studies into mathematical physics and enabled him to work on the theoretical aspects of physics and chemistry in which he was destined to make major scientific contributions in his career. He was awarded the PhD in 1924 and shortly afterwards appointed Reader in Mathematical Physics at Bristol University. In 1925 he married Kathleen Mary Lennard and changed his name to Lennard-Jones following his wife's desire to keep the family name alive after the death of her brothers in the First World War. He was promoted to Professor of Theoretical Physics at Bristol University in 1927. A turning point in his academic career came in 1929, when he spent the year as a Rockefeller Foundation Fellow at the University of Göttingen in Germany. There he studied quantum mechanics with some of the leading German scientists in this emerging field of physics. He brought this knowledge back to Bristol University.

Above: Professor Lennard-Jones with his colleagues and research students in 1953. J Pople was awarded the Nobel Prize in 1998 and S F Boys used the EDSACs for his research in computational chemistry.

Left: The Department of Theoretical Chemistry occupied the top two floors of a building in the New Museums Site, which was part of the building seen through the trees. The Meccano Differential Analyser used by Maurice Wilkes was located in the Department.

Sciences on behalf of the Mathematics Faculty. It made a comprehensive case for a computing laboratory in the University. Not only had the idea of establishing a laboratory originated with Lennard-Jones but he was undoubtedly also the principal architect of the report.

Following established procedures, the General Board published the report in the *Cambridge University Reporter*, the University's internal newspaper. The preamble stated that the Faculty of Mathematics had circulated the report to other faculties for their comments before approaching the General Board. All these faculties had given their formal blessing. This was a wise move because in 1936 the idea of creating a laboratory for mathematical computation would have appeared quite extraordinary. Opponents of the scheme for founding a computer laboratory could easily have argued that mathematical calculations could be carried out in college rooms or offices. The report from the School of Physical Sciences, mindful of the need to justify its proposal to found a laboratory, therefore went to great pains to explain why it was needed.

Chapter Two: The Genesis of the Computer Laboratory

Post-war Career in Cambridge

After working for the government during the Second World War Lennard-Jones returned to Cambridge in 1946 to take up his Chair again, and in the same year he was awarded the ScD degree by Cambridge University. He continued to hold government advisory posts, and from 1942 to 1947 he was a member of the Advisory Council of the Department of Scientific and Industrial Research.

His exceptional service to the nation was recognised in 1946 when he was appointed KBE. In 1947 he became Chairman of the Scientific Advisory Council of the Ministry of Supply and also served as President of the Faraday Society. More scientific honours followed. In 1953 he was awarded the Davy Medal of the Royal Society and an honorary Doctorate of Science from Oxford University. He was a candidate for the Mastership of his college, Corpus Christi, in 1953 but failed in his bid against the Nobel Laureate, Sir George Thomson. He then accepted the position of Principal of the University College of North Staffordshire (later Keele University). Sadly he died within a year of his appointment. Today he is commemorated in Keele University, where the Chemistry Department is named after him.

In his career as a theoretical chemist Lennard-Jones created and established a prominent school of research specialising in the application of quantum mechanics to the properties of molecules. Both before and after the Second World War a number of exceptionally able students worked with him and many became leaders in the field that he had pioneered. In his research group he rarely had fewer than 15 research students under his supervision. Today he is frequently described as the 'Father of Computational Chemistry'.

His work on theoretical chemistry continued to flourish in Cambridge and a succession of distinguished professors of theoretical chemistry built upon his pioneering work. Today the research is based in a newly refurbished part of the Chemical Laboratory of Cambridge University; the Cambridge Centre for Computational Chemistry and some 50 research workers actively continue the work that Lennard-Jones had initiated. His contributions were recognised again in 2011 when the Lennard-Jones Centre for Computational Materials Science was inaugurated in Cambridge University.

This silver salver was presented to Lennard-Jones on his departure from Cambridge in 1953. After his death it was returned to the Chemistry Department by his son and is now on display in the Centre for Computational Chemistry.

In making the case for a computer laboratory the report gives a fascinating insight into the state of computing before the outbreak of the Second World War. It noted that there had been significant developments in mechanical and electrical devices for calculations. Not only mathematicians but also scientists from across a wide range of disciplines were making use of machines for numerical work. Three types of machines were mentioned: mechanical Brunsviga machines of German origin, which were operated by cranking a handle, and Monroe and National machines, which were electrically operated. The National machine was considered the most efficient for tabulating a function and its successive differences. Scientists operated these machines themselves or employed 'computers'. The machines were decidedly a great improvement on carrying out numerical calculations on paper by hand, but some calculations were still very time-consuming and difficult to carry out with sufficient accuracy. It was noted that the machines were inadequate for some complex problems which remained intractable, implying the need to develop or acquire better machines in the future.

Cambridge Computing: The First 75 Years

R R M MALLOCK AND THE MALLOCK MACHINE

Rawlyn Richard Manconchy Mallock (1885–1959) was born in Devon and educated at Winchester College and Trinity College, Cambridge, where he was admitted in 1904. He studied Mathematics with distinction, winning the College mathematics prize in 1906. He went on to read Mechanical Sciences (Engineering) and graduated with a first-class degree in 1908. Following graduation he went into industry and travelled to Canada before returning to work in the UK for the Admiralty.

He returned to Cambridge University on his appointment to a lectureship in the Engineering Department. He became interested in electro-mechanical aids for computation and constructed a machine for solving up to six simultaneous linear algebraic equations. He transferred his ideas to the Cambridge Instrument Company (founded in 1881 by Horace Darwin, son of the renowned Charles Darwin) where a more advanced version was built in 1933. Unfortunately the machine was not a commercial success and the only working model ended up in the Mathematical Laboratory and was eventually dismantled. Mallock published a paper describing his work and Wilkes published one of his early papers describing the use of the Mallock Machine to solve second order simultaneous linear differential equations. Mallock retired at the age of 52 and did not contribute any further to the development of computational techniques but he had played a small part in the history of Cambridge computing and reinforced Wilkes's interest in numerical methods.

The Mallock Machine was invented by R R M Mallock of the Cambridge University Engineering Department. Only one machine was built, and it was used by Wilkes for some of his early work. It was not developed commercially and the prototype was eventually scrapped to make room for EDSAC.

In the report from the School of Physical Sciences, the Mallock machine was specifically recommended for installation in the proposed laboratory, and it was suggested that it should be developed in a University research laboratory. It was noted that the machine had been invented in Cambridge and used successfully by members of the Mathematics Faculty to solve important problems. This emphasis was an early indication that the proposed computer laboratory would be expected not only to provide a service but would also be required to undertake research leading to the invention and development of advanced computing machines.

The Cambridge Differential Analyser

An important part of the report was a reference to the emergence of instruments capable of carrying out the process of integration. It pointed out that Lord Kelvin and his brother James Thomson had proposed a method

Max Bennett, age nine, a boy of the iPad era, examining the Brunsviga machine used by Professor Sir John Lennard-Jones in the 1930s, occasionally with the assistance of his ten-year-old son John, who was allowed to wind the handle.

Chapter Two: The Genesis of the Computer Laboratory

The Double Brunsviga comprised two single machines coupled together with the facility to both exchange numbers and compute with complex numbers. This machine was installed in the Mathematical Laboratory in the 1940s.

for solving differential equations by successive integration but had not been able to build a working machine because of mechanical difficulties. Their most significant problem had been the lack of torque necessary to drive successive sections of the integrator, and torque amplifiers were not invented until well after the Thomson brothers had failed in their attempts. The report stated that, since then, Vannevar Bush at MIT in the USA had overcome the problems that had frustrated the Thomsons by using modern engineering devices and had constructed a machine capable of solving differential equations of one variable of any order up to the sixth. This remarkable advance had enabled Bush and his co-workers to solve problems in physics, chemistry and engineering hitherto regarded as impossible to solve. The Board noted that Professor Lennard-Jones had followed the example of Vannevar Bush and constructed such a machine for research in the Chemical Laboratory.

Lennard-Jones had constructed his machine with the help of the mathematician Douglas Hartree, who was then working at Manchester University. Hartree's help in this instance was the first of his many invaluable contributions which aided the foundation and development of the

DOUGLAS RAYNER HARTREE (1897–1958)

Douglas Rayner Hartree was very much a Cambridge man. He was born in Cambridge and graduated in Mathematics from St John's College. He became involved in numerical computation from the beginning of his professional life; his father, himself an academic working on numerical methods at the Engineering Department of Cambridge, encouraged the young Hartree's interest in numerical techniques and in later life collaborated with him professionally. Hartree's PhD work in physics brought him considerable distinction and he was appointed to the Chair of Applied Mathematics at Manchester University. He derived the Hartree equations for the distribution of electrons around an atom, with further work by Vladimir Fock leading to the Hartree–Fock equations, which are well established in physics.

Hartree followed the pioneering work of Vannevar Bush in the USA and made a Meccano differential analyser. Shortly afterwards, the Second World War intervened and he diverted his energies to wartime work and became responsible for groups working on computational methods. He also worked for the government and was assigned as a liaison officer in the USA. He was involved in computer projects in America as well, and transferred much of his experience in this field to groups working on computational methods in the UK.

He played a significant part in the creation and evolution of the Mathematical Laboratory on a number of occasions. He gave Lennard-Jones the details of the differential analyser he had built. Subsequently he was invited by the Cambridge Philosophical Society to lecture on the applications of the differential analyser in his laboratory in Manchester. Wilkes was in the audience and immediately recognised that the differential analyser could help him to solve the intractable equations he was encountering in his own research. Hartree moved to Cambridge in 1946 when he was appointed Plummer Professor of Theoretical Physics, and his career in Cambridge is described in the next chapter.

Computer Laboratory in Cambridge. He had been given access to design details of the differential analyser while he was visiting Bush in the USA, and on returning to Manchester he had not only constructed a simple machine using mainly Meccano parts but had also commissioned

Cambridge Computing: The First 75 Years

Below: The Millionaire Machine was highly regarded because it used multiplication rather than repeated addition. It was invented by Leon Bollée and patented by Otto Steiger. Two thousand machines were sold and a motor-driven version was developed. The Millionaire Machine shown here was installed in the Mathematical Laboratory.

Above: The first differential analyser in Cambridge was constructed by J B Bratt using largely Meccano parts. It was used extensively by Wilkes before the Second World War but removed to New Zealand after it was no longer required in the Mathematical Laboratory. It is now in a museum in Auckland, New Zealand.

Below: The children's toy Meccano played a significant part in the early days of the development of analogue computers. It consisted of metallic strips of different lengths, plates of different sizes and angled pieces all pre-prepared with drilled holes through which nuts and bolts could be used to attach the pieces to each other. A selection of pulleys, wheels, belts and driving gears were also included. The range of parts available provided the user with great flexibility in design and construction. Many standard designs were offered in the instruction leaflets which came with the toy and new designs could be created by the experienced user.

the Manchester-based company, Metropolitan Vickers, to manufacture a robust and fully engineered machine. He had published accounts of the operation of his machine and had been generous in giving other scientists access to it.

Lennard-Jones, on learning of the Manchester machine and its capabilities, contacted Hartree, who made the construction details available, and he commissioned his assistant J B Bratt to construct a differential analyser. Although Bratt also used Meccano parts in the main, he designed and constructed some critical sections himself and these performed more effectively than Meccano parts.

In the report the General Board stated that the speed with which definitive answers could be produced was a particularly impressive feature of the machine. Results which would have taken months using conventional adding and multiplying machines could be produced in a few days. The Bush machine had enabled scientists in many branches of science to attempt solutions to problems that had hitherto been insoluble. This remarkably detailed report made a compelling case for the establishment of a computer laboratory in Cambridge University.

Chapter Two: The Genesis of the Computer Laboratory

Funding and Space

The cost of the various machines was as follows: the Bush machine with eight integrating units would cost £5,000. Four additional units would add £2,000 to the cost. The Mallock machine would cost £2,000. The National tabulating machine would cost £500. Sundry other items would cost anything between £50 and £150. The total equipment cost was estimated at £10,000 (about £580,000 today).

The report made recommendations that a Director should be appointed for the proper supervision and operation of the Computer Laboratory, and that the Laboratory would not be subservient to the needs of an existing department but would operate independently to serve the whole of the scientific community in Cambridge. This recommendation had far-reaching consequences in the long term.

The report proposed that the Director should be an existing professor, which made it possible for Lennard-Jones to be appointed and thereby reduced the overall cost of the enterprise. It was suggested that there should be a Lecturer associated with the Mathematics Faculty capable of teaching modern methods of computation and of applying the machines to solve problems. A technician would be required to ensure that the more sophisticated Bush and Mallock machines could be kept in proper order for operation by users. Recurrent expenditure was expected to be a modest £600 per annum (£35,000 today).

Another part of the proposal suggested that the Computer Laboratory would carry out research projects from the outset, and a sum of £400 per annum (£23,000 today) was allocated for this purpose. The provision was of very great significance because ten years on the Computer Laboratory would use these funds to create new computing machines.

Finally the question of providing adequate space for the new laboratory was addressed. Several sites were considered and it was noted that Lord Rutherford could make space available in the Cavendish Laboratory in the former drawing office of the Engineering Department. Another proposed site was the top floor of the Chemical Laboratory, where the differential analyser was housed. Eventually the new laboratory was located in space vacated by the Anatomy Laboratory, which moved to a new site in 1938.

Formal Approval and Name Change

Almost a year after receiving the proposal from the School of Physical Sciences the General Board responded in a report to the University published in the *Reporter* in January 1937. No doubt Lennard-Jones and his colleagues were beginning to feel impatient over this long passage of time but to their gratification the response was entirely positive. The Board felt that the time was ripe for the establishment of a Computer Laboratory and in the Board's opinion computing machines had passed through their early experimental stages and reached a stage of development which made them essential for the development of applied mathematics.

The report revealed a need for numerical work in faculties other than those that had been consulted. The faculties of Economics and Politics, the faculties of Biology A, of Biology B and of Agriculture all expressed their desire for the establishment of a Computer Laboratory because they would find its services of great assistance in their research activities. This was not surprising, because analytical and statistical mathematical methods were beginning to be widely used in these subjects. For example in economics statistical analysis and econometrics were becoming prominent, and are now well established as essential disciplines.

In an important respect the General Board went beyond the proposal from the School of Physical Sciences. It proposed that a person with the rank of University teaching officer should take charge of the machines and be held responsible for the supervision of the Laboratory.

There were still some formal stages to go through. First the Financial Board needed to be consulted to confirm that funding was available. Secondly, a discussion had to be held in Senate House before the passing of a 'grace'. The grace is normally a formality at a ceremonial event in which the General Board's recommendations are put forward to all members of the University (Regent House) by designated officers of the University. If there is no dissent a 'placet' (it pleases) is pronounced. The General Board's recommendation becomes a binding decision. (A non-placet implies that the recommendation does not please some University members and the matter should be referred back to the Board.) A placet was duly received and it appeared now that the Computer Laboratory could be implemented – but there was to be another twist to the tale. The name was changed to the Mathematical Laboratory!

WHAT'S IN A NAME?

There has been a degree of speculation over the years on why the Computer Laboratory proposed by Lennard-Jones was renamed Mathematical Laboratory in 1937 and some 30 years later renamed the Computer Laboratory. The Lennard-Jones papers in the Churchill archives provide an account of what took place 75 years ago. Two months after the 'placet' (it pleases) for the proposal had been accomplished, the General Board produced another report in which the name of the Laboratory was changed from the Computer Laboratory to the Mathematical Laboratory on the grounds that the name should be more general than the meaning implied by the word 'computer'.

The name Mathematical Laboratory was a compromise to counteract a suggestion to the General Board that 'Calculating Laboratory' was a more appropriate name for the Laboratory. It is not clear where this suggestion had come from but Lennard-Jones did not like the idea at all and argued against it. In his opinion the word 'calculate' is applied when it is possible to come to an exact answer by mathematical means. For example it is possible to calculate the area of the circle exactly by integral calculus. Whereas, he wrote, we compute when the area enclosed by a curve cannot be calculated exactly. He stated that the name Computer Laboratory was more in keeping with customary usage (c.1936) than the proposed name 'Calculating Laboratory'.

He then suggested a compromise. It would be safer to adopt the more general title of Mathematical Laboratory than either of the names that had been put forward. He knew well how committees worked in the University, and he probably feared that if he insisted upon 'Computer Laboratory' the foundation of the Laboratory might be delayed. In support of the compromise he argued that the Bush machine (differential analyser) could not be adequately described by either 'compute' or 'calculate'. He wrote that it dealt with curves and produced an answer in graphical form. Its features went well beyond producing a set of numbers and there was no question of producing an exact answer with it. He argued that Mathematical Laboratory would match Physics Laboratory or Chemical Laboratory. Some 30 years later the name was changed back to the Computer Laboratory and the then Director, Maurice Wilkes, remarked that the name change in 1937 had been ill-advised! By then of course computers were ubiquitous and the meaning of the word had changed completely from its connotations in 1937. In retrospect a Computer Laboratory in 1937 would have been the first in the UK if not anywhere in the world.

Portrait of Professor Sir John Lennard-Jones, 'Father of Computational Chemistry' and founder of the Mathematical Laboratory.

Founding Director, Early Years and the Second World War

Professor Lennard-Jones was named the first Director of the Mathematical Laboratory for a period of five years. It was suggested that future appointments to the position of Director should be made by a committee in which the several faculties interested in computation and the development of the Laboratory would be represented. The report recommended that a relatively junior University officer known in Cambridge then as a University Demonstrator (a post with a limited tenure of five years) should work under the Director. Lennard-Jones asked Wilkes to apply, promising his strong support, and Wilkes was duly appointed University Demonstrator in the Mathematical Laboratory. Lennard-Jones was obviously a good judge of men for Wilkes was destined to lead the Laboratory to worldwide prominence over the next 35 years.

J B Bratt, who had built the differential analyser and was also its principal operator, left the employment of the University in 1936 and Wilkes took over his role. He became expert in the operation of the machine and in assisting others to use it to solve research problems.

Chapter Two: The Genesis of the Computer Laboratory

In particular he assisted Elizabeth Monroe, an American who was doing a PhD under the supervision of Lennard-Jones. He and Monroe added an extra integrating section to the analyser. Later in life, Monroe became well known in the USA for her work with children with disabilities.

The analyser was the centrepiece of the Mathematical Laboratory's work in this formative period. It occupied the largest amount of space in the Laboratory and was in considerable demand from users. Recognising its significance, Lennard-Jones followed Hartree's example and approached Metropolitan Vickers Ltd to build a more robust and better-engineered machine. Work began but progress was slow because the company had received a large number of contracts from the government as war was imminent and war-related equipment needed to be given high priority. It was eventually delivered to the Mathematical Laboratory at the commencement of hostilities and diverted to use on wartime projects.

Other machines destined for the Mathematical Laboratory were spread around the University and could not be brought together until the space allocated in the old Anatomy School had been refurbished. Wilkes demonstrated at this early stage of his career his ability to get things done. Realising that the University Building Syndicate was being somewhat tardy in preparing the space for the analyser, and that Metropolitan Vickers were waiting for the space to be ready before delivering it, he decided upon an arbitrary date on which the space had to be ready, and informed both parties of this date. Neither party realised that Wilkes had chosen a date to give each party some sense of urgency and they met the deadline. Nevertheless it was not until October 1939 that the new differential analyser could be installed.

The Ministry of Supply, which had been set up by the government to supply *inter alia* research facilities for the war effort, took over the Mathematical Laboratory on a lease negotiated by Lennard-Jones. The erstwhile academic scientist now turned his attention to ballistics research and tried to use the new differential analyser for calculations required to predict shell trajectories. In the event the machine proved to be inadequate for this purpose and it was diverted to research on other wartime armaments requirements. Lennard-Jones became increasingly involved with the Ministry of Supply, where he showed a talent for administration and scientific leadership, and was appointed Chief Superintendent of Armament Research. Although he left Cambridge he continued to direct the wartime work of the Mathematical Laboratory. Wilkes had also left Cambridge and did not return until 1945. After the war Lennard-Jones decided to leave the service of the government and to take up his chair again in the Chemistry Laboratory, but he retained advisory positions on important government committees. He resigned from the Directorship of the Mathematical Laboratory and the University placed on record its appreciation of the valuable pioneering work on computation done during his tenure as Director.

Below: The Metropolitan Vickers differential analyser at Manchester University. Douglas Hartree is standing on the right.

Below right: From left to right: A F Devonshire, J Corner and M V Wilkes operating the Meccano Differential Analyser in the Theoretical Chemistry Laboratory in the 1930s.

TURING, CAMBRIDGE, KING'S COLLEGE AND THE TURING MACHINE

In a remarkable coincidence, at almost exactly the same time at which Lennard-Jones was planning the foundation of the Computer Laboratory in his rooms in Corpus Christi College, no more than 100 yards away in King's College a young mathematician, Alan Turing, was working on his paper which would lay down the foundations of computer science and computability.

Early Life in Cambridge

'If only Turing could have stayed at King's' – the remark was heard more than once as the 100th anniversary of Turing's birth was celebrated in Cambridge and across the nation in 2012 with lectures, seminars and exhibitions.

Alan Mathison Turing (1912–54) entered King's as an undergraduate in 1931 to read Mathematics and immediately felt at home in the College, where he was absorbed comfortably into the society. King's prides itself on being 'different' from other Cambridge colleges and a facet of this 'difference' is that the collegiate community is extremely tolerant. Turing's sexuality would not have been remarked upon; indeed most members of the College would have been entirely indifferent on the matter. Turing enjoyed his first year at the College, taking part in a number of extracurricular activities. He was perhaps distracted, obtaining only a second class in Part I of the Mathematical Tripos, but after two more years he graduated with a first class and distinction, having taken Part II Schedule B of the

King's College, Cambridge, founded 1441 by King Henry VI, where Turing was an undergraduate and later a Fellow.

Chapter Two: The Genesis of the Computer Laboratory

Mathematical Tripos, Part II, 1934

MODERATORS:
- GODFREY HAROLD HARDY, M.A., *Trinity College.*
- JOHN EDENSOR LITTLEWOOD, M.A., *Trinity College.*

EXAMINERS:
- SYDNEY GOLDSTEIN, Ph.D., *St John's College.*
- WILLIAM REGINALD DEAN, M.A., *Trinity College.*
- WILLIAM VALLANCE DOUGLAS HODGE, M.A., *St John's College.*
- NEVILL FRANCIS MOTT, M.A., *Gonville and Caius College.*

The names in each class are arranged in alphabetical order.

The mark (b) is attached to the names of those candidates who have satisfied the Moderators and Examiners in subjects of Schedule B.

The mark (b*) is attached to the names of those candidates who in the opinion of the Moderators and Examiners deserve special credit in subjects of Schedule B.

Wranglers

Barton, A.	Trin.	Hardie, C. D. (b*)	Magd.	Shiveshwarkar, S. W. (b*)	Sid. Suss.
Bennett, A. J. (b)	Joh.	Head, J. W. (b)	Trin.	Sibson, R.	Magd.
Black, J. A. E. (b)	Pemb.	Houston, T. J.	Christ's	Slater, N. B.	Cai.
Blanco White, T. A.	Trin.	Kerawala, S. M.	Pemb.	Smith, G. A. W.	Jes.
Brown, B. M. (b*)	Christ's	Leggett, D. M. A. (b*)	Trin.	Sutherland, J. W.	Magd.
Clark, G. E.	Joh.	Manisty, J. C. (b)	Sid. Suss.	Trevaldwyn, J. R.	Joh.
Cork, L. G.	Trin.	Mead, H. M.	Sid. Suss.	Turing, A. M. (b*)	King's
Craddock, J. M.	Magd.	Melton, M. W. (b)	Jes.	Walton, S. R.	Joh.
Cundy, H. M.	Trin.	Newbold, L. F.	Trin. H.	Westwater, F. L. (b*)	Emm.
Daniels, H. E.	Cla.	Pitt, H. R.	Pet.	Whittuck, G. S. (b)	Cla.
Goodwin, E. T. (b*)	Pet.	Porter, R. I.	Queens'	Wilkes, M. V. (b*)	Joh.
Green, A. E. (b*)	Jes.	Rowland, E. N. (b)	Cai.		
Haddow, T. D. (b*)	Trin.	Sachse, K. H.	Cai.		

Mathematical Tripos results for 1934 showing Turing and Wilkes in the list.

Mathematical Tripos (re-designated Part III in 1934). In the same list in which Turing's name was entered is that of Maurice Wilkes of St John's College, also with a first class and a distinction in Part II of the Mathematical Tripos, having obtained a first class earlier in Part I. It is an interesting coincidence that these two men who would make such a mark on computing were contemporaries at Cambridge.

In 1935 Turing was elected to a Fellowship at King's College and at the age of 22 entered its inner sanctums, becoming a colleague of the many distinguished members of King's in the 1930s. Among these were the Provost John Sheppard, the economist John Maynard Keynes and the writer E M Forster. It was an outstanding achievement to be elected to a College Fellowship so young and so soon after graduation. He lived in great style in a set of Fellows' rooms free of charge, cared for by loyal College servants with all his meals provided in his rooms or in the College Hall. His rooms were X8 in the College court known as Bodleys, with delightful views of 'The Backs' and the River Cam. It was an idyllic lifestyle. Rooms in this unusual two-sided court are much prized by undergaduates who aspire to spend at least one year of their residence in Bodleys. Nevertheless he did not neglect his work and in 1936 he successfully submitted a thesis for the highly regarded Smith's Prize.

Turing conceived 'The Turing Machine' and published his remarkable paper 'On Computable Numbers with an application to the Entscheidungsproblem' (Decision Problem) in September 1936. The paper introduced for the first time a formal description of the notions of computation needed to show that some questions are not decidable by an algorithm. In other words not all mathematical problems can be solved by computers, not even computers with unlimited memory and time. Although his publication was preceded by a few months by a paper published by Alonzo Church, there is no question that Turing had worked independently and taken an entirely different approach.

Although no digital computer had been built or even described at the time, Turing arrived at the notion of the Turing Machine, a conceptualised computer described in physical terms as an approach to resolving questions as to what could be 'systematically decided'. The machine he conceived had only two components, a 'head' and an indefinitely extensible paper-tape that could be interrogated by the head. The machine had a finite set of different states that determined its behaviour. The head – depending on its state – could either read or write discrete symbols on the tape, moving along the tape either to the left or to the right, and had the ability to erase a symbol in the position addressed by the head. After each operation, an 'action table' determined whether the machine had changed its 'state' or not, thus determining the actions of the next step. Quite remarkably, all of the computational power of a modern computer could be encoded in such a simple machine. He also introduced the idea of a 'universal machine', one that could emulate any other Turing Machine when given a description on its paper-tape. This concept proved to be deeply influential, foreshadowing the development of programmable computers. Today this paper by Turing is considered to have laid the theoretical foundation of computing.

Employment in Post-War Cambridge

Turing went to Princeton University for his PhD. After graduating he declined an opportunity to stay at Princeton and returned to King's to take up his Fellowship, which had been held in abeyance. Turing tried to obtain a post in the University but there were no vacancies (Cambridge University appoints people to fill vacancies and does not create posts for individuals). At this juncture the Second World War intervened and Turing went on to make his remarkable contributions at Bletchley Park which are the stuff of legends and which, four decades later, made him a national hero.

Cambridge Computing: The First 75 Years

At the end of the war Turing returned to Cambridge and King's but his Fellowship was of limited tenure and he could not remain there for long. He obtained a position at the National Physical Laboratory (NPL) and there he designed the ACE computer. Unfortunately he was not in a position to supervise the building of the computer to his design and had to leave all details of construction in the hands of other members of the NPL. He became frustrated by slow progress and redesigns of his computer by others and in 1947 he returned to King's on leave and settled down again in his College. He developed a circle of friends and acquired a lover in King's.

At this time he was well aware that Maurice Wilkes had been appointed to a permanent position in the University as Director of the Mathematical Laboratory and was building a computer following the design described by John von Neumann. Wilkes invited Turing to visit him at the Mathematical Laboratory to inspect the computer he was building, but although Turing was living just a few hundred yards away, for almost a year he could not bring himself to walk the short distance to the Mathematical Laboratory. When he did eventually go he found himself unable to listen to Wilkes, and completely ignored what he was saying.

This was a significant encounter through which Turing recognised that Wilkes was making excellent progress while his ACE was languishing at NPL. He also convinced himself that he could not possibly work at the Mathematical Laboratory under Wilkes, nor could he stay at King's because his temporary Fellowship was due to expire. The subject of computing was then in its infancy and there was no prospect that the University would create a second senior position in the subject. Turing was left with no alternative but to leave Cambridge and took an academic position at Manchester University. He continued to make contributions to computing but was not central to the work in Manchester, as established members of the local team were in charge. Personal recognition did come at this stage and he was elected a Fellow of the Royal Society in 1951. He settled in Manchester but must have been deeply unhappy in his personal life and no doubt hankered after his privileged existence at King's. In 1950s Manchester the conflicts between Turing's sexuality and society's expectations were irreconcilable, and his sexual indiscretion with a local man led to a prosecution and to the ultimate tragedy, when he took his life at the age of just 41.

Alan Turing's statue showing him seated on a bench in Whitworth Park (aka Sackville Park), Manchester, England.

Chapter Two: The Genesis of the Computer Laboratory

Turing's Worldwide Fame

In some of the lectures on Alan Turing in his centenary year (2012) he was described as the equal of such Cambridge luminaries as Newton, Darwin and Keynes. If this claim appears to be somewhat exaggerated today many would claim that posterity might see Turing as an even more important figure in another 100 years. The all-pervasive computer and its many applications which are changing society may well become more significant than many other remarkable contributions to science and technology. Turing's contributions to artificial intelligence, cryptography and natural science, when added to his contributions in computing, reinforce his standing as a scientific genius.

Turing was one of the founding fathers of computer science and is decidedly the best-known name among those who feature prominently in its history. His reputation is of such significance that the 'Nobel Prize' equivalent for computing is named after him: the 'ACM Turing Prize'. He is included among the greatest thinkers of the 20th century and commemorated and honoured across the world. Research centres, auditoria, buildings and lecture series on computing are named after him. King's College maintains an archive of his papers and memorabilia, and many biographical books and papers have been published on his life and work. At Princeton University he is ranked among its most eminent alumni, second only to James Madison, fourth President of the USA of America, and architect of the American constitution. *Time* magazine ranked Turing among the 100 most influential people of the 20th century. In the UK he now has the status of a national hero for his work on code breaking during the Second World War at Bletchley Park. He led the scientific work which broke the Enigma Machine cipher and enabled British intelligence to pinpoint the movement of enemy submarines, thus saving countless lives and making a significant contribution to the eventual defeat of Germany and its allies. In 2009 Prime Minister Gordon Brown made a public apology on behalf of the nation for the persecution and subsequent prosecution of Turing which led him to take his own life.

Right: A blue plaque was unveiled in King's College on 23 June 2012 to mark the 100th anniversary of Alan Turing's birth. The plaque is installed on the wall of Keynes Building, King's Parade.

Alan Turing 1912 – 1954
mathematician, computer pioneer and code breaker

Brief Encounters

Turing and Wilkes may not have liked each other but they maintained a civilised professional relationship and conversed amiably when they met in Cambridge, without discussing computing in any depth. Wilkes invited Turing to give a lecture in the regular series he had instituted in the Mathematical Laboratory, and this lecture was well received. Turing invited Wilkes to travel to Manchester to examine one of his PhD students and Wilkes duly obliged. They met at the anniversary of the first operation of the Manchester computer where they were both among the lecturers. Turing had very little new work to report but Wilkes gave a lecture on microprogramming which was new and exciting and he was highly praised for his achievement. Wilkes and the EDSAC project moved from success to success and in due course Wilkes was appointed Professor of Computer Technology. He took a title, Professor of Computing Technology, which distinguished him from Turing and also from the Engineering Department of the University. In a twist of irony, Wilkes was awarded the ACM Turing Prize in 1967.

A prominent and highly influential figure in Turing's life was Max Newman, Lecturer in Mathematics at Cambridge University and Fellow of St John's College. It is believed that his lectures on the foundations of mathematics, which included Gödel's Theorem, inspired Turing to write his remarkable paper on 'computable numbers'. Newman also suggested that Turing should go to Princeton University for his PhD studies, and in the course of the Second World War, Newman encouraged Turing to move to Bletchley Park to work on code breaking. He continued to influence Turing's life right up to its tragic end. In 1948 he helped Turing obtain a position as Reader in Mathematics at Manchester University and in 1949 assisted him to gain a position as Deputy Director of the Manchester University Computer Laboratory.

CHAPTER THREE

Maurice Wilkes: Computer Pioneer

Wilkes Returns to Cambridge in a Period of Post-War Reconstruction

Maurice Wilkes returned to Cambridge in 1945 for a brief visit before he was formally discharged from his wartime post at the Telecommunications Research Establishment (TRE). He had been appointed Demonstrator in the Mathematical Laboratory in 1938 and his post had been put in abeyance for the duration of his absence on wartime duties. He could not return immediately to work in the Laboratory because it had been leased to the Ministry of Supply and was still occupied by government scientists. The purpose of his visit was to investigate alternative employment possibilities in the University.

At this time, Wilkes believed that Lennard-Jones, who had founded the Laboratory, would continue as its Director and that he, Wilkes, would have to serve under him in a relatively junior position charged with re-establishing the Laboratory for academic use. After six years on wartime work, during which he had held a number of responsible positions, he did not relish this task. He therefore approached Professor Bragg, Head of the Cavendish Laboratory and asked for a post in the Physics Department but Bragg would not agree to his request. Wilkes was disappointed and began to contemplate a career in industry, unaware that he was in fact the perfect man – in the right place, at the right time – to take charge of the Mathematical Laboratory.

Acting Director of the Mathematical Laboratory

Unknown to Wilkes, Lennard-Jones had accepted a senior government position and had informed the University authorities that, in these circumstances, he could no longer continue his Directorship of the Mathematical Laboratory. The University authorities were left in a quandary. They were aware that the Laboratory, which had been founded just before the outbreak of the Second World War, was an important development for Cambridge, but it had not become fully operational for University purposes before it was transferred to the government. The Ministry of Supply had used the Laboratory for wartime research directed by Lennard-Jones, and its main asset, the differential analyser, had been heavily employed. In peacetime Cambridge, all those who had had the experience of using the machine were leaving and the University needed to find a suitably qualified replacement for Lennard-Jones with the necessary skills to establish the Laboratory for academic use.

The return of Wilkes from war service provided the University administrators with the perfect opportunity to overcome their problems. The Faculty Board of Mathematics interviewed Wilkes for the now vacant position of Director and offered it to him with the designation Acting Director, and to his immense gratification informed him that he would also be promoted from Demonstrator to Temporary Lecturer. It was decided that he would hold the position of Acting Director for one year only, as an interim measure, while more permanent arrangements for the future of the Mathematical Laboratory were considered by the University. Wilkes was delighted and accepted with alacrity. The Secretary-General of the Faculties, the University's senior administrator, informed him of the duties of the Acting Director and in the spirit of urgent post-war reconstruction the whole matter was settled very rapidly.

From the lowly post of University Demonstrator he was not only promoted to Lecturer but also appointed to the coveted position of Acting Director of a University department, albeit a small department. The relieved University authorities charged Wilkes with establishing the Mathematical Laboratory in accordance with the

Chapter Three: Maurice Wilkes: Computer Pioneer

PROFESSOR SIR MAURICE VINCENT WILKES (1913–2010)

Maurice Vincent Wilkes was born in Dudley, Staffordshire, in the UK, and went to the King Edward VI School in Stourbridge. He was admitted to St John's College, Cambridge, in 1931 to read Mathematics and graduated in 1934 with a first-class honours degree with distinction (Part II Schedule B). Wilkes went to the Cavendish Laboratory to study for a PhD. His degree subject was the propagation of radio waves in the ionosphere – an unsurprising choice because he had been interested in radio and wireless communication as a boy and had become a radio enthusiast as a young man. He received the PhD in November 1938.

In 1937 he attended a lecture by the mathematician Douglas Hartree which was delivered at a meeting of the Cambridge Philosophical Society, and there he learned about the differential analyser that was in use at the Theoretical Chemistry Department of Cambridge University for solving equations numerically. During his PhD work Wilkes had encountered similar equations and approached the Laboratory Head, Professor Lennard-Jones, who gave him permission to use the analyser, and Wilkes began his lifetime fascination with computing. In 1937 he started work at the newly founded Mathematical Laboratory as assistant to Professor Lennard-Jones. His main responsibility was to operate the differential analyser on behalf of students working under Lennard-Jones. He found this task unfulfilling and, wishing to pursue independent research in basic science, asked Lennard-Jones if he could find him projects in theoretical chemistry based on using the analyser. Before he could make any progress in this direction the Second World War broke out and Wilkes was obliged to leave Cambridge for wartime duties.

After the war ended, he built up a dedicated team around himself to design and construct the first stored-program computer to come into general service to a user community. The machine served a large number of Cambridge scientists including some who went on to win Nobel prizes. Wilkes was responsible for many important contributions to computer science. He was elected a Fellow of St John's College, Cambridge, in 1950. In 1965 he was promoted to Professor of Computer Technology. In 1980 he reached retirement age and went to work in the USA. He worked as a senior consulting engineer with the Digital Equipment Corporation and he was Adjunct Professor of Electrical Engineering and Computer Science at MIT from 1981 to 1985. He eventually returned to England to become a member of the Olivetti Research Laboratory in Cambridge. He was elected a Fellow of the Royal Society in 1956 and was the first President of the newly formed British Computer Society from 1957 to 1960. He was elected a Fellow of the Royal Academy of Engineering in 1976 and awarded the Kyoto Prize in 1992 and the ACM Turing Prize in 1967.

Wilkes was admitted to St John's College, Cambridge (founded 1511), as an undergraduate in 1931, and was elected a Fellow in 1950. His private papers are deposited in the College archives.

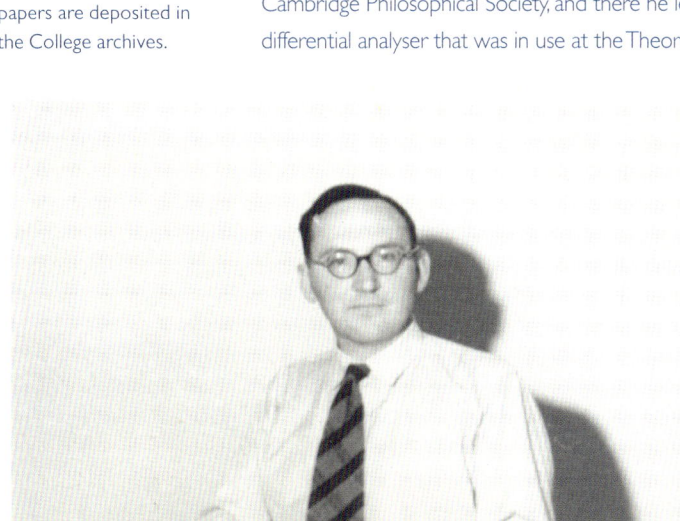

decisions taken in 1937 to provide a computing service in the University.

With his innate sense of self-belief, Wilkes grasped the opportunity he had been given and asked the University to make an application to the government to release him from his service at TRE and to foreclose on the lease of the Mathematical Laboratory to the Ministry of Supply.

With characteristic decisiveness, even before leaving TRE, Wilkes set about recruiting staff and appointed P F Farmer, who was also working at TRE, as his first staff member. He contacted L J Comrie, who had set up a consultancy service, Scientific Computing Services Ltd, and purchased mathematical tables, books and calculating machines from him for the Laboratory.

35

Cambridge Computing: The First 75 Years

LESLIE JOHN COMRIE (1893–1950)

Leslie John Comrie was born in New Zealand and graduated from Auckland University College and later from University College, London. He served with the New Zealand Expeditionary Force in France and lost a leg in action adding another disability to the deafness from which he suffered all his life. He came to Cambridge to take a PhD in Astronomy and was admitted to St John's College as a postgraduate student. He taught numerical analysis in the USA before returning to England to take up a post at the Nautical Almanac Office of the Royal Greenwich Observatory, where he became Superintendent in 1930. After disagreements with his employers he left the Nautical Almanac Office to found the first private company dedicated to scientific computing, Scientific Computing Service Ltd, which did valuable work during the Second World War.

Comrie, rather fortuitously, played a significant role in the early days of the Computer Laboratory in Cambridge when he gave Wilkes the report by von Neumann on the EDVAC. On another occasion Comrie sold books on computing, tables of data and calculating equipment to Wilkes for the Laboratory. His principal contribution to computing was to apply punched card methods to mechanical computers for the preparation of tables for scientific studies. He was elected a Fellow of the Royal Society in 1950 shortly before his death, and the Computer Laboratory in Auckland University is named after him.

Right: Miniature Brunsviga.

Right: Monroe Electric Calculators were made in New Jersey, USA. This machine and the Marchant were both discontinued as cheap electronic calculators became available.

Chapter Three: Maurice Wilkes: Computer Pioneer

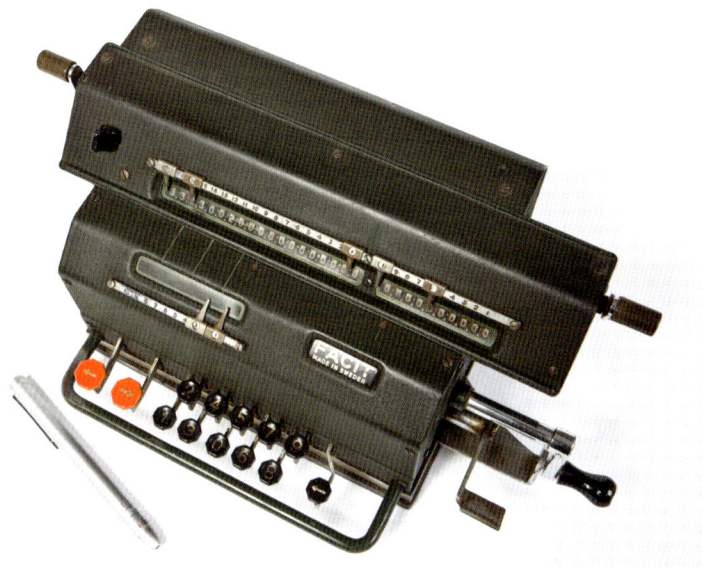

Facit LX mechanical calculator (**above**) and Facit ESA electric mechanical calculator (**right**) were purchased in 1948 for teaching numerical analysis in the Mathematical Laboratory.

Wilkes Reports to the University

Wilkes started full-time work at the University in September 1945 and by January of the following year had not only managed to recover premises for the Mathematical Laboratory but had also started to equip it with 'computing machines'. He worked briskly, and just a month or two later, in February 1946, reported to the Faculty Board of Mathematics outlining his achievements. He had procured a number of mechanical calculating machines and was in the process of acquiring modern electrical calculators. He had also installed two differential analysers (Bush machines). One was the Meccano machine built by Bratt and used extensively by Wilkes before the war and the other was the full-scale version built by Metropolitan Vickers. He had acquired a Mallock machine which needed a complete overhaul in order to work effectively, and he had built up a library of more than 100 books. He planned to initiate teaching activities and therefore needed more space. This was remarkable progress by any standards and particularly noteworthy in view of the restrictions placed by post-war shortages and regulations. The Board was duly impressed.

In 1946, approximately the tenth anniversary of the proposal to found a computer laboratory, the two-man team of Wilkes and his assistant were busy setting up their equipment. They had a number of mechanical calculating machines arranged on benches and two differential analysers which dominated the Laboratory space. Sundry other pieces of equipment such as the Mallock machine were distributed around the Laboratory. There was also an embryonic library. At that stage there was still no teaching or research activity.

In his report Wilkes stated that teaching would be provided when the Laboratory was fully operational and proposed that there should be a 'thoroughly practical' course in computational methods for selected undergraduates and for research students in their first year of study. Students would be taught how to make the best use of calculating machines to solve numerical problems. He stressed that lectures in the Mathematical Laboratory should be focused on practical computing rather than on the theory of finite differences and that there should always be practical work to support these lectures. He viewed himself very much as a utilitarian and saw computing as a hands-on activity.

In the report he discussed the service to be provided by the Mathematical Laboratory to users from other University departments. He placed on record his view that all University members would be welcome to come to the Laboratory to make use of its facilities but that the Laboratory staff would be responsible only for teaching new users how to use standard equipment. An exception would be made for those wishing to use the differential analyser. For this particular machine the Laboratory would provide operators but the 'client' would be expected to keep in close touch and provide all the necessary formulae as well as the mathematical background required for the calculations. The Mallock machine was also cited as a special case for which extraordinary provisions would be needed. Finally he stated forthrightly that access would not be allowed to applicants

JOHN VON NEUMANN (1903–57)

John von Neumann was born in Budapest, and from an early age showed enormous ability as a mathematician. He obtained his PhD at the age of 22 and lived in Germany, publishing some remarkable papers which brought him great acclaim. In 1930 he went to Princeton University in the USA, joined the faculty of the Institute for Advanced Study and held this position until his death in 1957. He became a naturalised citizen of the USA and in the course of his career worked on many defence projects. Although mathematics was his speciality, he was a gifted polymath and made remarkable contributions in a wide variety of scientific and mathematical subjects. Among his many achievements he is credited with having created the architecture of the stored-program computer so that he is often referred to, somewhat controversially, as the 'Father of Computing'.

Von Neumann wrote the report entitled 'First Draft of a Report on the EDVAC', which gave a detailed account of the stored-program computer in clear and easily comprehensible terms. In the modern Computer Laboratory's library there is a somewhat battered and marked-up copy with interesting marginalia by members of the Computer Laboratory who must have consulted it frequently in the early years. Wilkes always believed a grave injustice was done to John Mauchly and J Presper Eckert at the Moore School of Engineering when von Neumann was named as the sole author of the report. Because it was very widely circulated it became impossible for others to protest and to claim to be the inventors of the stored-program computer. Whatever the rights and wrongs of the ownership of the content it is entirely certain that if the report had not been circulated widely and a copy had not fallen into the hands of Wilkes, the construction of EDSAC would have been much delayed or perhaps the computer might never have been built at all. John von Neumann, somewhat inadvertently, had a considerable impact on the early days and direction of the work of the Mathematical Laboratory.

John von Neumann was a distinguished mathematician and scientist. He was also the author of the EDVAC report on the stored-program computer.

from outside the University. He argued that resources would be fully stretched in serving just the Cambridge University clients. Outside parties interested in numerical computation should seek resources elsewhere.

Early Research Proposals

The most intriguing part of the report was presented as an extended appendix entitled 'Development of New Computing Machines'. This section was introduced cautiously and linked to the service element. Wilkes was not certain at this stage that his remit included independent research activities in computing on the scale he envisaged. He did, however, make his ambitions very clear. He was planning to enter what he describes as the 'big field' of electronic computing and would try to catch up on the lead that the Americans had taken in designing electronic computing machines. He was aware of the automatic sequence calculators under construction in the USA but was uncertain of the direction he himself should take. He suggested to the Mathematical Laboratory Committee that he should recruit either a research student or a research assistant to build a demonstration machine which could carry out arithmetic operations at high speed. He planned to use electronics because he had acquired a good deal of experience in the subject during his wartime work on radar.

In his report Wilkes compared analogue computers to mechanical and electrical calculating machines which could perform arithmetic operations using finite difference methods for solving problems involving a continuous variable. He argued that, by using electronic devices, a sequence of operations could be performed automatically without the intervention of an operator who would only be required to give the initial instructions. The machine was likened to a female 'computer' working 168 hours a week without tiring, trustworthy enough to do as she is told and totally infallible. Furthermore the electronic version of the 'computer' could carry out arithmetic operations at phenomenally high speeds, easily outpacing a human operator.

He argued that analogue machines were limited in two ways: firstly the precision with which a physical system may be designed was limited to one part in 1,000, but this level of accuracy would be lost through the accumulation of errors when a long sequence of operations was carried out. A second limitation of an analogue machine would be that variables in the calculation needed to lie within close limits to prevent the error becoming unacceptably large. He argued that the accuracy of adding and multiplying machines could be increased at will by simply allowing for a large number of digits in each register of the machine. In the end he decided to sit on the fence by concluding that there was room for analogue as well as adding and multiplying types of machines in a well-equipped laboratory. He already had two analogue machines, the Meccano differential analyser and the Metropolitan Vickers differential analyser with eight integrating sections, which should suffice for all analogue computing needs within the University. Since he did not have a machine of the adding and multiplying type he needed to build or purchase an automatic sequence calculator. Exactly which machine he would be able to acquire was not clear to him at this stage.

Director of the Mathematical Laboratory

The Faculty Board of Mathematics reported to the General Board in May 1946, with some degree of self-satisfaction, that the Mathematical Laboratory was operational. Dr Wilkes, then Temporary University Lecturer and Acting Director, had installed modern calculating machines, including the Bush and Mallock machines, built up a library and workshop facilities and recruited staff – all this in just a few months. The General Board in its report to the University noted that the Mathematical Laboratory would be expected to serve a number of departments across the University and appointed a Management Committee with University-wide representation to oversee the operation of the Laboratory and to act formally as Head of Department. The Board also proposed that Dr Wilkes, who had successfully established the Laboratory, should be appointed its Director for a period of five years. His stipend was fixed at £750 per annum (with a bonus of £50 for the year 1946 to 1947) subject to a deduction of £250 if he were to be elected to a Fellowship at a college which paid a dividend. (Until the 1960s it was common practice for colleges to pay dividends annually to College Fellows.) Wilkes was expected to provide up to 48 hours of lecturing per annum on behalf of the University and he was debarred from taking on any significant college posts but allowed to teach for his college for up to six hours per week. His office as Director of the Mathematical Laboratory was recognised formally as a University teaching position.

The duties assigned to Wilkes were to 'advance knowledge of the science of mathematical computation, to promote and direct research in it, and to supervise the work of the Mathematical Laboratory under the general supervision of the Mathematical Laboratory Committee'. It is interesting to note that by this time Douglas Hartree had moved from Manchester to the Plummer Chair in Theoretical Physics at Cambridge University. He was one of the members appointed to the Mathematical Laboratory Committee and was known to support attempts to improve facilities in the University for numerical computation. He also knew Wilkes through interacting with him on the use of the differential analyser and he took this opportunity to help him to establish the Mathematical Laboratory. Wilkes now had five years of secure employment ahead of him, and every prospect that he would be given a permanent position in Cambridge. He felt that he had received tacit approval to go ahead with the suggestion included in his report, to build a prototype of an automatic sequencing machine.

St John's College, founded in 1511, where Wilkes was a student and later a Fellow for more than 50 years.

Chapter Three: Maurice Wilkes: Computer Pioneer

The 'Big Field' of Electronic Computing

Any uncertainty on the part of Wilkes regarding the direction he should take in his research was entirely dispelled three months later by a chance encounter with Comrie, who had helped him earlier to set up the Laboratory. At this encounter in May 1946, Comrie gave Wilkes a copy of a report by John von Neumann on work in progress at the Moore School of Electrical Engineering in Pennsylvania. Although this project had been funded by the American Department of Defense the report was not classified. Winston Churchill's famous 'iron curtain' speech to the American people in March of that year had not yet had its effect and Cold War espionage had not created a culture of secrecy among scientists. Wilkes understood immediately the implications of the report which he read during the one night for which he had possession of the document. As he wrote 30 years later, he did not have the benefit of a 'Xerox machine' with which he could have photocopied it.

Later in the year he had another stroke of luck when he received an invitation to visit the Moore School of Engineering to learn about the ENIAC project. This was probably a consequence of Hartree's official visit to the USA to learn about the advances in mathematical computation in American organisations. Hartree was acting as a liaison officer between the UK and the USA on scientific matters and knew of Wilkes's ambition to build a computer in Cambridge.

In 1946 Wilkes went on an extended visit to the USA to attend a lecture series on the 'Theory and Techniques for the Design of Electronic Digital Computers' and during this visit learned a great deal about the ENIAC and EDVAC projects. He was able to have detailed discussions with the two key figures responsible for the work at the University of Pennsylvania, John Mauchly and J Presper Eckert. Wilkes now had a clear understanding of the operation of the stored-program computer. Even as he was making his way back to the UK he was planning his research projects, his stored-program computer and its name: 'Electronic Delay Storage Automatic Calculator (EDSAC)'. Wilkes's transformation from mathematics

Wilkes was aware that giant calculating machines were under construction in the USA, and ENIAC at the Moore School was the best known of these developments. It is shown here with some of its designers.

DOUGLAS RAYNER HARTREE, WARTIME AND CAMBRIDGE CAREER

Douglas Hartree had already played a significant part in the foundation of the Computer Laboratory when he introduced Lennard-Jones to the differential analyser in 1937, and his influence continued for many years beyond this first interaction. During the war Douglas Hartree was deputed by the British government to interact with the USA on scientific matters of mutual benefit to the war effort. As part of this work he visited the Moore School of the University of Pennsylvania and was introduced to the ENIAC project. He saw immediately the potential of the machine and was invited by the Americans to advise on its use in scientific projects.

In England after the war Hartree was an influential figure serving on government committees charged with post-war reconstruction. He gave the strongest possible support to the development of computing in the UK, helping to identify three main centres where electronic computers could be developed: the University of Manchester, Cambridge University and the National Physical Laboratory at Teddington. Shortly after the war Hartree moved from Manchester to take up the Plummer Chair of Theoretical Physics at Cambridge University and came into regular contact with Maurice Wilkes, who had recently been appointed Director of the Mathematical Laboratory. He influenced Wilkes's thinking and was almost certainly the person who engineered an invitation to Wilkes to attend the remarkable series of lectures given at the Moore School of Engineering with the purpose of disseminating computing advances across the world. Wilkes went on to build EDSAC at Cambridge. Hartree, although based formally in the Mathematics Faculty, spent a great deal of his time in the Mathematical Laboratory and contributed to the applications of EDSAC by helping to build a library of subroutines.

Douglas Hartree, Plummer Professor of Theoretical Physics, supported the Mathematical Laboratory and made contributions to EDSAC.

to physics and finally into a proponent of computer technology was now complete.

Wilkes had also begun to think that more subtle approaches than those employed by the Americans could be used in building the computer in Cambridge. At this stage he was still Acting Director of the Mathematical Laboratory and his future was uncertain, but Lennard-Jones, with great foresight, had founded the Mathematical Laboratory as a department of the University, which gave Wilkes a number of advantages he would not have enjoyed had the Laboratory just been part of another department.

Wilkes had the right to receive resources from the University in his position as Director through his Head of Department, formally the Mathematical Laboratory Committee. These resources comprised funding for research and teaching and the manpower required to implement these activities. He did not have to ask permission or seek funds to build an electronic machine for computation. Furthermore he had the support of his Management Committee, which was impressed by the progress of the Mathematical Laboratory, and gave its full backing to its Director and to his plans to build a

Chapter Three: Maurice Wilkes: Computer Pioneer

Above: Vannevar Bush designed the first working differential analyser at MIT in the USA c.1928. It had six integrating sections and it filled a large room. This remarkable analog computer was used to solve problems arising in many different branches of science and technology before the advent of digital computers.

Right: The EDVAC report belonging to Hartree, now in the library of the Computer Laboratory.

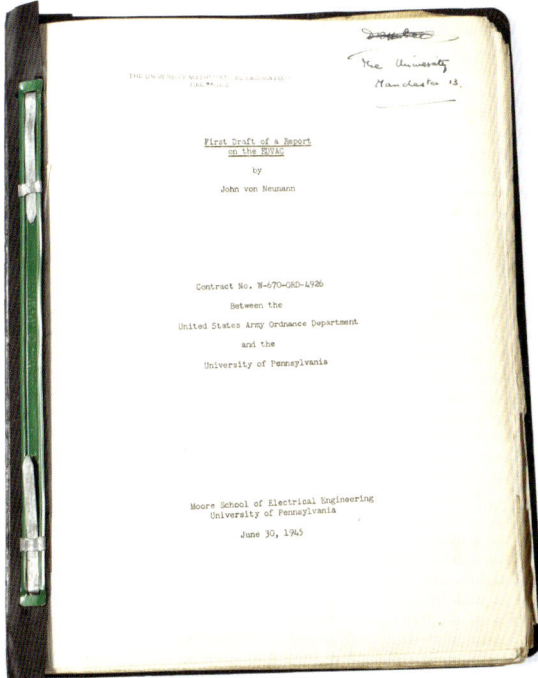

computer. Wilkes was now very much in charge, and in a postscript the role of Professor Lennard-Jones in founding the Laboratory was acknowledged formally by Professor Hodge, Head of the Mathematics Faculty, at a discussion in Senate House in November 1946. He noted that Professor Lennard-Jones had served the full term of his appointment of five years and had installed two differential analysers in the Mathematical Laboratory before relinquishing the post.

In another report submitted in July 1947, the Committee asked the Faculty Board of Mathematics to provide Wilkes with the resources needed for his research projects. In this report the first of the objectives set out for the Mathematical Laboratory was 'research in computational methods and on all kinds of calculating machines'. This became the mission statement of the Laboratory and the report ended with a preliminary description of EDSAC.

CHAPTER FOUR

Maurice Wilkes and the EDSACs

'THE PLAN IS TO BUILD A COMPUTER'

By his own admission Wilkes had moments of good fortune at critical stages of his long and illustrious career, but in the construction and commissioning of his two famous computers, EDSAC (Electronic Delay Storage Automatic Calculator) and EDSAC 2, there was little or no element of luck. To build these computers he needed to possess an intimate knowledge of state-of-the-art computing, outstanding technological skills, great determination and exceptional qualities of leadership over a sustained period of time. Wilkes possessed all these qualities in abundance. He built a team around himself and inspired its members to share his single-minded vision, 'we will make a computer that works'. When he started building EDSAC he was in charge of the Mathematical Laboratory; he had gained access to the EDVAC report and seen the ENIAC project in America. Most importantly he had sufficient funding from the University to start building a computer without delay.

During his time at the Moore School in the USA Wilkes had paid close attention to the ENIAC and had been impressed by the size and complexity of the computer as well as by the large team of engineers and scientists working on its construction and commissioning. The computer filled a room 12m x 6m with 18,000 valves (vacuum tubes) glowing in dozens of racks of electronics which generated a massive 150kW of power. This must have been a daunting experience for Wilkes but his determination to build his own computer in Cambridge remained unshaken. He wrote that 'only a handful (of people), of whom I was fortunate enough to be one, had the necessary engineering qualifications and experience to embark on a (computer) construction project'. He might have added that the construction project required considerable expertise in the emerging field of electronics, which he had acquired in the course of his wartime work on radar.

Wilkes attended part of a course on computing held at the Moore School in Pennsylvania, USA, and was able to examine the ENIAC machine then under construction at the School.

Almost 30 years after the EDSAC machines had been retired and replaced by commercially manufactured machines Wilkes wrote that decisions concerning the EDSAC project had been taken on three levels. The first level was the overall policy to be adopted for the project. The master plan was to build a computer, learn how to use it effectively and then put it to work on solving scientific problems. The second decision he had to make concerned the architecture of the computer. Wilkes took the view that the computer had to be 'user-friendly', in today's jargon, and not a research project in itself. Finally there was the question of implementation. Wilkes decided to take a very conservative approach in the design and construction of the electronics. He did not wish to design state-of-the-art electronic circuits. His purpose above all was to build a reliable computer. With this objective constantly in mind he decided that there should be no frills in the electronic design and insisted that the operating frequency would not be pushed to the limit. He fixed the clock frequency at 500kHz although he knew that circuit designs were available that could operate at double this frequency.

Wilkes was also aware that other projects were underway to build computers not only in the USA but also in the UK at Manchester University and at the National Physical Laboratory. In the early stages of the project, Hartree gave Wilkes his personal copy of the invaluable report by von Neumann on the EDVAC. The report was much consulted by Wilkes and others and the slightly battered copy in the Computer Laboratory's library has a number of marginalia probably in Wilkes's own hand. There are both corrections and comments on the text. Its existence, and Wilkes's determination to follow its directions and to eschew the temptation to re-invent what was already available, almost certainly gave Wilkes an advantage over his competitors.

Once Wilkes had decided to enter the race to build the first computer he launched a crash programme for the construction of EDSAC. His working methodology was based on his experience with the crash programmes for constructing radar equipment in which he had participated during the war. The construction of EDSAC began in a room on the top floor of the Mathematical Laboratory which had previously been occupied by the Anatomy School. John Bennett (Research Student 1947–50) recalled it was uncomfortable 'in the summer when the formalin (used to preserve cadavers) that had impregnated the floorboards over the years was vaporised by the heat. The smell of the formalin vapour is very penetrating.' (From *In the Beginning – Recollections of Software Pioneers*, Robert L Glass.)

'How Can We Make a Memory for the Computer? Everything Else We Can Do by Hard Work and Determination.'

In the mid-1940s, a few years before magnetic core memories were invented, by far the most novel and demanding part of any plan to build a computer lay in the design and construction of the memory. Wilkes wrote: 'Orders [instructions] expressed in [binary] coded form as a train of electrical pulses, are stored in the memory until required.' He made an early decision to use an ultrasonic delay line memory in EDSAC. The principle of operation was well understood by him because he had had experience in the use of delay lines in wartime ground radar. In this application radar pulses were transmitted with a time interval introduced between them by the delay line. Echoes were received after a time lapse which depended upon the distance of the approaching aircraft from the radar station and this time changed as the distance decreased. All echo signals returning to the receiver without a time lapse could be discarded as spurious effects from stationary objects.

In a delay line memory, a train of electrical pulses defined a number in coded form. This electrical signal was converted into a sound wave at ultrasonic frequency. Transformations into sound and vice versa were carried out by transducers, usually quartz crystals. The ultrasonic signal was fed into the delay line at one end and when the ultrasonic pulses reached the far end of the delay line, another quartz crystal converted the sound wave back into an electrical signal. At this stage it was normally necessary to amplify the signal and to restore the pulse shape. The restored signal was sent back to the input and the cycle of events was repeated for as long as was necessary. Many such pulse trains, representing 'orders' circulated in the memory tube at any one time until they were extracted. Wilkes needed to build a device in which a train of pulses could be delayed for a time interval longer than the duration of the train. He also noted that the particular group of pulses that were needed for the computer's operation might not be available at the output

Right: The principle of the delay line memory is illustrated in this diagram. Electrical signals are converted into sound waves which travel along the mercury-filled tube until required. They are then converted back into electrical pulses before passing into the computer through gating circuits.

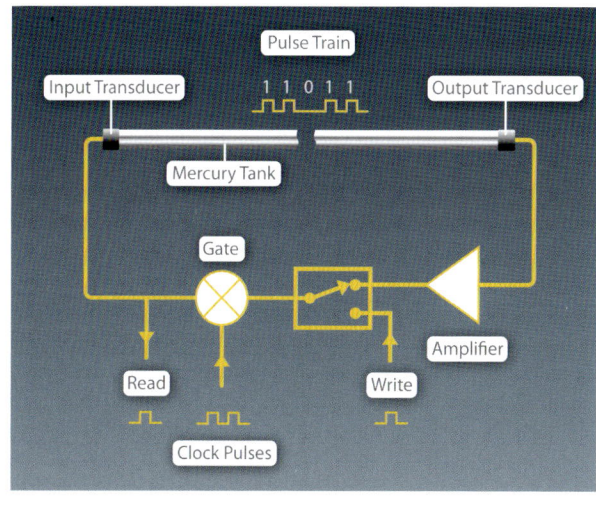

Cambridge Computing: The First 75 Years

when required and one would inevitably have to wait for their appearance at the output. This time interval was a fundamental limitation of this type of memory device and the consequential loss in operating speed was accepted by Wilkes as a necessary limitation of the memory device that he had selected.

The delay line memory required a 'gating circuit' to ensure that information in the memory would not be lost through deterioration in the shape of the group of pulses as they circulated within the memory. Output pulses from the delay line were not passed direct to the input. Instead the pulses were amplified and passed to an electronic gate which controlled the passage into the delay line of clock pulses generated by a continuously running pulse generator. Each pulse appearing at the output of the delay unit enabled a clock pulse to pass into the input. If a pulse failed to appear then a clock pulse did not pass into the input. Thus well-shaped pulses replaced distorted pulses and the whole of the pulse train was replaced by a well-formed sequence of pulses for the next transit along the delay line. Gates were also used at the input and output of the delay line to inject and extract data pulses.

The Mercury Delay Line Memory

Although the operating principle of the ultrasonic delay line was well understood by Wilkes he needed a detailed and dimensioned mechanical design of the mercury delay line. He was considering the possibility of making prototypes and carrying out trials until he could devise a suitable design, but before embarking upon this time-consuming exercise he had another of his strokes of luck. He met Tommy Gold, who had been a research student with him at the Cavendish Laboratory in Cambridge University and had subsequently worked with him on radar. Gold had used mercury tanks (the word tank was used instead of tube to avoid confusion with the American vacuum tube) in his experiments on an experimental radar project for the cancellation of spurious signals and Gold, in Wilkes's own words; 'laid before my wondering eyes a dimensioned drawing of a mercury tank'. Wilkes seized his opportunity and passed on the drawings forthwith to the workshops of the Cambridge University Engineering Department for the construction of the mercury delay line.

A complete memory battery, seen here in April 1948, consisted of 16 tubes (tanks) filled with mercury and sealed at each end with a metal plate into which quartz crystals (transducers) were embedded in intimate contact with the mercury.

The physical structure of the delay line was a mercury-filled tube. The ends of the tube were sealed with caps with a quartz crystal embedded in contact with mercury. This element was chosen as the medium for the acoustic waves because it offered a number of advantages over other materials. The first advantage was that the acoustic impedances of mercury and quartz are similar and impedance matching ensured good energy transfer in the conversions from acoustic waves to electrical signals and vice versa. The material also gave the required bandwidth for transmission of the signal pulse. Variation with temperature of the velocity of sound in mercury is relatively small around room temperature. It is possible therefore to avoid the expense and difficulty of placing the Mercury Delay Line memory in a tightly controlled, constant-temperature environment. For EDSAC the mercury memory was kept in a cabinet with cooling fans which were kept on at all times. A home-built thermostat kept the temperature of the tanks within prescribed limits. As mercury is not corrosive with steel, low-cost

Chapter Four: Maurice Wilkes and the EDSACs

Right: Several short delay lines, as shown here, were also designed and used as necessary in EDSAC.

Below: End cap showing the 16 tranducers embedded into the metal plate which was attached to the delay line tanks to make up a battery.

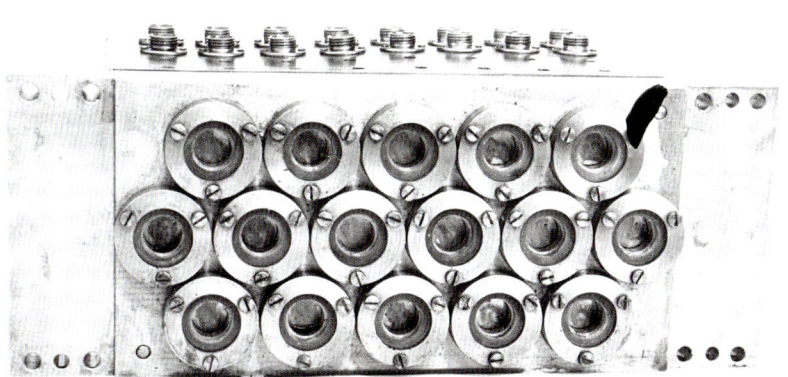

and easily machined mild steel was used for the tubes. During filling some mercury inevitably escaped onto the floor but nobody paid any attention to this health hazard; many years later Herbert Norris (Technician 1951–63) wondered 'what would health and safety say now to the mercury globules in the floorboards'.

The length of each tube or tank was approximately 1.6m, the diameter was about 25mm and a group of 16 tubes was packaged together with metal end plates to hold them in place. Each metal plate had 16 embedded tube end caps. A group of 16 tanks formed a 'tank battery'. Two tank batteries with 32 tubes in total were needed to provide the main memory capacity specified by Wilkes for EDSAC.

Computer Architecture and Electronics

The storage capacity of the mercury delay line was determined (a) by the length of the tube used to make the memory and (b) the time interval between successive pulses. Wilkes used pulses with amplitude of 18V, 0.9µs in length with a space between pulses of 1.0µs for the main memory. Each tube could hold 576 pulses and each battery could hold 256 numbers. Wilkes decided upon 34 binary digits to represent a number (ten digits in decimal scale). An additional digit was used to define the sign of the number. This made it necessary to have 35 pulses to represent a single number. A space equivalent to one pulse width was needed to separate numbers from each other, thus the total length of the pulse train was equal to 36 pulses. The memory was capable of storing 1,024 17–bit words. There were also some subsidiary memory tubes which could hold just one word of 35 bits.

The memory was coupled to an arithmetic logic unit which was designed to be capable of accepting 650 instructions per second. The input to EDSAC was by paper-tape and the output was received in a Creed teleprinter at a rate of about six characters per second. The operating system, named 'initial orders', occupied 31 words of read-only memory which was hard wired. At a later stage the operating system occupied 41 words of read-only memory and included the possibility of using subroutines. In operation the average order time was 1.5ms, multiplication took 4.5ms and division required software for implementation and took 200ms.

Although Wilkes claimed that he knew exactly what he had to do with the electronics, a great deal of hard

Cambridge Computing: The First 75 Years

EARLY COMPUTER ELECTRONICS

There was considerable experience and expertise in electronics in the Cavendish Laboratory of Cambridge University before the Second World War and research scientists were using electronic circuits extensively for sensitive measurements. The laboratory was known worldwide for the discovery of the electron by J J Thomson who was awarded the Nobel Prize in 1906. Later Owen Richardson had postulated the theoretical basis of electron emission (Nobel Prize, 1928) and another Cavendish scientist, Ambrose Fleming, invented the diode valve.

In the early 1930s, the Cavendish Professor, Ernest Rutherford, was leading research in nuclear physics. Among his research students was C E Wynn-Williams (**left**) who had been admitted to Trinity College in 1925 to study for a PhD. Before coming to the Cavendish, he had acquired expertise in electronics through his work on instrumentation at Bangor University and through his personal interest in wireless communication. Rutherford tasked him with devising an electronic means of counting electrical pulses generated by particles emitted during nuclear reactions and in 1926 Wynn-Williams invented electronic circuits known as scale-of-two counters which proved highly successful. He used thyratron valves (hard vacuum triodes were used later) and his designs could count pulses arriving at any rate from one to tens of thousands per minute. Each successive stage of the scale-of-two counter divided the counting rate by two which enabled the circuit to count reliably at high particle arrival rates.

It was later recognised that the scale-of-two counter also had more general applications, particularly for circuits used in the electronic computers developed during and after the Second World War. The scale-of-two counter was described as one of the 'most influential of all inventions' related to modern computing and Wynn-Williams is now considered to be one of the pioneers of computing although his original work was carried out for a very different purpose.

The mercury delay memory was vital to the operation of EDSAC, and each tube (tank) was tested before installation on a special test bench, as seen here in June 1947. It took several months to commission and install the full complement of tanks into the two batteries.

work was necessary to implement arithmetic operations in the computer. The circuits were designed by Wilkes while members of his team soldered the components and wiring by hand in specially designed, 762mm-long (30in) chassis which were built by an external contractor. The standard 17-inch racks which were commonplace at that time were eschewed for reasons that are not clear. In all, 12 racks were needed and 3,000 valves were used. The entire team worked on constructing electronics including Wilkes. Don Hunter (Research Assistant 1949–51) recalls that he found Wilkes working 'late one evening with a unit propped between two chairs'.

Wilkes was determined to make the computer as reliable as possible and it is apparent that a great deal of thought was put into the construction of the electronics. Again with reliability in mind he made sure that only new components of good quality were purchased for the construction of the electronic circuits. The procurement of the electronic valves was a different story, and an interesting illustration of the spirit of post-war reconstruction prevalent in the country. Wilkes was the beneficiary of a friendly telephone call from a 'helpful

Several versions of EDSAC chassis were designed and constructed (*c.*June 1947). Chassis were placed in racks each of which could hold up to 12 chassis. There were 15 racks altogether.

man in the Ministry of Defence'. This 'angel' offered a truckload of valves free of charge as they were surplus to requirements now that the war had ended. Wilkes accepted the offer with delight and did not subsequently encounter any shortage of valves for EDSAC. He was not the only beneficiary of this post-war largesse from the government. Just a short distance from the Mathematical Laboratory Charles Oatley, later Professor Sir Charles Oatley, under whom Wilkes had worked during the war, received a similar phone call at the Engineering Department. The truckloads of electronic equipment were weighed as they left the defence establishment and the tonnage delivered to each university was recorded! Oatley used these gifts for his pioneering research on scanning electron microscopes which are now ubiquitous across the world. At the Cavendish Laboratory, a stone's throw from the Mathematical Laboratory, Martin Ryle, later Professor Sir Martin Ryle and Nobel Laureate, was able to use wartime electronic components to construct the circuits he needed for aperture synthesis research and to build his first radio telescopes. Ryle used EDSAC for his calculations and acknowledged the contribution of EDSAC when receiving his Nobel Prize.

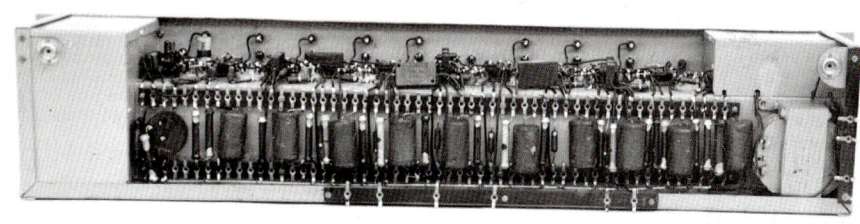

Each of the electronics chassis in EDSAC had its own power transformer for heating the valves. The total power consumption was 12kW and a sizeable room 5m x 4m was required to house the computer. Although this size was vast compared with the computers we have today it was very much smaller than the gigantic ENIAC room which Wilkes had seen in America!

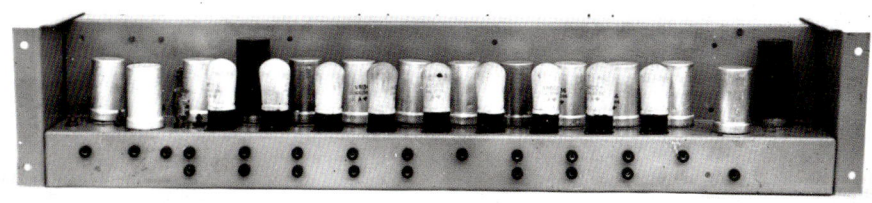

EDSAC is Operational – 6 May 1949

The development of EDSAC into a fully operational, stored-program computer was marked by a series of intermediate milestones. First of all there was a successful demonstration of patterns of pulses circulating in the memory tube for hundreds of hours without significant deterioration in quality. Much to everyone's relief the principle and practice of the mercury delay line memory was proven and the mechanical design and construction of the tank battery had been found to be satisfactory. A little later some of the electronics were tested and gave a satisfactory demonstration of binary counting in operation. This was another cause for celebration. As construction proceeded it was demonstrated that the more complicated sections of EDSAC, such as the multiplier section, were also working satisfactorily and an instruction

Cambridge Computing: The First 75 Years

to the computer could be executed from memory. Each of these discrete events was regarded as a significant step towards eventual success. The team celebrated these minor triumphs with, as Wilkes describes, a journey to the local pub known as the 'Bun Shop' where he treated his colleagues to pints of beer.

By the autumn of 1948 most parts of the machine were working as designed, when tested independently. The tape reader for inputting the data was connected to the machine and instructions could be read into the memory and at this stage the output teleprinter was attached to the machine. The computer did not work immediately and there followed a period of several months during which many necessary modifications were carried out. The timing of pulse transmissions needed to be adjusted, logical errors in the design had to be identified and eliminated and circuits were improved when necessary to ensure better performance and greater reliability. This was a frustrating period for Wilkes and his colleagues. The construction of EDSAC had been a journey into the unknown and Wilkes and his team were uncertain whether they would ever be able to make the computer work.

Time spent on the computer during this period was by no means wasted, as all the parties involved in attempting to make EDSAC come to life were gaining insights into the strengths and weaknesses of their creation. They were also establishing test methods and checking procedures which were very useful activities and gave them valuable experience for the days when the computer would have to be maintained under heavy usage. Wilkes names Bill Renwick, the Chief Engineer,

as the key person at this stage. On him fell the heaviest burden and he patiently stuck to the task and made steady progress in eliminating problems and making improvements. During this period another important activity was research into programming methods.

In the course of a test on 6 May 1949, the program tape for computing a table of squares of the numbers zero to 99, written by David Wheeler, was fed into the computer and to everyone's elation the results were printed out correctly on the printer. EDSAC was operational. Wheeler, true to his nature, immediately set about writing another program for EDSAC aimed at

Above: Wilkes considered this image the official view of EDSAC in October 1947, 18 months before the computer operated for the first time.

The tape reader with its cover removed (far left) and teleprinter (left) used on EDSAC in 1949.

50

Chapter Four: Maurice Wilkes and the EDSACs

Right: Each successful step in the construction and commissioning of EDSAC was celebrated by a trip to a local pub, the 'Bun Shop'. The tradition of celebrating successful projects continued as long as the Bun Shop existed.

Below right: Margaret Marrs, who worked with EDSAC 2 in the 1950s, holding the paper-tape used to feed data.

computing prime numbers. The team could hardly wait to start using the computer that they had been building for more than two years.

EDSAC could now claim to be the first complete and fully operational electronic digital computer with an internally stored-program and it was capable of providing a comprehensive service to users. Manchester's Small-scale Experimental Machine started to work before EDSAC but it had been built more to validate the innovative CRT memory technology created by F C Williams rather than to serve as a general-purpose computer. Although several computer projects were underway in the USA there is no evidence of a stored-program computer working before the date on which EDSAC became operational.

The team's efforts were now directed towards improving the operational characteristics of the computer. Wilkes and his colleagues realised that they could make EDSAC more user-friendly if subroutines could be made available to the user, thus saving the time and effort otherwise required to write independent software for routine operations. By 1951 nearly 100 subroutines were available for general use including *inter alia* floating point arithmetic, operations with complex numbers, differential equations, power series, logarithms and trigonometric functions. The consequence of these amenities created by Wilkes and the Laboratory staff was that the computer became extraordinarily user-friendly. Users multiplied and scientific work across the whole of the University began to benefit. Within a short while it was widely acknowledged that major scientific advances were taking place as a result of calculations carried out with EDSAC. Users had to become accustomed to the vagaries of EDSAC. It broke down frequently in a working day but a dedicated repair team went into action immediately and it was normally restored into operation very quickly. On a few occasions it worked for more than 24 hours, much to the relief of users, and the queue disappeared quickly.

A semi-formal user service was now initiated and every effort was made to obtain maximum use of the computer. An operator was available to run the programs throughout the day but during the night only authorised users could operate the computer. Some authorised users could work independently but others were only permitted to use the computer under the close supervision of a high-level user. If a computer problem occurred during the night all work was suspended until the morning, when the maintenance staff returned to work and repaired the computer. Apparently there were very few nights during which the computer was still active when dawn broke! On these particular occasions the maintenance staff would find one or two dedicated users, who had worked through the night, still inputting their tapes lest they miss the opportunity to complete their project before the inevitable breakdown of the computer. The tradition of running the computer throughout the night under the auspices of authorised users was retained right up to the mid-1960s. There is a story of a research student

Cambridge Computing: The First 75 Years

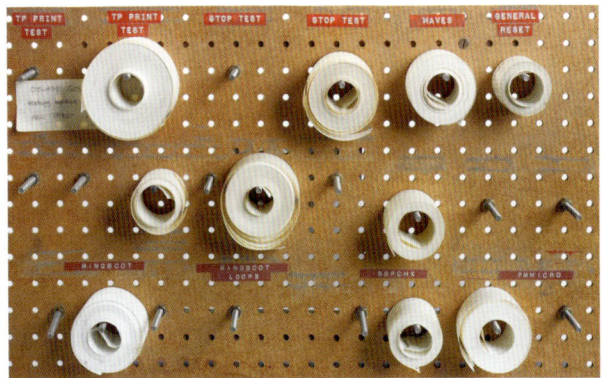

going to sleep while EDSAC continued to run for an unprecedented period of time, producing reams of tape. The sleeping student woke up to find that most of his tapes had been cleared away by an over-zealous cleaning lady arriving early in the morning!

In June 1949, following precedents in the USA, a conference was held in Cambridge on 'High Speed Automatic Calculating Machines'. This was the first conference on computing to be held outside America, and there were more than 100 participants. EDSAC was successfully demonstrated and a report published. Wilkes also attended conferences in the USA on computing and during one of his visits showed a film in Philadelphia of EDSAC in operation. This film had been made under the direction of E N Mutch. The cameraman was Alexis Brookes, a Lecturer at the Cambridge University Engineering Department and Fellow of St John's College. The film told the story of a scientific problem solved by EDSAC. A committee first of all reviewed the problem presented by a scientist and gave its approval for the use of EDSAC to solve the problem. A programmer then took up the task of writing the code for the computer. Various stages of the program running on the computer and the results being printed out were filmed. The film was silent but a commentary was provided when the film

Left: Paper-tape spools for the EDSAC subroutine library.

Below: The Mathematical Laboratory staff in July 1948. Top row, from left: D Willis, L Foreman, G Stevens, R Piggott, P Farmer, P Chamberlain. Middle row, from left: D Wheeler, E Lanaerts, J Steel, R Bonham-Carter, C Mumford, S Barton. Bottom row, from left: E McKee (later Breakwell), J Bennett, B Noble, M Wilkes, W Renwick, E Mutch, H Gordon.

The operator's console of the LEO I electronic computer in the 1960s.

was shown. Many years later sound was added to the film by Wilkes. EDSAC became widely known and captured the imagination of the astronomer turned science-fiction writer, Fred Hoyle, who described its use by one of his characters in his science fiction novel *The Black Cloud*.

The University recognised the notable achievements of the Mathematical Laboratory. Wilkes was appointed Head of Department and freed from having to report to the committee that had hitherto acted as his Department Head. Renwick was appointed to the academic position of University Demonstrator. The commissioning of EDSAC as a general-purpose computer and its sustained and successful use by Cambridge scientists were outstanding achievements and Wilkes was recognised as a major international figure in computing.

The Lyons Story and LEO Computers

In July 1947 visitors from the catering company J Lyons arrived at the Mathematical Laboratory for a meeting with Wilkes. The company had 200 cafes distributed across the country and four vast and very popular Lyons Corner Houses in London. It also manufactured and distributed bakery products to thousands of shops across the nation and employed an army of clerical staff in its administrative offices to deal with the flood of receipts, vouchers and invoices received daily from its outlets.

The management of the company was forward-looking and became aware of the 'giant brains' under development in the USA which were said to be capable of doing the work of thousands of men and women. Lyons sent a delegation to America to learn more about these calculating machines, and, among other centres, they visited Princeton University, where they met Herman Goldstine. He gave them Hartree's name as a British computer expert who had recently moved to the Plummer Chair of Theoretical Physics at Cambridge University. Lyons contacted Hartree, who in turn pointed them towards Wilkes and the EDSAC project. The Lyons management was delighted to find work on computers at the Mathematical Laboratory and came to

DAVID JOHN WHEELER (1927–2004)

David Wheeler was a critically important member of Wilkes's team when the EDSAC computers were being built and commissioned in the Mathematical Laboratory. He was very young, just 21, when he took up, almost casually as part of his research project, the heavy responsibility of programming for EDSAC. He had grants from the government and Trinity College to study for a PhD and registered as Wilkes's second research student but was the first to graduate from the Mathematical Laboratory. His dissertation was entitled, very appropriately, *Automatic Computing with the EDSAC*. He displayed such skill and ingenuity that he became vital to the team effort that brought the computer into service. Later in life he was deeply involved in all of Wilkes's major building projects, *viz.* the Titan project, the CAP computer and the Cambridge Digital Ring. Throughout his period of service in the Laboratory he was considered the 'intellectual' in the Laboratory who could solve seemingly intractable problems but at the same time he was a practical engineer who could design computers and systems that worked – a rare gift.

He wrote many of the programs for EDSAC that made up the remarkable library of subroutines that was so invaluable to users. His description of the subroutine is a classic in the precise use of language. In his words: 'A subroutine … is an entity of its own within a program.' After EDSAC was operational Wheeler worked in the USA for two years at the University of Illinois at Urbana-Champaign and wrote the early programs for the Illiac computer and helped to commission it. He returned to the Mathematical Laboratory in time to play another vitally important role in the construction and commissioning of EDSAC 2.

Away from his computer-building skills he was extremely well known for his work on algorithms and two of them are widely recognised to this day, *viz.* The Burrows–Wheeler Transform for data compression and the Tiny Encryption Algorithm (TEA). His ideas on data compression were first formulated in 1978, some ten years before the topic was re-visited by his research student Mike Burrows for his PhD research project. Later Burrows and Wheeler worked together at the Digital Equipment Corporation's Systems Research Centre where they tested the algorithm comprehensively and published it as a company research report. Following this exposure the Burrows–Wheeler transformation received more and more attention and is recognised today as an outstanding contribution to computer science. Later, working with Needham, he developed an encryption technique known as the Tiny Encryption Algorithm (TEA), and made it freely available to anyone who wished to use it provided they informed the inventors of the nature of the application for which it was being considered. The algorithm, with just eight lines of code, was so simple to use that it was widely adopted and it continues to be used to this day. Another example of Wheeler's seemingly effortless but highly original contributions arose in the field of radio astronomy. In his Nobel Prize lecture Professor Sir Martin Ryle wrote 'the development by Dr David Wheeler of the Mathematical Laboratory of the fast Fourier transform (incidentally some six years before these methods came into general use) made possible the efficient reduction of the 7.9m and 1.7m surveys….'

In his academic career he worked on a wide variety of projects and did not follow any unifying theme of research. He had an unquenchable enthusiasm for 'solving problems' – on most occasions other people's problems. He said of himself that

Wedding photograph of David and Joyce (née Blackler) Wheeler taken in 1957.

Chapter Four: Maurice Wilkes and the EDSACs

he had spent most of his life helping people to use computers, improving programs, doing hardware design and occasionally writing clever algorithms. Most of his contributions were developed from first principles and were entirely unique and some were minor works of sheer genius. One of his former students, later a distinguished professor himself, remarked that supervision from David Wheeler left him in a haze in his first year, but in the second year every word Wheeler spoke brought wisdom and clarity. Wheeler supervised a number of exceptionally gifted students and brought out the best in them. They included Roger Needham, Andy Hopper, Bjarne Stroustrup and Michael Burrows, to name just a few. He wrote very few papers in his long career but each one of these is a model of originality and precision. The mathematician Sir Peter Swinnerton-Dyer asserted in a recent interview that 'Wheeler was a genius with the remarkable ability to be ahead of the field in his thinking'. He also remarked that Wheeler had published the smallest number of papers among those elected to a Fellowship of the Royal Society in modern times.

Wheeler was elected to a Research Fellowship at Trinity College, Cambridge, after he had completed his PhD. He was appointed an Assistant Director of Research at the Mathematical Laboratory in 1956 and promoted to Reader in Computer Science in 1966. In 1977 he was promoted to Professor of Computer Science and in 1981 he was elected to a Fellowship of the Royal Society. He was awarded the 1985 Computer Pioneer Award for Assembly Language Programming. In 2003 he was inducted into the Hall of Fellows at the Computer History Museum in California. He died in 2004.

David Wheeler (right) and Bill Gates on the occasion of the announcement of the benefaction of £12 million from the William H Gates Foundation to the University on 7 October 1998. The glass brick, engraved with the first program written by David Wheeler, was presented to Bill Gates.

inspect EDSAC which was still under construction. The company came to the conclusion that the Cambridge project had great potential and backed their judgment with an offer of a grant to Wilkes of £3,000 with no strings attached as well as the services of an engineer paid for by the company. Ernest Lanaerts was sent to assist Wilkes and to give Lyons up-to-date information on the progress of EDSAC. A cheque for £3,000 from Lyons was sent promptly. The University rewarded Wilkes by increasing the resources provided to the Mathematical Laboratory, increasing his salary and appointing him to the much-coveted 'permanent position' of Director of the Mathematical Laboratory. This increase in support enabled Wilkes to press ahead at an even greater pace with the construction of EDSAC.

The Lyons Board of Directors came to the conclusion that there would be commercial benefit to the company in manufacturing and selling computers designed for use in business. They decided to make computers themselves with EDSAC as the prototype and thus LEO Computers (Lyons Electronic Office) was established. The company recruited John Pinkerton, a Cambridge graduate who knew Wilkes, and he became the key figure in the company's aspirations to create a computer business based on EDSAC. From the beginning the plan was that LEO Computers would make a modified version of EDSAC appropriate for commercial and clerical operations, though the Board of Directors hesitated from giving formal authority to proceed until they had witnessed a demonstration of EDSAC in operation. This happened in May 1949 and J Lyons immediately decided to go ahead with constructing a computer and launching LEO Computers Ltd. This interaction between the Mathematical Laboratory and industry set a precedent for collaboration with industry which continues to this day in the Computer Laboratory.

During the construction phases of the Lyons computer there was a great deal of collaboration between LEO Computers and the Mathematical Laboratory. The key people in the Mathematical Laboratory were Eric Mutch, who was recruited by Wilkes to be the principal administrator in the Laboratory, and David Wheeler. They had very significant roles in the effective transfer of EDSAC technology to industry. This transfer of know-how to Lyons ensured that EDSAC was the first research computer to become a prototype for a commercial machine.

LEO Computers built and marketed machines based on the EDSAC architecture in a series designated LEO I, LEO II and LEO III until it merged with the English Electric Co in 1963 to form English Electric LEO Computers Ltd. This company eventually became part of ICL, which manufactured computers in the UK until it was acquired by the Japanese company, Fujitsu.

WILKES AND THE EDSAC TEAM

Maurice Wilkes needed a team of many talents to construct and commission EDSAC as a working computer for general use. He had to employ electronic and mechanical engineers to build the machine and maintenance engineers to keep the machine operational despite the inherent unreliability of electronic components in the 1950s. He needed mathematicians to write the software for the computer and staff to manage the growing complexity of the project and assist inexperienced users.

He began with P F Farmer, who was capable of doing some of the mechanical construction, and with his friend Tommy Gold, who was helping with the design of the mercury delay lines. A little later he obtained a grant from the Department of Scientific and Industrial Research (DSIR) which enabled him to appoint W (Bill) Renwick in May 1947. Renwick had worked with Tommy Gold and was an experienced electronic engineer and he made a major contribution to the construction and commissioning of EDSAC. G J Stevens was employed as an instrument maker and shortly afterwards S A Barton was appointed as an electronic technician. R S Piggott, L J Foreman and P Chamberlain were some of the other technicians in the group. All of them made significant contributions to the construction of EDSAC. A number of women worked in the laboratory. C Mumford was a Brunsviga machine operator. E McKee, later Breakwell was a Senior EDSAC operator, V Webber and R Hill were also trained EDSAC operators. J Steel, R Bonham-Carter and H Gordon provided invaluable support to the burgeoning research staff. For Wilkes and his team the years 1947 and 1948 were full of hard work on the construction of EDSAC with no assurance of a successful outcome. The scale and nature of the project was such that it became well known and many visitors came to see what was going on in the Mathematical Laboratory. As the complexity of the enterprise increased Wilkes felt the need for more careful record-keeping and more thorough project management and so he appointed E N (Eric) Mutch to manage the project. Another member of the staff was Donald (D W) Willis, who worked on the magnetic tape deck with Wilkes before leaving to join the commercial company, Decca Radar. The project attracted a small number of student volunteers who helped with the construction of the computer. Among them was David (D J) Wheeler, who joined the Mathematical Laboratory as a research student in September 1948.

While construction was the first priority Wilkes did not neglect other academic duties and started a colloquia series which were attended by increasingly large numbers. One of the important roles played by the Mathematical Laboratory was to disseminate the ideas and news of progress in computing as widely as possible. The colloquia also brought groups of computer scientists in other universities and in industry into contact with each other and created new activity in computer science. This initiative by Wilkes was an important contribution nationally and internationally. Ben Noble, who was responsible for the operation of the differential analyser and the Mallock machine, also organised coloquia. Other than Wheeler, the student volunteers working on the construction of the computer were V Hale and B Haselgrove. There were also two unestablished 'boys' (I quote), a part-time cleaner and, unofficially, Professor Hartree.

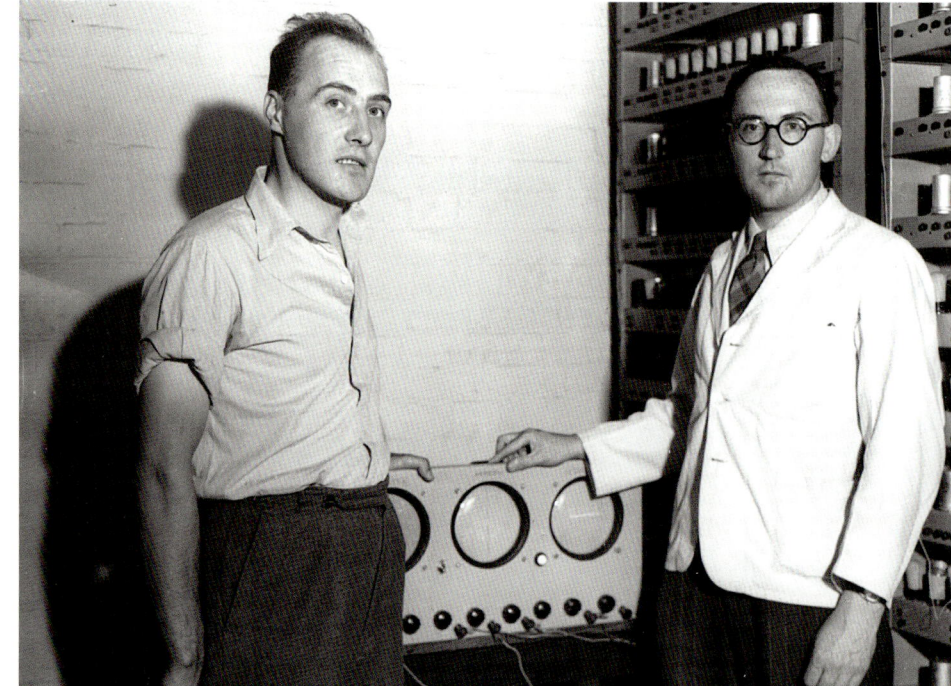

Bill Renwick and Wilkes with EDSAC. Renwick was a key member of Wilkes's team and supervised the design and construction of the EDSAC machines.

Chapter Four: Maurice Wilkes and the EDSACs

Posed photograph of Wilkes (kneeling) and his team working on EDSAC. The group on the left are G J Stevens, J Bennett and S A Barton. On the right with Wilkes are P Farmer, W Rennick and R Piggott.

In 1950, research students working in the Laboratory included S Gill, A S Douglas, B Worseley and E S Page, although they were not all registered with the Mathematical Laboratory. Willis left the Laboratory and R A Brooker joined the staff in the same year. Members of the Laboratory and users were given the responsibility to care for the machine and to help each other to use the machine effectively. Personal reminiscences of those who worked on EDSAC, EDSAC 2 and Titan were recorded in 1999, when the 50th anniversary of the birth of EDSAC was celebrated. There is a booklet entitled 'EDSAC 99' which includes the reminiscences and they are also recorded on the website of the Computer Laboratory. The entries make interesting and amusing reading and demonstrate the relaxed and welcoming atmosphere in the Mathematical Laboratory in the 1950s.

Let Us Build Another Computer and Call It EDSAC 2

The successful operation of EDSAC in 1949 confirmed that the stored-program concept was sound and that its design was the proper basis for the development of computers. Wilkes and his team immediately started to think of making a second-generation computer. Wilkes also noted that the availability of EDSAC in day-to-day operation had varied considerably. At times the machine had given an excellent service but overall there were too many occasions when it had failed to work for more than a few hours. He argued that this was not surprising considering that EDSAC had been built as an experimental machine. He believed that a computer could be constructed which would not only perform to a higher technical specification than EDSAC but would also be more reliable. His team was confident that the methods used for manufacturing the electronics for EDSAC had been satisfactory and could be used again with only a few improvements. After some debate they decided that the mercury delay line memory with which they had acquired considerable experience should be used in the new computer.

Unlike his experience with EDSAC Wilkes realised that before he could embark upon a new project he would need a considerable sum of money. He consulted his ally, Douglas Hartree, and following a suggestion from him obtained a grant of £25,000 from the Nuffield Foundation in 1951. The sum was sufficient for the team to make a start on EDSAC 2.

57

'THE BEST WAY TO DESIGN AN AUTOMATIC CALCULATING MACHINE'

The problem of poor overall reliability was inherent in any large and complex system built with the electronics available in the 1950s. The active components, thermionic valves, were much more prone to failure than the transistors and integrated circuits that were used later to make computers. Discrete passive components such as resistors and capacitors soldered together by hand to form circuits were also prone to frequent failure. Their nominal values could change with time and the components could also fail catastrophically by becoming either open-circuit or short-circuit. Poorly soldered joints caused serious problems because the failure was particularly hard to detect. Wilkes came to the conclusion that a solution to the problem of poor reliability would be a substantial breakthrough for computers and he argued in a lecture entitled 'The Best Way to Design an Automatic Calculating Machine' that 'the first consideration for the designer [of a computer] at the present time, is how he is to achieve the maximum degree of reliability in a machine'. He could do little to make the individual components more reliable, and therefore proposed that the problem could be greatly alleviated by using a parallel design of arithmetic units with a repetition of identical units of electronics. He stated that exactly the same arithmetic units could be built in separate chassis, each containing, for example, one stage of an adder and one flip-flop for each of the various registers which could be coupled together as necessary. Other parts of the circuitry could be organised in a similar manner. In effect he had proposed a new configuration for computer electronic hardware as a means of overcoming the lack of reliability. His approach was not of great relevance to commercial computers and its significance was not recognised. However, many years after he had proposed it and used it to construct EDSAC 2, it was used in microprocessors as a simplification of the design of computer logic. In this context the technique was called the 'bit-sliced principle'.

Wilkes and his chief engineer Renwick started designing the computer just as Wheeler returned, after an absence of two years in the USA, to join the EDSAC 2 team. Renwick was given the responsibility for the project

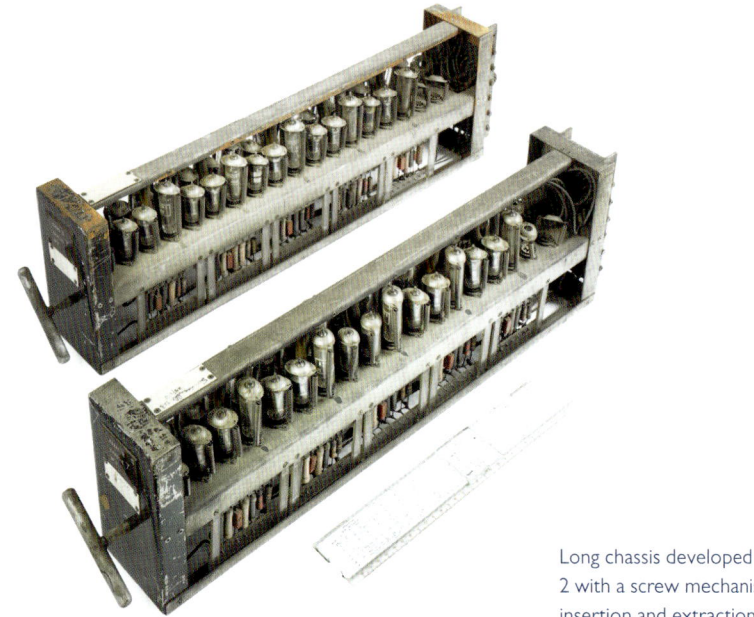

Long chassis developed for EDSAC 2 with a screw mechanism for rapid insertion and extraction.

engineering while Wheeler was made responsible for all programming activities. Wilkes had created the ideal partnership and EDSAC 2 began to take shape. EDSAC was used to design some elements of the new computer and also for devising the wiring schedules of the electronics. This was probably the first example of a computer being used to design its replacement! Some of the technical problems identified in EDSAC were overcome by careful redesign and better construction. Others, such as the gradual deterioration with time of the performance of the thermionic valves and discrete components such as resistors, were compensated for by designing circuits conservatively

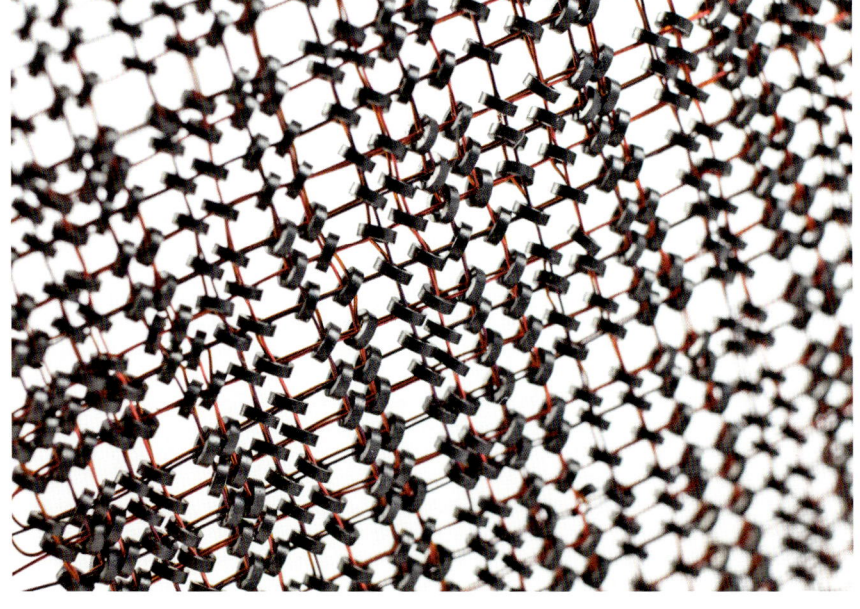

Ferrite cores used in the memory for EDSAC 2.

with large operating margins. Stability of power supplies was improved and Wilkes insisted that the purpose of the project was to build a computer that could provide a reliable service rather than to optimise the design of computers.

Microprogramming and the Magnetic Core Memory

The designers of the new computer recognised that the fast parallel arithmetic unit for EDSAC 2 would be truly beneficial only if it could be matched with memory of compatible speed. They knew from their experience with EDSAC that the mercury delay line memory was too slow for their plans. Fortunately magnetic core memories became available just in time and the electronics company Mullard Ltd was interested in manufacturing and supplying ferrite cores to the Mathematical Laboratory. Wilkes purchased the memory for a sum of £5,000 and in addition to the main memory of 1,024 words, a read-only memory – in which information was permanently wired – was constructed as a 'reserved store'. The reserved store contained 768 read-only words and an additional 64 words that were read/write. This subsidiary memory contributed significantly to the speed of operation of EDSAC 2 by eliminating the loading times for frequently used library subroutines.

Microprogramming was the most important of the many contributions made by Wilkes to computer science and technology. In planning the control sections of EDSAC it was apparent to him that a good deal of random logic was needed for these operations. He came to the conclusion that by turning a control unit into a miniature computer controlled by conditional microinstructions he could greatly enhance the operating speed of the computer and increase the set of instructions it would perform. This 'microprogramming' was separated from the main programming and became a strikingly original feature of EDSAC 2. Almost all parts of the machine, the input by paper-tape, the output, the magnetic tape decks, floating-point arithmetic, the read/write cycle in the main memory and much more could be controlled by a single microprogram. In fact some 80 sets of gates in the machine were controlled in this manner. A magnetic core memory of 1,024 words was used for storing the microprogram in EDSAC 2. Wilkes's concept of microprogramming was implemented by David Wheeler with meticulous care and attention to detail.

Magnetic core panels used in EDSAC 2 displayed by Chris Hadley, standing beside the Relics display cabinet. He is responsible for the care of the relics retained in the Computer Laboratory.

Above: EDSAC 2 in operation in October 1959. V Webber (later Barron) seated at the console. M Mutch standing in the background and E Swann (later Howe) punching input tape.

Cambridge Computing: The First 75 Years

Implementing microprogramming with circuits built using thermionic valves was a difficult task for the team. It was therefore necessary to make the maximum possible use of the microprogram in order to obtain full value from the investment of time and effort in Wilkes's innovation.

Naming the Computers

Once the decision had been made to make a second computer it was necessary to find a name for it. In the end it was designated, rather unimaginatively, EDSAC 2. Opinions have been expressed that EDSAC 2 did not receive the publicity and acclaim that it deserved and its novel features, particularly microprogramming, were not recognised because outside observers thought it to be merely an enhanced version of EDSAC. A new acronym incorporating microprogramming might have been more appropriate.

It is worth noting that there was also an EDSAC 1.5 which became operational before EDSAC 2 was completed. This version lasted for only a few months but served some useful purposes. The design of EDSAC 2 was checked by loading a small microprogram matrix with just 48 cores. This machine was used by Dr Joyce Wheeler (née Blackler) for her PhD research in astronomy under the supervision of Professor Fred Hoyle.

Arithmetic Unit, Instruction Set, Input of Instructions and Tape Readers

The word length for EDSAC 2 was 40 bits, with 20-bit instructions. Seven bits in an instruction constituted the operation, two bits specified a modifier register and 11 bits the address. The computer was designed to have floating point operations, and a substantial part of the microprogram consisted of microinstructions for implementing the individual steps of floating point addition, multiplication and division. The instruction set and input routine were both designed by David Wheeler. A program could be read into the computer at one of two locally developed paper-tape readers. These had a continuously rotating capstan drive which could read tapes at speeds up to 1,000 rows of holes per second and come to an instant stop when required. High speed was essential because input and output were not buffered and the time for which they were operational interrupted valuable computing time. Magnetic tape decks

Left: The commercial Elliot machine was developed from the tape reader designed in the Mathematical Laboratory.

Below: Valve extractor used to speed up the repair of defective chassis removed from the racks.

60

purchased from a commercial company, Decca Radar, were also attached to EDSAC 2. These improvements, together with the 16K memory store, meant that bigger jobs could be carried out and a high-level computer language could be implemented on the computer. The basic research for these magnetic tape decks had been carried out in the Mathematical Laboratory by D W Willis before he left Cambridge to join Decca Radar. In the course of EDSAC 2's life more output devices were added. These included a line printer, curve plotter, photographic imager and high-speed paper-tape punches.

Speed of Operation, Program Diagnostics and Hardware Maintenance

EDSAC 2 was a good deal faster than EDSAC. Wilkes stated that an indication of the speed of EDSAC 2 can be obtained from the following measurements made on the computer. An add or subtract instruction took between 17 and 42µs (fixed point) and between 100 and 270µs (floating point) while an add-product instruction took between 270 and 330µs (fixed point) and between 210 and 340µs (floating point). These times were up to ten times shorter than those for comparable operations with EDSAC.

Wheeler built a number of program diagnostic aids into the operating system which were invaluable to programmers for debugging their programs and essential to the machine maintenance staff for diagnosing machine malfunctions. A fault-tracing routine was implemented for EDSAC 2 partly in the microprogram and partly in the reserved store.

The problem of hardware maintenance in a machine that was expected to operate for 24 hours a day, seven days a week was also addressed by the designers. The greater part of the electronics for EDSAC 2 consisted of circuits built in a bit-sliced configuration. There were 40 arithmetic slices and 11 control slices, each packaged in a single plug-in unit. When a fault was detected in a unit it could be replaced promptly with a spare unit while the original unit was sent off to be repaired. Fault finding was not easy in those days when the only test equipment available was a multimeter

The Mathematical Laboratory staff in May 1949. Top row, from left: D Willis, J Stanley, L Foreman, G Stevens, S Barton, P Farmer, P Chamberlain. Middle row, from left: H Smith, C Mumford, H Pye, A Thomas, E McKee, J Steel. Bottom row, from left: R Bonham-Carter, E Mutch, W Renwick, M Wilkes, J Bennett, D Wheeler, B Worsley.

and an oscilloscope. Thermionic valves were often changed sequentially until the faulty device was located. Experience with the running of EDSAC 2 confirmed that this attention to hardware maintenance greatly enhanced the time for which the computer was available to users.

By 1958 EDSAC 2 was beginning to take over much of the load from EDSAC and on 11 July 1958 EDSAC was formally shut down without much ceremony. Because of the shortage of space in the Laboratory, the computer was dismantled and most of its parts were sold as scrap; very little remains today of this historic machine. Wilkes was not to know how famous he and his computer would become in the fullness of time.

As soon as it became available EDSAC 2 was heavily used by members of the University and its limitations began to be exposed as more demanding applications came to the fore. One significant limitation was the size of the memory compared with the memory sizes available in computers elsewhere. It was difficult to expand the memory in EDSAC 2 because the computer had been designed specifically for the small size of memory available in 1958, *viz.*: 1,024 words together with a read-only memory of 768 words plus 64 normal words (read and write). After much effort by Wheeler and Wilkes a comparatively large memory extension of 16K words was patched on to EDSAC 2 in 1962. The new memory was bought from Ampex with a grant of £10,000 obtained from the Nuffield Foundation.

A somewhat unusual contribution from Cambridge arose out of the work of the diploma student, Jeff Hillmore, who wrote a business game to run on EDSAC 2. This program attracted many users, including Her Majesty's Treasury! EDSAC 2 continued to serve the University until 1965 when it was switched off, thus ending an important phase in the history of the Mathematical Laboratory when it concentrated largely on building computers. In retrospect the principal historical importance of EDSAC 2 is that it established beyond doubt the advantages of microprogramming as a basis for computer design. In time microprogramming would be used very widely in computers built with transistors. The giant computer company IBM learned of microprogramming from Wilkes and adopted it in its System 360 range of computers.

Applications of EDSAC and EDSAC 2

The EDSACs were designed and constructed to be used by scientists and mathematicians. Cambridge academics working in astronomy, wave mechanics, economics, crystallography, biological molecule structure determination and radio astronomy sought access to the computers, and many research projects benefited significantly from calculations carried out on them. John Bennett, Wilkes's first research student, who had earlier played a major part in the design and construction of the main control unit, developed a system that employed Stanley Gill's Runge–Kutta subroutine to solve differential equations, using an interpretive program structure to save space. Bennett also started to work on the programs necessary for x-ray crystallography patterns to be interpreted in terms of crystalline structure. Equally as important as access to computers was the helpful attitude of the programmers in the Mathematical Laboratory who generously made their services available to inexperienced users.

Ronald Fisher, later Sir Ronald Fisher, a statistician working in the field of genetics, was an influential figure in the University and a member of the committee which was appointed to oversee the activities of the Mathematical Laboratory. Following a presentation at which Wilkes described the capability of EDSAC Fisher challenged Wilkes to find a solution to a problem that he had encountered. He was trying to determine gene frequencies and the problem gave rise to a seemingly intractable differential equation. This was a difficult problem but Wilkes was anxious to impress Fisher and accepted the challenge. He passed the problem to Wheeler as part of his PhD research. Wheeler succeeded in solving the problem and Fisher was duly impressed when shown the results. The publication describing Fisher's work on genetics with the aid of EDSAC is now regarded as one of the seminal papers in genetics. Another scientist, Peter Naur, used numerical integration to find the equations of motion for a minor planet. He compared the work done by hand taking two hours for each step to working with EDSAC which required just five seconds once the initial programs had been written. He remarked 'the memory of the machine is so large'.

When the Mathematical Laboratory was founded in 1937 it had been anticipated that economists would wish to use computational techniques and this proved to be the case. The EDSACs were used by a number of economists; among them was Richard Stone, later Professor Sir Richard Stone, who produced a model for the first British National Accounts. He was awarded the Nobel Prize in 1984. The x-ray crystallography group in the Cavendish Laboratory was another user of the EDSACs. John Kendrew, later Sir John Kendrew, used EDSAC for the complex calculations which were required for his research on the structure of myoglobin. He was awarded the Nobel Prize in 1962. In the field of radio astronomy Martin Ryle, later Professor Sir Martin Ryle, used the EDSACs for his work on the technique of aperture synthesis and remarked that progress in his field of work closely followed the progress of computing power. Ryle was awarded the Nobel Prize in 1974. Another major user of the EDSACs was the theoretical chemist Frank (S F) Boys. He had been sceptical about the value of digital computers in solving the types of mathematical functions that he was encountering. Later he used EDSAC to some extent but it was not until more powerful computers had become available that he benefited from their use in his work.

The number of applications to use EDSAC began to increase once its capabilities were widely recognised. Research students told supervisors of the benefits of carrying out calculations by using a computer. Supervisors moved from scepticism to encouraging more of their students to explore the benefits of computation. One of the early users, Dr Joyce Wheeler, asserted that 'the Cambridge college system, which has people working in different disciplines meet regularly, helped to spread the news of EDSAC's possibilities and aroused the interest of academics'. Eventually it became necessary to find some way of allocating time on the computer in an orderly manner. A Priorities Committee was set up with Mutch as Secretary. It acted more as a technical committee than a time-allocating body and approved projects on scientific merit giving a time allocation to the approved user. It is said that it did not reject a single application in the course of its existence. Hartree was a key member of this committee who assessed most of the projects and gave sound advice on numerical methods and computational strategy. Expertise in programming increased across the University and programmers were recruited onto the staff of larger departments to work on scientific projects. The computers became more and more a 'service' to the University and numerous scientific papers were published in which the EDSACs had played some part. A queue of users would form each morning and waited patiently for their turn to feed their tape into the computer. If the computer broke down the atmosphere became rather tense, as users worried about finishing on time. Mutch managed the whole enterprise with great efficiency and was appointed to the position of Superintendent of Computing Services in 1961.

From the very early days of the operation of EDSAC, Wilkes had realised that programming a computer was not a straightforward matter. He wrote 'that the good part of the remainder of my life was going to be spent in finding errors in my own programs'. In the summer of 1950 the Mathematical Laboratory prepared a comprehensive report on the methods and the experiences of users of EDSAC. Mutch was charged with carrying out most of the work necessary to prepare the report. Copies were circulated to users and became cherished possessions because of the help they provided in preparing programs to run on EDSAC. This report was later published together with additional material as a book by the then small American publishing company Addison-Wesley under the title *The Preparation of Programs for an Electronic Digital Computer* by Wilkes, Wheeler and Gill. It is recognised today as the first book to have been published on computer programming and it was used for many years to teach programming in Cambridge.

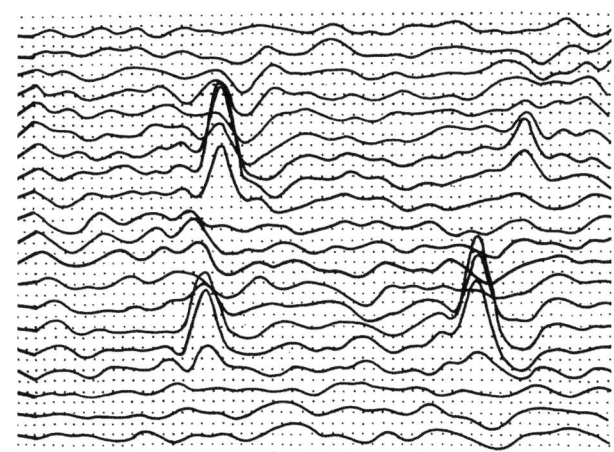

An example of embryonic computer graphics on EDSAC 2: a radio-astronomy map showing two radio sources displayed as cross-sections of the sky brightness distribution and photographed from a CRT screen. (Elizabeth Waldram, Research Assistant, 1962)

Cambridge Computing: The First 75 Years

Peter Crofts putting up a plaque to commemorate EDSAC on the Arup Building during the EDSAC 50th anniversary celebration.

1965 – 20TH ANNIVERSARY OF WILKES'S APPOINTMENT AS DIRECTOR

Wilkes had been Director of the Mathematical Laboratory for 20 years when EDSAC 2 was retired. His contributions were internationally recognised and belatedly acknowledged by the University of Cambridge. Nine years after he had been elected a Fellow of the Royal Society he was promoted to the Chair of Computer Technology. He chose the title to describe his perception of his contributions to the subject of computing. He felt that he had advanced computer technology very significantly, whereas others had worked on the theoretical side of the subject. He avoided 'Engineering' in his title to differentiate his Laboratory and its work from the University's Engineering Department. In making the case for his promotion, the Faculty Board of Mathematics stated 'that there can be no doubt that the importance of computer technology, both for mathematics and for science and learning generally, fully justifies the establishment of a Professorship, and that it is indeed anomalous that Cambridge has hitherto had no such Chair'. The Board added that 'Dr Wilkes's services to computer design and technology have earned him a worldwide reputation … He had contributed greatly to the theory of programming and originated many basic concepts that are now common knowledge.' The academic subject of computing and the man who had pioneered it in Cambridge were both given the acknowledgement they had long deserved.

By 1965 the Mathematical Laboratory had grown substantially. David Wheeler, J P C Miller, Peter Swinnerton-Dyer, Eric Mutch, Margaret Mutch, David Barron, Roger Needham and David Hartley were now on the academic staff. There were also ten engineers employed to maintain the equipment. Seven PhD students and ten diploma students were carrying out research in the Laboratory and the number of users was more than 50. But it still operated with a relatively informal management structure. Today, users recall with some disbelief the dangers from bare wires at high voltage and unguarded electronics racks operating at 350 volts in the 1940s. Jennifer Leech recalls being 'woken sharply by an electric shock. A little investigation revealed an unprotected rheostat, at mains voltage, under the table. My bare knee had been pressing against it!'

64

Chapter Four: Maurice Wilkes and the EDSACs

There were still long queues of users waiting to load their programs when EDSAC 2 was in its last few days of existence and a new computer, Titan, was in operation. Eventually, on 1 November 1965, EDSAC 2 was switched off with due ceremony. The abiding memory of the moment for members of the Laboratory present on the occasion was a roomful of people all dressed in black or wearing black ties, a funeral wreath made from paper-tapes, a funeral oration, and a final program punched on black tape caused EDSAC 2 to play 'The Last Post'. There was even a display of emotion from some as EDSAC 2 was closed down.

Speaking at the 50th anniversary of the birth of EDSAC, Robin Milner, Head of the Computer Laboratory, said of the early achievements, 'This was a miracle, for so it now seems.' In 2012 Andy Hopper recalled Wilkes's thoughts on those early days in a conversation in his office a few years before Wilkes's death in 2009. 'The Mathematical Laboratory was a pioneering research centre which made available to users the fruits of its research as a service. In those days users had no idea of the computing facilities that could be created for them.'

The Mathematical Laboratory Staff in 1956.

The University Mathematical Laboratory, Cambridge
June 1956

R.W.Farmer, H.Goodman, A.C.Smith, I.Reynolds, J.Leech, D.Fairburn, D.F.Mayers, H.G.Martin, J.Jones, B.G.Millis, I.Shavitt, D.Monsey, R.Gaenserich,
J.E.A.Barter, R.Benn, J.Blacker, V.Webber, P.W.Waldock, S.A.Barton, G.J.Stevens, V.Claydon, H.L.Norris, N.W.P.Unwin, R.Kimpton, M.Brown, A.Gladwell, K.Covill,
C.Froese, A.S.Douglas, V.E.Treasure, M.O.Mutch, E.N.Mutch, D.J.Wheeler, M.V.Wilkes, W.Renwick, C.B.Haselgrove, J.Haselgrove, C.M.Munford, S.Wilkinson, C.H.Lindsay.

Absent: Lady Hoskyns, G.K.Letellier, J.C.P.Miller, C.E.Phelps, S.W.Rossiter.

CHAPTER FIVE

Maurice Wilkes

New Directions of Research and the End of an Era

The Titan Deal

The Mathematical Laboratory went through a period of transition following the successful commissioning of EDSAC 2. Its predecessor, EDSAC, had created a University-wide demand for computing and by 1960 there was increasing pressure on the Laboratory to provide a better service to users. Numbers had grown steadily to almost 200 users of EDSAC 2. Wilkes was aware that a significantly more powerful computer would shortly be needed, and he was conscious that either he would have to build a computer using transistors in place of the outdated valves (electron tubes) or he would have to purchase a machine from a commercial company.

The timing was propitious for purchasing a commercial machine because the University Grants Committee (a government-funded body which allocated resources to universities in the UK) had announced an initiative encouraging applications from universities wishing to install general-purpose computers. Wilkes's application to purchase a computer for the service was successful and he decided to purchase the Atlas computer which had been developed by a team at Manchester University and was marketed by Ferranti Ltd. Unfortunately Ferranti's asking price (believed to be in the region of £2 million) far exceeded the £250,000 that the University Grants Committee was able to allocate to Cambridge University. The University authorities agreed to supplement this sum with a grant of £100,000 from general funds, but despite this subvention the total amount available was wholly inadequate. Wilkes had received representations from some of the major users of the service that he should purchase an IBM machine to make it easier for them to collaborate with their scientific peers in the USA but he did not consider this option feasible because of the high cost of an IBM system.

Ferranti's management learned, with regret, that Wilkes could not raise the money to purchase the Atlas machine but the company did not wish to forego the possibility of collaborating with the outstanding team of computer experts at the Mathematical Laboratory. As a consequence the two parties negotiated a somewhat unusual compromise. Ferranti offered to supply the standard units of the Atlas, comprising the basic central processor, at an affordable price, providing they could take part in a project to design and commission a 'reduced performance' version of the Atlas for the University. Ferranti's expectation was that the Cambridge machine would serve as a prototype for a commercial computer which the company could manufacture and sell as Atlas 2, a low-cost, reduced-specification model of Atlas 1. The proposal was a nice compromise, giving the Mathematical Laboratory the opportunity to apply its acknowledged expertise on behalf of Ferranti while acquiring, in return, a powerful computer for the University. The deal was sealed, and ICT (International Computers and Tabulators), which had acquired Ferranti's computer business, suggested that the collaboration should be called the 'Titan project'. Wilkes recruited W S (Bill) Elliot as Senior Project Engineer to coordinate the project and to deliver it successfully within the approved budget.

The project's objective was to develop a batch-processing, multi-processing computer in which users would load their programs using either cards or tape, and return later to collect the results. The machine was optimised to handle a variety of jobs of different sizes and complexities concurrently. It had a relatively small main memory but this was supplemented with a large magnetic tape backing store. The most significant and demanding part of the Titan project was a new operating system to

Chapter Five: Maurice Wilkes: New Directions of Research and the End of an Era

Titan under construction, viewed from the public gallery.

be designed *ab initio* because the memory organisations of the Titan and the Atlas were very different. It was agreed that two teams would work simultaneously on the Titan project, one based at ICT, and the other, a relatively small team, based at the Mathematical Laboratory. The principal members of the Cambridge team under Maurice Wilkes comprised: David Wheeler, who was in charge of the hardware design and also responsible for day-to-day negotiations with ICT; Roger Needham, who was responsible for writing programs to optimise the printed wiring of the equipment rack's backplane and also for the wiring schedules needed by ICT to build the rack; and David Barron, who was responsible for designing the operating system and software development until he left the Laboratory part-way through the project, at which point Needham assumed his responsibilities. At a later stage, Needham was also responsible for the design and implementation of the user subsystem as well as the user interface. Neil Wiseman was the Chief Engineer for the project. Other members of the team who made significant contributions were David Hartley, Barry Landy, Mike Guy, Sandy Fraser and Peter Swinnerton-Dyer. The two teams made good progress but their aims began to diverge as the project proceeded. ICT felt that their customers would not benefit from the multi-programming system that the Cambridge group was intent upon designing. As a consequence two different but equally successful operating systems were designed using identical hardware and software engineering.

Time-Sharing Titan – A Change of Direction

The Titan project was making good progress but, in the event, went through a dramatic change. In 1963 Wilkes proposed a radical revision of the design of Titan and the project was dramatically interrupted and diverted in a different direction. Wilkes's intervention followed his extended visit to the USA, where he was able to use the Compatible Time-Sharing System (CTSS) that MIT had developed. He recognised, with his usual unerring judgment, that simultaneous multiple-user access and time-sharing systems would be the future of computing with a mainframe computer. He explained to his colleagues that with the CTSS the user could sit at a terminal in his office at MIT to enter the program directly into the computer, edit and run it. Programs would then be immediately executed and the results received back on the same terminal. Dozens of users were able to work simultaneously without having to leave their offices or laboratories. Convenience to the user was so extraordinary compared with the batch-processing approach that there was no doubt in his mind that time-sharing would very rapidly replace the batch-entry method. He argued that in the environment of Cambridge University in which large numbers of users could work on terminals in many different locations on a diversity of projects, a time-sharing system would be ideal. It would utilise the full capacity of the powerful Titan computer. He therefore proposed that the batch-processing system under development for Titan should be abandoned in favour of a time-sharing system.

The initial reaction of Wilkes's colleagues was consternation and some degree of apprehension. At least one strongly dissenting voice was raised arguing that there would be considerable delay in implementing the project and there was a serious risk of total failure. It was argued that resources in Cambridge for writing software were limited compared with the resources that MIT had been able to provide. It was also asserted that the user service had not been satisfactory in the final stages of operating EDSAC 2 and delays in implementing Titan would make the service totally unacceptable to users. In the end, however, all objections were put aside and Wilkes's colleagues were persuaded that he was foreseeing the future of computing and, notwithstanding the formidable challenges that would inevitably arise, they changed the design of Titan to accommodate time-sharing. Their willingness to adopt this new direction was based, to

The Titan memory unit rack. The inset shows more detail.

Chapter Five: Maurice Wilkes: New Directions of Research and the End of an Era

some extent, on their belief that they, as a research-driven group, should always be trying to do something better and different. In other words they just could not resist a challenge! Needham now became the de facto leader of the project under Wilkes. The collaborative relationship with ICT totally collapsed.

The change of direction affected both hardware and software architectures. A large disc store, capable of storing 40 million characters, was now essential and it was purchased for a sum of £75,000. A memory protection system which would enable many user programs to coexist safely in the memory of the computer was needed, and David Wheeler rose to the challenge, designing an elegant and cost-effective scheme for the purpose. It was also necessary to provide a multiplexer to connect dozens of terminals to the computer and for this task the well-established partnership between Wilkes and Wheeler again proved very effective. Wilkes sketched out a preliminary design which Wheeler and the rest of the team transformed into a detailed hardware design. The core of the Cambridge team consisted originally of David Barron, David Hartley and Barry Landy. Needham replaced Barron as team leader, and the team was augmented as work progressed by additional staff (Sandy Fraser and Mike Guy) and a number of research students, all contributing significant parts of the software. Hartley wrote the kernel of the operating system and later the user control mechanism. Landy developed many of the internal parts as well as establishing a low-fault maintenance regime. Fraser conceived and designed the automatic filing system with a provision for backup and archiving on magnetic tape; he also worked on controlling the privacy of files in a time-sharing system. Needham and Barry Landy wrote the disc control interface. Contributions from research students included the magnetic-tape scheduler by Peter Radford and the interactive text editor by Steve Bourne.

The development of Titan was proceeding at a relatively slow pace and Wilkes suggested to Peter Swinnerton-Dyer that he should write a Temporary Supervisor (Operating System) to enable the computer to come into service. Swinnerton-Dyer wrote the complete operating system with assembler and compiler over the Long Vacation period, and when it was installed it worked almost immediately. Just four 'slips of the pen' were noticed and easily corrected. The computer was operational in 1964 and in November 1965 EDSAC 2 was switched off.

The Temporary Supervisor designed by Swinnerton-Dyer was replaced a few months later by a new Titan Main Supervisor. Needham invented a system of scrambling and

Below right: Peter Swinnerton-Dyer (later Sir Peter Swinnerton-Dyer) worked on EDSAC 2 and later on Titan. Initially opposed to Wilkes's proposal to adopt time-sharing on Titan, he later helped to ensure the success of the project.

Below: The original building of the Mathematical Laboratory was demolished and a new building known as the Arup Building was constructed in 1969. Titan was lifted by a crane into its new location.

69

storing passwords for the Titan computer which has since been widely adopted elsewhere. All members of the team made significant and timely contributions and the huge engineering challenge to build a general-purpose computer in the Mathematical Laboratory was successfully met. High-level languages such as Autocode and Fortran were installed on Titan to the benefit of the multitude of users who now had access to the machine. From 1967 Titan operated as a multiple-access system, 24 hours a day, seven days a week, serving the whole of the University community. The Mathematical Laboratory could now justifiably claim that Cambridge University had one of the best computing services anywhere in the country. In 1968 the Superintendent of the service, E N (Eric) Mutch, reported that there were 200 registered users of the multiple-access system. The Atlas 2 computer, of which Titan was the prototype, was developed by ICL (the successor of ICT) but only two other machines were sold before ICL introduced a new range of mainframe computers.

New Directions of Research

Once Titan had been successfully commissioned Wilkes decided to explore new directions of research, and four major projects occupied his time and his leadership for the final 15 years of his career at the University: Computer Graphics and Computer-Aided Design, the CAP computer, the Cambridge Digital Ring and the Cambridge Distributed System. Right up to the end of his working life in the University he was active in leading research into new areas of computer science and technology.

Computer Graphics and Computer-Aided Design

In 1965 the newly commissioned Titan computer was the centrepiece of the Laboratory's assets. It was working well and serving the community of users satisfactorily. In this year Wilkes received a sizeable grant from the Science Research Council to exploit the computing resources and expertise that he had built up over two decades. Funding was awarded for 'Research in Computer Science', leaving the choice of research topics entirely to Wilkes, which created a golden opportunity for him and his team to branch out into new directions of research. Speaking about the grant, at the 50th anniversary celebrations of the commissioning of EDSAC in 1999, Roger Needham, the then recently retired Head of the Computer Laboratory, described the flexibility given to Wilkes as a 'contrast with the Swindon bureaucracy of today with its deliverables, beneficiaries, progress charts, milestones, millstones, and you have to go into industry to avoid that now – *experto crede*'. Wilkes used some of the money to buy a DEC PDP 7 computer and Type 340 display, and the Chief Engineer, Neil Wiseman, designed a data link from the PDP 7 to the Titan and worked on screen editors using this link. This modus operandi, where a small computer accessed a much larger machine, was an early example of distributed computing.

Wilkes decided to expand the programme of research in computer science in the Mathematical Laboratory by using Titan rather than by building another bigger and better computer. In the course of a visit to the USA he had been impressed by the work on computer graphics by Ivan Sutherland, who had created the iconic 'Sketchpad', and by the interactive graphics work at Lincoln Labs and MIT which had led to the innovative computer game 'Space War'. In his laboratory in Cambridge he made the PDP 7 system available to William Newman, the son of Max Newman, who had taught him mathematics while he was an undergraduate at St John's College. William Newman was a PhD student at Imperial College, London, working on an experimental system which would enable architects to design public buildings using standard building modules. The project was a good example of the power of computer graphics and Wilkes wanted to build on the experience to move into Computer-Aided Design (CAD). He was fortunate that he met Charles Lang at MIT and discovered that he was already working

ERIC (E N) MUTCH (1921–69)

Eric Mutch was employed at TRE during the Second World War and worked closely with Wilkes from time to time. In 1947 he left TRE at Wilkes's invitation and joined the EDSAC team in Cambridge. Wilkes approached him because he had realised that better administration was required for the EDSAC project, particularly with regard to documentation and record keeping. Mutch took over the detailed management of the project and soon made his mark as an administrator. Wilkes described him as 'a man of great parts, and I came to rely very heavily on him'. Examples of the variety of tasks entrusted to Mutch give credence to Wilkes's comment.

In the summer of 1950 Wilkes prepared a draft report on EDSAC before leaving on a trip to Canada and the USA. He left the document with Mutch and asked him to complete the work. Mutch worked on the report and by the time Wilkes returned it was ready for duplication. It was published under the names of Wilkes, Wheeler and Gill. For some inexplicable reason Mutch was not included as an author.

By 1951 the number of applications to use EDSAC had increased sharply. Wilkes set up a committee with Mutch as Secretary to manage the process of allocating time on EDSAC to users. It was called the Priorities Committee but in reality it was a technical committee charged with judging the suitability of applications. The applications gave Wilkes and his colleagues a comprehensive perspective into how EDSAC was influencing scientific research in Cambridge. Mutch managed the committee with great skill and patience. Wilkes wrote: 'The efficient but unobtrusive administrative support that Mutch provided, along with good documentation of the facilities available, enabled informal collaboration to flourish between those inside the Laboratory and those outside it.' It is believed that no application was rejected during the life of the committee, and some way was always found to help those who wished to use EDSAC.

A little later Mutch was involved in the making of a film which showed the operation of EDSAC. As he had had some experience of film-making while at TRE he was appointed director of the production. Alexis Brookes, a Fellow of St John's College, provided further expertise as an experienced cameraman, and Wilkes wrote the script. The film was shown by Wilkes on a number of occasions.

In the summer of 1952 Mutch went to MIT in the USA to participate in a group discussion on constructing a comprehensive programming system, and later in his career he became involved in EDSAC 2. When the decision was taken to move away from the mercury tank memory to a ferrite core memory he wrote a memorandum on which the decision was taken to adopt the ferrite core memory for EDSAC 2. In 1961 the extensive contributions made by Mutch in the Mathematical Laboratory were recognised by the University and he was given the title of Superintendent of Computing Services.

By 1969 it became necessary for the Mathematical Laboratory to expand into an adjoining site. Mutch was placed in charge of organising the move. One of the dramatic moments of the move came when Titan was airlifted by crane into the new building. A research student then, Keith Van Rijsbergen claims 'the students watched and prayed that Titan would fall out of the sky and be replaced with an IBM computer'. Titan survived. Sadly, while the move was in progress, Mutch died suddenly at the age of 47. He was sorely missed by his many friends and the legion of users he had helped in the course of his life. It is impossible to overestimate the contribution of Eric Mutch to the success of the Mathematical Laboratory in its early years.

Right: Eric Mutch was recruited by Wilkes to help with administration and became a key figure in the Mathematical Laboratory until his untimely death during the move to the Arup Building.

on computer graphics and CAD, and he recruited him to work at the Mathematical Laboratory.

Charles Lang's first task was to write software for the data link between the PDP 7 and Titan. He then began to establish a CAD group working under his supervision to develop tools for computer graphics and CAD. He needed programs for the software system components, computer graphics and computational geometry, and his research student Robin Forrest did the initial work on two- and three-dimensional curves and surfaces. Other research students carried out initial experiments on solid modelling, and Lang recruited Ian Braid in 1969 as his research student. Braid developed BUILD, a boundary-representation 3D solid modeller which was a major advance on the software available at that time, and later he devised a more advanced modeller, BUILD 2.

Lang recognised that the most important application of CAD was in CAD/CAE/CAM (E for engineering and M for manufacturing). The data structure of an object was created by the designer in the computer's memory as a complete model of the object to be manufactured. The model served as the common link among the many processes occurring between initial design and manufacturing, with instructions generated from the model being fed into machines, transforming the design into a viable product. The intermediate stages of producing and interpreting drawings were eliminated, saving time and the cost of manufacture.

In 1971 Alan Grayer joined the group and developed algorithms for automatic machining of parts modelled by BUILD. The group was able to build 3D design systems and to tackle tasks downstream of initial design, including finite element analysis of shell structures and numerically controlled machining of objects with doubly curved shapes.

Following a visit to Pierre Bézier at the Renault car company in Paris, Lang showed Wilkes a model of a curved surface that had been cut in rigid foam material using a specially adapted, numerically controlled machine tool. Lang's group developed this technique by designing a cutting machine which was restricted in use to cutting soft materials at high speed. The first one, built in 1971, was known as a '3D plotter' or 'model-making machine', assuming that such machines would be in design offices rather than workshops. Foam models were also used for making prototype parts.

Lang's group also developed a display with an A0 sized screen in conjunction with Laser-Scan Ltd, a spinout from the Cavendish Laboratory. This was used for making maps and designing banknotes. Wilkes remarked that its remarkably high resolution made it the only display where he could see more detail if he looked closer.

When Lang left the Mathematical Laboratory Braid took his place and supervised a number of research students. The group made significant advances in computer-based solid modelling and its applications. Pioneering work was done on dimensioning and tolerancing, generating tetrahedra to represent modelled solids for finite element analysis, classifying mechanical components by characteristics of their shape, and on geometry for representing and performing computations on increasingly complex shapes. Work on CAD continued

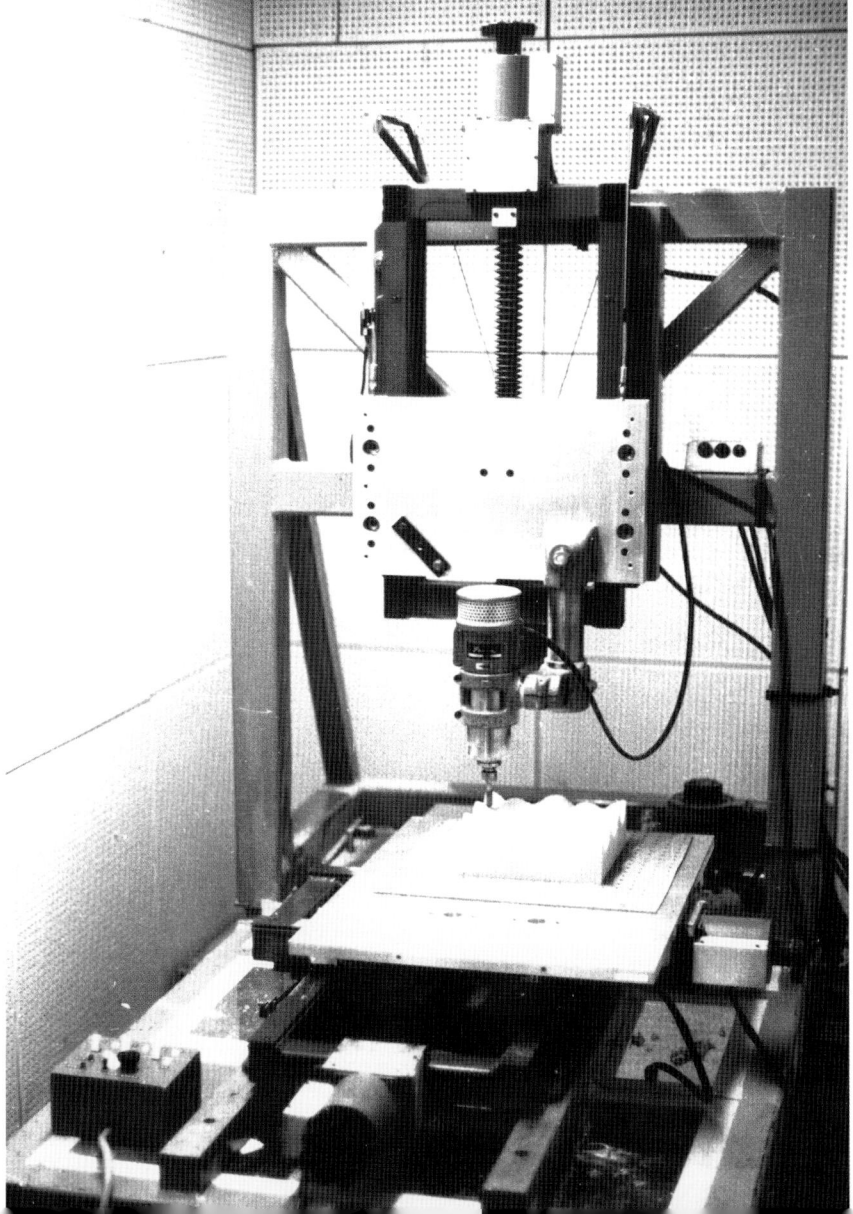

CAD Group 'model-making machine', or '3D plotter', driven from a PDP 11/45 computer and designed by Robin Forrest in 1972. Built for high-speed cutting of soft materials, it had three computer-controlled linear axes and two manually controlled rotational axes. It was used for visualising 3D shapes and for rapid prototyping.

COMPUTER LANGUAGES AT THE MATHEMATICAL LABORATORY

By the time EDSAC 2 came into operation it had become clear that direct programming of the computer in machine language was a major obstacle to users' progress, and work towards a more general computer language was begun. In 1961 David Hartley developed Autocode for EDSAC 2. His work was stimulated by advances at Manchester University, and Cambridge Autocode proved a great success.

At the same time Wilkes began to consider what high-level language should be provided on Titan, which had just come into service. In computing circles the view was now universally held that languages should be independent of machines. The languages ALGOL 60 and Fortran had been widely adopted outside the Mathematical Laboratory and even in some Cambridge University departments. After some deliberation, Wilkes, in consultation with his colleagues, David Hartley and David Barron, decided that a new language should be developed, without the limitations of ALGOL 60 and Fortran, and work on language development was initiated at the Mathematical Laboratory. It was at this point that Christopher Strachey joined the group.

The name initially chosen for the language was Cambridge Programming Language (CPL), though it was changed to Combined Programming Language when a wider collaboration was set up between Cambridge and the University of London, Institute of Computer Science. CPL was based on ALGOL 60 and used many concepts of the language but had a number of additional features. These included extended data description command and expression structures, provision for manipulating non-numerical objects and functions, and comprehensive input/output facilities. The language development group (Hartley, Strachey, his assistant Peter Landin, Park, Barron and Richards) decided to design CPL from first principles in a logically coherent structure rather than basing it on extensions of ALGOL 60.

In the end, very disappointingly for Wilkes, CPL was not fit for the purpose of running on Titan. According to Wilkes 'the project was a complete failure'. He claimed that the protagonists had lost sight of their goal of producing a language suitable for use on Titan and instead became involved in research into language design and implementation. Wilkes claimed that part of the reason for the failure of CPL was the appointment of Strachey to the staff of the Mathematical Laboratory. Strachey had worked as a schoolmaster in his early career but had developed a reputation for programming and this ability was widely recognised. Later in his career he had joined the staff of the National Research and Development Corporation (NRDC), where he met and impressed Wilkes. On leaving NRDC he practised as a private consultant in London for a while until Wilkes invited him to work in Cambridge, and Strachey's reputation was greatly enhanced because of his appointment to a post at the University.

Unfortunately, on his arrival at the Mathematical Laboratory he proved to be difficult to work with and was, according to Wilkes, unnecessarily argumentative on minor issues. His ambition was to lead research on language theory and implementation but this did not suit Wilkes, who persuaded him to leave the Laboratory. Strachey obtained an academic post at Oxford University, where he set up a research group and made a very considerable name for himself. From Wilkes's perspective the move was of mutual benefit, as the Mathematical Laboratory had escaped from an awkward situation while Strachey was free to work on theoretical research at Oxford. CPL was never used to any significant extent but it is regarded today as the core of some important computer languages.

The setback of the CPL project might have been the end of all language-related projects at Cambridge but in 1966 Martin Richards, who had worked on a CPL compiler in the Mathematics Laboratory, went on an extended secondment to MIT, where he invented a derivative of CPL which he named Basic Combined Programming Language (BCPL). It was described by him as 'a procedural imperative and structured computer language' and he stated that he had developed it by 'removing those features of the full language which make compilation difficult'. As the first successful portable systems programming language, BCPL was implemented on more than 25 computer architectures, and intensively used for many years. In 2003 Martin Richards was awarded the USA IEEE Computer Pioneer Award for his work on BCPL. The language is no longer in wide use but it is recognised as having led to the development of the industrial standard programming languages C and C++.

There was very little research work on theoretical or mathematical aspects of computing in Wilkes's time. A line of research was started on automated algebra under D Barton and continued by J P Fitch and others for some years.

in the Laboratory for 15 years until the retirement of Maurice Wilkes, when Braid also left the Laboratory, and the development work moved to the Cambridge University Engineering Department.

The government recognised the importance of Computer-Aided Design, opening the CAD Centre in Cambridge in 1968. Several commercial companies also emerged out of the CAD activity. These were early examples of technology transfer from University to industry and there is still tangible evidence of the benefits from the 'no strings attached' grant to Wilkes.

More CAP – the 'Capabilities' Computer

In 1970 there were detailed discussions, usually on Saturday mornings, between Wilkes and Needham on the future direction of research in the Mathematical Laboratory. It was already obvious to them that there was no need to build another computer to serve the University. Future University service needs would be best met by purchasing a suitable computer from a commercial company, and IBM was the preferred choice despite pressure from the government in favour of ICL.

Nevertheless the three senior academics in the Computer Laboratory – Wilkes, Wheeler and Needham – were committed to doing what they knew best, making computers, and contemplated making a novel computer using an array of microprocessors coupled to a large memory store. They rejected this idea when they could not think of an elegant solution to the problem of the inherent time delay when a large memory is accessed by a multiplicity of microprocessors.

They decided to revert to the established line of research in the Mathematical Laboratory, which was building a novel machine and developing a new operating system for it. Computers had advanced from executing one program at a time to multiple-user, time-sharing systems. In this configuration the memory was shared by all users and it was therefore necessary to ensure that no user could either invade or steal information from another user's memory space. The problem was being addressed by a number of research groups using different philosophies. Among these was the 'capability' concept, which could be configured in either hardware or software to prevent attempts to defeat memory protection. They were aware that Titan, in common with other computers across the world, lacked adequate memory protection.

Wilkes and his colleagues decided to build a computer based on the capability concept, with an emphasis on hardware implementation. Initially Wilkes and Needham devised the basic system architecture and David Wheeler produced the hardware design. The computer was built in the Laboratory with Vic Claydon responsible for the mechanical details and Ken Cox for the electronics. The design automation for CAP was carried out by Robin Fairbairns using Titan – another early example of a computer helping to design another machine! Roger Needham and his team including, notably, Andrew Birrell, developed the CAP operating system. The machine was constructed using integrated circuits, which had replaced transistors, and was located in the space vacated by Titan when it was replaced by the new IBM 370/165. This included a water-cooled system which proved to be a hazard to the CAP sitting underneath it on the floor below. Frequent leaks rained water onto CAP and a tray had to be suspended above to protect it!

A 'capability' (also called a key or a token) is an encoded data structure which gives authority to reference an object and also gives a set of access rights. In the

Charles Lang holding a 'portrait' of his wife Brendel 'sculptured' on the CAD Group's model-making machine.

Chapter Five: Maurice Wilkes: New Directions of Research and the End of an Era

The internal construction of the CAP computer shown here is an example of the complex construction techniques in use in the 1970s. Bjarne Stroustrup (left) and Andrew Herbert used the CAP extensively as research students in the Computer Laboratory.

CAP machine capabilities could be assigned for a region of memory (segment capabilities), for an ability to call another domain (enter capabilities), or for use of operating system resources such as files (software capabilities). The design prevented users from creating new capabilities or editing those they already held, thus preventing both accidental and deliberate attempts to defeat the protection. The Cambridge ideas followed the work of J B Dennis and E Van Horne at MIT and Bob Fabry at the University of Chicago, which Wilkes had seen during one of his visits to the USA, and he believed that this work had been abandoned prematurely.

The machine had a 4K 16-bit micro control store which was used to implement the implicit loading of capabilities. The non-capability part of the machine was conventional. Initially the machine had 192K of 32-bit memory, some salvaged from Titan, and a tape reader and teleprinter were connected directly to the computer. Later 1Mb of semiconductor memory was added and peripherals were replaced by servers which were accessed through the Cambridge Digital Ring.

The local variant of the programming language ALGOL 68C was chosen for the computer by Needham, and Wheeler designed the machine imaginatively around a clever microprogram which enabled users to reconfigure the computer into different forms using only a few micro-orders. His subtle design also meant that the computer architecture was flexible, so that different 'capability' approaches could be tested with it. The feature of the machine was that it did not have program-loadable capability registers. Instead the registers were invisible to the programmer and would be automatically loaded with a program-specified capability.

Research student users of the CAP. From left to right: Bjarne Stroustrup, Mark Pezzaro, Andy Hopper and Bruce Croft.

BJARNE STROUSTRUP AND C++

Bjarne Stroustrup was awarded a PhD in Computer Science from Cambridge University in 1979; immediately afterwards he went to work for AT&T Bell Laboratories, where he stayed for 24 years. There he worked in the highly acclaimed Computer Science Research Centre of the laboratory, which he described as – 'no place like it on Earth'. After rising to become Head of the Large-Scale Programming Research Department he 'escaped' from industry in 2003 to avoid a promotion which would have made him a full-time manager. Instead he decided to seek an academic position and was appointed to a chair at Texas A&M University, where he is now Distinguished Professor in Computer Science (the highest professorial rank accorded by the university).

Stroustrup is famous throughout the world for his invention and implementation of C++, which has been the most widely used computer language for two decades. Its popularity has been enhanced by Stroustrup's definitive textbook on the language, *The C++ Programming Language*, published in 1985 while he was at Bell Laboratories. Since then there have been three further editions and the book has been translated into 19 languages. It is without question the most widely read book on computer programming. He has written three further books on C++ which have also been highly successful, and C++ has been an important influence on a number of computer languages which have been developed since it was invented. On his research philosophy he comments, 'I believe in supporting my abstractions through compiler technology on conventional architectures, carefully avoiding facilities that required "unusual" hardware interfaces.'

He is particularly proud of the spectacular uses to which C++ has been put: 'If it wasn't for the inspiration from the diverse uses of C++, I would not have stuck with the project this long.' The list of organisations and projects that have adopted Stroustrop's C++ is impressive and includes some of the most exciting scientific projects of our time; the higher levels of NASA's Mars Rover code is C++, as was the string-matching software for the human genome project. 'All related computing [is] done in C++' one of Bjarne's friends emailed from CERN on the morning of the announcement of the possible discovery of the Higgs boson. The development of C++ is nurtured and stimulated by a massive number of industrial applications. Examples included Google's search engine, Adobe Photoshop for image manipulation (including all the images from the Mars Rovers), and the engine controls for some of the world's most popular cars and largest ships. Much of the world's software infrastructure (e.g. telecommunications, banking and engine control) is in C++, and though you never see it, if it failed we would all be in deep trouble.

More than three decades after leaving Cambridge with a doctorate Stroustrup returned to the Computer Laboratory for a sabbatical. He recalled that he had been supervised by David Wheeler and guided informally by Roger Needham. In the overcrowded Computer Laboratory of the 1970s he had shared an office with six other research students, including Andy Hopper, now Head of the Computer Laboratory. His thesis was entitled *Communications and Control in Distributed Computer Systems*.

He writes with affection and pride of his time as a research student and claims that 'Cambridge is still the best place for computer science in Europe'. In the 1970s it was an intimate Laboratory, with a handful of academics under Professor Maurice Wilkes and only 40 graduate students. He learned his trade in this laboratory and recalls the advice from his mentors to be intellectually ambitious and to 'keep a high external profile'.

Today he is acknowledged as one of the most famous of the PhD students to have graduated from the Computer Laboratory, and his fame has eclipsed that of most of his peers. He was elected a member of the American National Academy of Engineering in 2004 and was the first computer scientist to be awarded the William Proctor Prize for Scientific Achievement. He has won innumerable awards and prizes across the world and received much acclaim, yet he remains modest, unassuming and dedicated to his chosen profession.

Bjarne Stroustrup, inventor of C++, former student and Visiting Professor at the Computer Labatory, 2012.

The project was a technical success and CAP continued in use in the Computer Laboratory for many years, from the early 1970s until it was decommissioned in 1985. During this time it supported a number of Laboratory projects, including the Cambridge Distributed System. Perhaps its most notable user was Bjarne Stroustrup. He used CAP extensively and came to the conclusion that the future belonged to software specifically designed for simpler and faster machine architectures – the language C++ is based on this conclusion. Andrew Herbert (later Chairman of Microsoft Research, UK) carried out research for his PhD on CAP. He explored different architectures for the computer, taking advantage of the flexibility that Wheeler had built into the original design.

CAP attracted a great deal of attention from research centres active in similar work, but the project did not lead to any further developments. The computer was evaluated by Douglas Cook, who found that systems without any kind of hardware support for capabilities were much less practical than CAP. In Wilkes's view the main drawback of CAP was that the computer required complex software and, as a consequence, did not operate at the speed the designers had anticipated. In effect the hope that 'capabilities' introduced through hardware would speed up the system compared with software-based implementation was not realised. It has also been argued that CAP's hardware may have been outdated even before it was operational, and that it was a serious practical problem that the CAP was unable to run 'legacy' software designed for conventional systems. Towards the end of the 1970s commercial computing systems were installed in University departments and the CAP project was abandoned. The computer itself was used as a server for some years before it was consigned to the Computer Laboratory's museum. Historically CAP was the second capability-based computer to operate in the UK. The Plessey 250, built by the company with the help of Maurice Wilkes, who was a consultant to the company, was the first to come into service.

Today, 25 years on, the capabilities concept is being re-examined because of the advent of server virtualisation and cloud computing. The need is for strong isolation between users and for robust operating systems. In this context CAP is an important point of reference. After huge advances in machine architecture over the last 40 years, research groups in the Computer Laboratory are now re-visiting CAP concepts, using state-of-the-art hardware to build a 'capabilities' computer in the Laboratory for the first time since the demise of CAP.

The Cambridge Digital Ring

By the mid-1970s Wilkes was in his sixties and approaching retirement, but his enthusiasm for introducing new areas of research in the Computer Laboratory had not dimmed. On a visit to Switzerland he saw a 'digital communication ring' in operation and immediately recognised the potential of the configuration for interconnecting computers. He was aware of research in a number of laboratories around the world on Local Area Networks (LANs), which enabled minicomputers, computer terminals and peripheral devices to be interconnected by high-speed digital data transmission links, but felt that he could do something novel and more advanced in the Computer Laboratory.

As a preliminary activity, Wheeler and Wilkes carried out a design study for a novel LAN which they called the 'Cambridge Digital Ring'. Wheeler then worked on the detailed design and constructed a ring system in the Computer Laboratory. The first objective of the project was to demonstrate that a number of computers in a local area could be interconnected in a ring purely using telecommunications techniques with high rates of data transmission and low rates of error. The second objective was to show that computational resources could be shared among all the computers connected in the ring. One practical objective was to prove that the system could operate with a high level of dependability, made possible by the availability of comparatively reliable integrated circuits. It was vitally important to demonstrate reliable operation because the whole ring was vulnerable to the failure of just one weak link in the overall system. Finally Wilkes addressed the question of cost. He showed that it was not excessive compared with the operational advantages and cost benefits that the ring structure could bring to the user community operating within a defined area.

The Cambridge Digital Ring was operational by the end of 1977 and it immediately became obvious that all the attributes and benefits that Wilkes and Wheeler

Cambridge Computing: The First 75 Years

Some of the PCBs used for the ring. The chips were designed in the Computer Laboratory with the support of a government grant.

had anticipated had been fully realised in practice. The operation of the Cambridge Digital Ring was based on the transmission of data in small 'packets' at 10Mb per second using twisted-pair transmission links between stations, in a manner that is known as 'slot-based' communication. Each station was connected to a computer or a peripheral device. A packet contained two bytes of data and two bytes of address information identifying a sender and a receiver station. Five further bits were used to control the transmission of packets. Slots were continually transmitted round the ring in an 'empty' state until a sender station chose to insert two bytes of data and the address of a receiver (a packet), thus marking the slot as 'full'. When it reached the receiver station, the two bytes were read and the slot was marked as 'received'. The slot continued on its way until it reached the sender, where its receipt was noted, and it was marked as 'empty' once again. Slots could also be marked as busy by the receiver for automatic 'retry' by the sender. The main applications of the Cambridge Digital Ring were peripheral sharing and file transfer which required only a moderate bandwidth, achievable with straightforward transmission links.

Wheeler designed the hardware and the associated protocols were designed by members of the Computer Laboratory working with Wheeler, including his research student Andy Hopper. The system design was taxing and required originality and ingenuity to implement; Wheeler and a team of people working under him provided the necessary engineering skills to ensure that there was perfect transmission of packets of data. A monitoring station kept a log of corrupt packets, which enabled maintenance engineers to identify faulty equipment. Wheeler and Hopper explored the operation of the ring in meticulous detail and devised alternative approaches. Hopper went on to design and implement one of these as an integrated circuit version of the ring, which in turn led to further developments. The performance of the ring improved as the functionality and speed of integrated circuits continued to advance along the roadmap predicted by Gordon Moore of Intel in 1965.

As more and more computers were added to the ring, the time taken for the slots to rotate increased. Not only was the delay undesirable but serious reliability issues were also raised. Ian Leslie, as a PhD student, designed a bridge that enabled the ring to be divided into two, with inter-ring traffic crossing the bridge. Another split took place, with two bridges connecting three rings, known as Ruby, Emerald and Sapphire respectively. The Sapphire ring used two fibre-optic links and extended under Downing Street in Cambridge to the University's Old Music School, which was then in use by the expanding Computer Laboratory. It housed the Rainbow and Systems Research groups. The Computer Laboratory had long outgrown the Arup Building and was scattered in buildings vacated by departments moving to new sites.

The Cambridge Ring was designed using eight-bit addresses because having more than 256 stations on a ring could not be envisioned. This eight-bit addressing was embedded in all protocol drivers. The bridges enabled this address space to be reused in the different connected rings using mappings, so that the eight-bit address was not a limitation to further expansion. This is closely mirrored in today's Internet, where Network Address Translation has been and remains a technique used to overcome the limits of the available 32-bit IP addresses.

The Cambridge Digital Ring became a national standard (ISO CR 82) in 1982. It was manufactured under licence by companies such as Logica, TopExpress and Orbis. In 1980 work began on developing a high-speed version of the ring, and in 1981 the Computer Laboratory was awarded the British Computer Society's technical award for 'the Cambridge Digital Communication Ring'.

In the 1980s general-purpose integrated circuits suitable for use in the ring were not available, and Hopper's team developed a CAD package which was used to simulate the ring's operation before the chips designed in the Computer Laboratory were manufactured by industry. A grant from the Advanced Computer Technology Initiative supported this research. The availability of high-speed integrated circuits enabled a 'fast ring' to come into operation in 1982 which operated at 100Mb per second. Later, in a collaborative project with Olivetti Research, an ultrafast ring working at 1Gb per second was developed with its range enlarged to become a 'metropolitan network'.

The huge commercial potential of the Cambridge Digital Ring was not realised, however, because of the competing 'ethernet' technology which was being developed in the laboratories of the American company Xerox. On purely technical grounds the Cambridge Digital Ring may have had an edge in performance over the ethernet approach but the commercial benefits of low-cost mass production favoured the ethernet, which used a different operating standard that was destined to be internationally adopted. The Cambridge Digital Ring continued to be used for a number of years until it was overtaken by other developments. Nevertheless the Computer Laboratory had made a seminal contribution to computer networking with its pioneering research.

The Cambridge Model Distributed System

In 1978 work began in the Computer Laboratory on the Cambridge Model Distributed System (CMDS) as a continuation of the Cambridge Digital Ring project. The project was based on the availability of inexpensive minicomputers which could be used to create a pool of processing servers. The server pool was made up of commercial LSI 4 machines. They were gradually replaced with microcomputers designed in the Computer Laboratory. The user was allocated one or more of these servers for exclusive use as long as it was needed, and multiple users could be accommodated on the system at any one time. The arrangement provided a facility very similar to that available from a time-sharing system on a mainframe computer, such that many users logging on to the simpler CMDS would be unaware that they were not using a central mainframe computer.

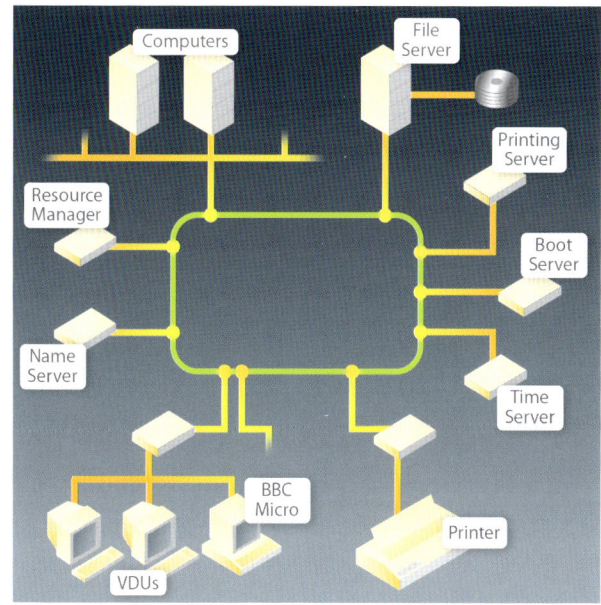

The Cambridge Distributed System developed in the Computer Laboratory.

The structure described by Wilkes and Needham in 1978 was based on the Cambridge Digital Ring. A number of visual display units (VDUs) were connected to a ring through a device called the terminal concentrator. Several servers were also connected to the ring with functions described as authentication server, file server, printing server, time server, name server, resource management server, etc. In the system built at the Computer Laboratory the microprocessor bank consisted of six Computer Automation LSI 4 minicomputers, each with 64K words of memory which provided the computing power. The 'name server' had a fundamental role in CMDS. It recognised the text name for a service, a computer or any other facility on the system and returned the appropriate ring address. It also operated in the reverse direction to allow machines to determine their logical names. The time server provided time and date information to its clients based on its internal digital clock, which was corrected from time to time by signals from a 'radio clock' broadcasting station. The name service was a precursor of the Domain Name System (DNS), on which the Internet is now heavily dependent, and the time server is reflected in the Internet's Network Time Service. Users gained access to the system by establishing their identity with the resource manager which allocated access to the servers.

It is interesting to note at this point that Roger Needham had a strong connection with the US-based Xerox PARC, where he was a regular visitor for extensive periods of time. Complementary distributed system projects were being carried out by Xerox, and Needham participated in these projects during his visits, which led to a great deal of cross-fertilisation between Cambridge and Xerox PARC, benefiting both parties.

The second-generation system comprised 50 linked computers and it was called the Cambridge Distributed System (being considered large enough for the word 'model' to be dropped from the name). The system was expanded to include locally constructed Motorola 68000 based systems, the Cambridge CAP computer, a group of DEC PDP 11 computers and some larger VAX computers. It was in daily use by members of the Computer Laboratory working on research projects who preferred it to the mainframe Laboratory computer. By 1988 the advance of high-performance personal workstations rendered the system out of date and it was closed down. It has been asserted that many of the ideas developed on the Cambridge Distributed Systems have survived in modern cloud computing data centres based on networked multiprocessor servers.

A Major Reorganisation

Towards the end of the 1960s Wilkes reappraised the remit and structure of the Mathematical Laboratory. So far he had been constrained by the terms of the General Board's report of 1938 which prescribed that his primary duty was to provide a computing service. Since then computing science and technology had developed considerably, and his Laboratory had gained worldwide recognition as a centre of excellence in computing research. He had provided an exemplary computing service for more than two decades by building and commissioning computers in an age when commercial suppliers did not exist, and he could look back with satisfaction on his achievements, but he was aware that the Mathematical Laboratory was losing some of its international pre-eminence.

Commercial computers were now available, most notably from IBM, who dominated the world market. In 1964 IBM had launched the 360 series of computers, the most successful mainframe computer ever marketed, and IBM computers were installed in universities, industrial laboratories, banks, large business enterprises and defence establishments across the world. National and international exchange of data for business and financial transactions and scientific collaborations requiring the sharing of programs and data needed to be IBM-compatible. In the course of a decade IBM had grown very rapidly and developed a virtual monopoly in supplying computer systems as the company became a dominant multinational computing giant. IBM computers were backwardly compatible so that customers could upgrade as technology advanced. Inexpensive integrated circuits with ever greater processing power and speed were becoming available, as were large-scale solid-state memory devices, and the booming semiconductor industry in Silicon Valley was driving advances in computing.

Towards the end of the decade Wilkes had accepted that Titan was unsuitable as a service computer. Although it had many advanced features and was much loved by

Chapter Five: Maurice Wilkes: New Directions of Research and the End of an Era

some users it was not IBM compatible, which was unacceptable to a number of major users in the University. They made it clear to Wilkes that Titan should be replaced by an IBM-compatible system, but the government of the day wished to support the UK computer industry, which was struggling against the might of IBM. ICL was the government's favoured provider even though user demand argued against this. A powerfully argued case for compatibility with IBM was put forward by the Head of the Department of Geodesy and Geophysics, who gave examples of the difficulty in collaborating with American organisations when there was a lack of compatibility across the whole system: in inputting the data, in outputting the data and even with the programming. He went on to demonstrate the ridiculous extent to which the Titan tapes had to be modified at many different locations across the country before they could be used successfully by a collaborator. His conclusion was that Cambridge had been overtaken by events, and that the world had moved on while Titan was being built and commissioned. He also argued that only with a commercial machine could new computer languages be accommodated and it was high time that the Cambridge Service tried to match the large installations in other parts of the world. This obviously placed Wilkes under a great deal of pressure; the Science Research Council also pressed the General Board of the University to reorganise its computing arrangements and Swinnerton-Dyer, a member of the Board, passed these concerns on to Wilkes.

Apart from the service element provided by the Mathematical Laboratory, Wilkes had become very aware that the focus of research in computing in major US industry and university research centres had shifted from the era of building computers. The Mathematical Laboratory was lagging behind the rest of the world in the newer 'computer sciences-related' research areas. There were, of course, pockets of outstanding research in the Mathematical Laboratory but overall it appeared impoverished, overcrowded and outdated compared with the magnificent computer research centres of IBM, Stanford and MIT in the US, to name a few.

Wilkes came to the conclusion that sweeping changes needed to be made to the remit and structure of the Mathematical Laboratory. These changes were so fundamental that they could not be made at his level, as a Department Head within the Faculty Board of Mathematics, but needed the support of the central University authorities. He drafted proposals to the General Board for the wholesale reform of his Department. Remarkably this was the first-re-examination of the remit given to the Mathematical Laboratory when it was founded in 1937. It was long overdue. Wilkes had rather belatedly come to the conclusion that the Laboratory should concentrate on research and teaching in computing science and technology, and give up the idea of building computers for the user service. He also decided that he needed more freedom of action, which could only be achieved by independence from the Mathematics Faculty. Finally he decided that the management of the user service was an unnecessary burden on him and his colleagues.

Wilkes's Proposals

Wilkes drafted wide-ranging proposals which were accepted by the General Board and summarised in a report to the University in 1969. This report was an important milestone in the history of the Computer

Maurice Wilkes receiving his knighthood in 2000 from Her Majesty, The Queen.

Laboratory, second only in significance to the 1938 General Board report which had proposed the foundation of the Mathematical Laboratory.

Wilkes proposed that the Computer Laboratory should become a department of the University independent of the Mathematics Faculty and placed within the departments designated as the University's School of Physical Sciences. The Mathematical Laboratory was now on an equal footing with other major University departments, and as Head of an independent department he could argue more effectively for a greater share of University resources. He could also bid for staff appointments and put forward proposals for an expansion of teaching in the Mathematical Laboratory.

The second significant proposal was that the user service should be separated from research and teaching. It should be a separate entity with its own Director of professorial or quasi-professorial rank who would manage it and report to a new body, the Computer Syndicate, on which the interests of users would be represented. Research and teaching would remain the core activity of the Mathematical Laboratory, but the Computer Syndicate would advise the University on the development of computer science teaching and administer the Diploma in Computer Science. It should be noted that Wilkes did not give up his authority over the user service, and maintained that it would remain under the aegis of the Mathematical Laboratory. He would remain in overall charge, although he conceded that the user service would develop and expand more effectively under a dedicated Director devoting all his time and energy to the management of the service. The first Director of the 'independent' Computing Service was David Hartley, who was then working in the Computer Laboratory as an ADR.

He proposed as well that the Mathematical Laboratory should be renamed the Computer Laboratory which gave him great satisfaction, as he had always been irked by the name agreed in 1938.

The report also noted that the University had applied to the Computer Board for Universities and Research Councils for funds to purchase a computer that would meet the needs of users for the foreseeable future. This grant was received in due course and, despite continuing government pressure in favour of ICL, an IBM computer system was purchased by the University.

Wilkes's Research Philosophy and Management

Wilkes's early research was constrained to some degree because he was obliged to provide a computing service to the University as his first priority. He later developed a philosophy for the function and prosecution of University research, arguing that projects should be long term, typically requiring ten years to reach a level of maturity where industry could develop the project into an industrial product or service. A University research project should either be transferred from the University to industry at some stage or abandoned if this was not possible. Projects should be designed in one of two ways, either for the training of graduate students or to satisfy the interests of a faculty member wishing to follow an intellectual enquiry. In many cases these aims would coincide. Whatever the nature of a project in the University at its inception, it should fall at some stage into the mainstream of computing and contribute to the field as a whole. In retrospect, one can see that projects such as CAD, the CAP computer, the Cambridge Digital Ring and the Cambridge Model Distributed System fall within his philosophy.

He maintained that he was not happy in his work unless he was leading research into new areas of computing. Speaking of the early days of computing, when EDSAC and EDSAC 2 had been built and commissioned, he claimed that in those days potential users simply did not know what benefits a digital computer could bring to their research, and that his own research projects were aimed entirely at building novel computers. Scientists in other disciplines realised that their research would benefit from these computers and became committed users. This is an entirely justifiable claim, because it was only when computers became available from commercial suppliers in the mid-1960s that users began to specify their needs.

Throughout his time at the Laboratory Wilkes was the dominant presence. He appointed Laboratory staff and eased out those with whom he could not work effectively. Not counting his two close colleagues, Needham and Wheeler, he appears to have made very few appointments to senior academic posts over a period of 20 years; Neil Wiseman in 1961, Martin Richards in 1971 and Frank King in 1976. Just before his retirement Andy Hopper and Andrew Herbert were appointed University Assistant Lecturers.

Chapter Five: Maurice Wilkes: New Directions of Research and the End of an Era

Except to Wheeler and Needham he was a remote figure who was always addressed as either Mr Wilkes or Dr Wilkes, never Maurice! After his promotion he was called Professor Wilkes by all members of the Laboratory. Life in the Computer Laboratory was very informal, but Professor Wilkes was always treated with a high degree of deference. His remoteness is exemplified by an account by a member of the academic staff, who said that he did not know the first names of his workshop and technical staff and always referred to them by their surnames. He was very definitely a man of the 1930s, always polite and formally dressed in a dark suit and tie. He was caring but firm towards staff members and was known to make the point that it was better for the careers of some people to move away from the Computer Laboratory after they had completed their PhD and occasionally after serving a short probationary period in a junior faculty position.

When asked to define himself within an academic discipline he denied firmly that he was a mathematician but was at a loss when asked to suggest an alternative. There is no doubt that his greatest expertise was in the technology of computers, but he also had a deep understanding of mathematical and theoretical concepts associated with computing.

He chose the title of the Chair created for him by the University – Professor of Computer Technology. (The University of Cambridge permits holders of personal chairs to suggest the name of the chair. The chair is supressed at the retirement or death of the incumbent.) The title was entirely appropriate because he had demonstrated his prowess in technology by building two computers in his Laboratory.

The End of an Era

Wilkes retired in 1980 at the age of 67. He had ruled over the Mathematical Laboratory for 35 years and was justifiably conscious of his own position as the first person to make a stored-program computer which could provide an extensive service to users.

To him retirement seemed premature and irrelevant, and he wrote that 'ordinances of Cambridge University require that a professor shall lay down his office (at age 67)' and he had no option but to leave the Computer Laboratory. (University ordinances in 1980 required all University officers to retire on 30th September in the year in which they reached the age of 67.) His retirement was marked by a splendid Retirement Dinner at St John's College which was attended by most of his colleagues and many of the great and good in the University and colleges.

Wilkes was immensely gratified that for several years before his death he once again had an office in the Computer Laboratory, and that he had a base in a laboratory. He was much respected and much cherished – an *éminence grise* of Cambridge Computing in his final years, before he died at the age of 97.

Wilkes in the Titan Room at the time of his retirement from his University position in 1980 at the age of 67.

CHAPTER SIX

Computing for All
Networking the University from EDSAC Users to Desktops and Laptops

David Hartley

Early History of the Computing Service

The main purpose of founding a Cambridge University Computer Laboratory in 1937 was to provide a service to scientific users. Indeed the founding Director, Lennard-Jones himself, was a theoretical chemist who saw himself very much as a user rather than a computing expert.

In those early days the most significant service provided by the Mathematical Laboratory was based around analogue computers known as the Bush Differential Analysers. These machines were operated by Lennard-Jones's assistant, Maurice Wilkes, on behalf of research students from Theoretical Chemistry and Physics who found it necessary to solve differential equations by numerical methods.

After the end of the Second World War, Wilkes built the remarkable EDSAC and from 1950 onwards used it to provide a formal computing service to Cambridge University scientists. It was totally unique, as no other organisation anywhere in the world had such a service. In the daytime operators helped scientists to load their programs and at night those users who could be trusted were allowed to run programs on their own. At its peak, the service had no fewer than 50 users who enthusiastically overcame difficulties with programming and cheerfully tolerated frequent breakdowns of the machine. Compared with the use of calculating machines it was certainly much better than what had been provided beforehand. Some of these early users managed to produce outstanding scientific results. The early EDSAC operators included Eileen Breakwell, Valerie Webber and Rosemary Hill. An historic film was made of the service in operation and is retained in the archives of the Computer Laboratory.

In 1958 EDSAC was replaced by EDSAC 2, which had more facilities than its predecessor and was easier to program. It again became a magnet for users whose numbers increased to no fewer than 200. EDSAC 2 Autocode programming language was developed by David Hartley following the work at Manchester University and made available in Cambridge. The service was skillfully managed by the Superintendent of Computing Services, Eric Mutch, who had been appointed by Maurice Wilkes in 1947. By the beginning of the 1960s, computers and computing services were widely available and, while the Cambridge computing service was no longer unique, it was certainly on a par with the rest of the world. IBM had not yet become a dominant force in the world of computing.

In 1964 Titan came into service and from 1967 operated as a multiple-access computing service operating, in principle, 24 hours a day and seven days a week. A film

Titan towards the end of its life. In the background are tape drives, memory, mainframe and peripheral controller; in the foreground are operator desks, a card reader and paper-tape readers; an engineers' oscilloscope can be seen on the far right.

Chapter Six: Computing for All: Networking the University from EDSAC Users to Desktops and Laptops

Engineers who variously built and maintained the early computers on stage at the 50th anniversary of EDSAC. Left to right: Vic Claydon, Roy Bailey, Herbert Norris, Ken Cox, David Prince and Peter Bennett.

David Hartley, BA Mathematics, Diploma in Numerical Analysis and Automatic Computing 1959, PhD 1963, Clare College, Founding Director of the University Computing Service and Fellow of Clare College.

of Titan in operation was made in 1968 and is stored in the archives of the Computer Laboratory. In 1969 Titan was moved to a new building and the full computing service was transferred without a break to the Atlas 2 computer at the CAD Centre in Cambridge while Titan was being re-commissioned.

During this period the first signs of criticism began to appear. The main complaint was that Titan was not compatible with other machines which were proliferating in research laboratories across the world. The development of the Titan system had run late and there was a long delay before a Fortran system was provided. At this point in the history of the Mathematical Laboratory users were no longer content with developing their own applications but had discovered the value of sharing data and programs with colleagues in other institutions. Indeed not only was this a growing national requirement, but – particularly in the case of Cambridge – increasingly an international affair. This created a need for a degree of compatibility between computing systems, which had become just as important as having adequate computational power and storage capacity.

His work and that of his colleagues laid the foundations of an organisation that believed in not only doing it right but doing it well. To have developed and built, both in hardware and software terms, not just two pioneering machines (EDSAC and EDSAC 2), but also to have worked with industry to develop the Titan created a lasting legacy providing advanced and innovative facilities both in quantity and quality.

In October 1970 the old computing service gave way to the new. The University Computing Service, as it was now called, became a separate organisation under its own 'Chief Executive' but remained within the Computer

DAVID HARTLEY

David Hartley was appointed Assistant Director of Research in 1966 and University Lecturer in the Mathematical Laboratory in 1967 and worked closely with Wilkes and Needham on a number of research projects connected with EDSAC 2 and Titan. He pioneered the mass teaching of computer programming to research students across the University.

He was appointed the founding Director of the independent University Computing Service in 1970, a post he held for 23 years, transforming the service from a mainframe computer service to a distributed computing environment connected by very high bandwidth networking. He created the Granta Backbone Network, a network of ducting and fibre-optic cables interconnecting all University and College sites in Cambridge.

He left Cambridge in 1994 to set up, and be Chief Executive of, the UK Education and Research Networking Association (UKERNA), a company created by the university funding councils to develop and operate the JANET network. He returned to Cambridge in 1997 to become Executive Director of the Cambridge Crystallographic Data Centre.

He was a member of the Computer Board for Universities and Research Councils (1979–83), a member of the Prime Minister's Information Technology Advisory Panel (1981–86), President of the British Computer Society (1999–2000) and Chairman of the Computer Conservation Society (2007–11). He is Museum Director of the National Museum of Computing at Bletchley Park (2012–).

Laboratory. David Hartley was appointed Director of the University Computing Service to manage the service under the direction of a Computer Syndicate which included representatives of users and served as a Board of Management. Maurice Wilkes as Head of Department retained overall responsibility for the administration of the Laboratory, but all operational and management issues became the responsibility of the new Director. This arrangement worked well for ten years until Maurice Wilkes retired in 1980 and continued equally successfully when Roger Needham became Head of Department. In 1994 David Hartley resigned to take up a national role in academic networking. He was succeeded as Director by Mike Sayers, who served for 11 years until his retirement from University duties. His successor, Ian Lewis, only the third Director of the University Computing Service in a history of 40 years, was appointed in 2005.

The Continuing Mainframe Era

This was still the time when a large mainframe system was an essential prerequisite to meet the need to maintain and support a complex system with a growing range of software. At the same time resources had to be shared among a large and expanding user population. Also, there was an emerging need for users in certain disciplines to share data and software with kindred groups in other institutions, and often those institutions would be worldwide. Thus compatibility of systems and systems software had become an essential requirement, which in those days simply equated to 'we must have an IBM mainframe'. Some of Cambridge's powerful and prestigious scientific research groups were particularly vocal on this point.

But this was contrary to the UK government's insistence to 'buy British'. There was a national policy, designed to protect the UK computer industry, which required that all large university systems had to be supplied by International Computers Limited (ICL), a company created by government from mergers of most of the UK's computer industry. (The fact that ICL was subsequently purchased by Fujitsu and is now a Japanese company adds a poignant epilogue to the story.) Two cards had to be played to get the IBM mainframe demanded by Cambridge users. The first was the need of many major Cambridge research groups for compatible facilities between themselves and their opposite numbers in the USA and elsewhere. The second was a proposal to meet similar needs, where they existed, in other UK institutions. An important institution in this regard was the Medical Research Council's (MRC) Laboratory of Molecular Biology, the home of the discovery of the structure of DNA, which was located in Cambridge. The Service had to 'sell' MRC the promise that a stable and technically competent service would be provided under a management discipline that would enforce this. MRC was a demanding organisation, and the deal gave them an entitlement to 11 per cent of the available resources for a contribution of 11 per cent of the costs.

A similar arrangement was made for those universities with a specific requirement for IBM-compatible resources, although the extra costs would be met directly by government. The Service, on behalf of the University, made some bold commitments which fortunately were in due course fulfilled. Success was owed not just to a management discipline of keeping new developments under tight control, but also to the 'doing it right and doing it well' tradition mentioned earlier.

The User Area with Output Tanks (one pocket for each user).

Chapter Six: Computing for All: Networking the University from EDSAC Users to Desktops and Laptops

David Hartley shuts down the IBM 370/165 in 1982.

Barry Landy, Head of Systems Software for many years and creator of Phoenix, is 'shown the door' by Maurice Wilkes in the traditional retirement ceremony.

An IBM 370 model 165, the newest but not quite the most powerful IBM mainframe of the day was duly approved by government and installed in 1971. The Titan, which was not very compatible with anything else although much loved by those that used it, was permitted to remain operational until 1973, giving breathing space to understand and adapt to the brave new world of IBM. The task was uncomfortable for several reasons. Unexpectedly the new machine was not as reliable as had been anticipated, it being an early model of a new product range, while the Multiple Virtual Tasks (MVT) operating system was something of a culture shock to service staff and users alike. In the words of a colleague from the other side of the Laboratory, the Director had the task of 'bringing users, kicking and screaming, backwards by about five years'.

Following the reorganisation of 1970 the Service had been endowed with a staff that was not only of high quality but sufficient in number. To ensure computers were well supported the government provided universities with both the capital to purchase new computers and additional recurrent funds for maintenance and staff, so that the inheritance of programming and support staff from the old Laboratory was supplemented with new money to enhance the dowry. In a period of only two years the total staff complement was doubled and the programming staff quadrupled.

From these exciting and challenging beginnings, the IBM mainframe service developed over a time into something of which the Laboratory and the University were justifiably proud. Two important achievements contributed to this.

Phoenix Rises from the Ashes

In those days, IBM had extended the MVT operating system to include time-sharing facilities which, thanks to the success of Titan, was by then a key requirement for Cambridge. But the Time Sharing Option, or TSO, as it was called, was initially something of a disaster. IBM had grafted time-sharing facilities on to the original batch operating system and had broken many of the principles of efficiency, utility and uniformity that had been established on Titan. The Service took measures to circumvent some of the more wasteful features and, at the same time, developed a new user interface as an alternative to both the infamous offline JCL interface and the online TSO system. Inevitably, the result had a strong resemblance to Titan. At the same time a discipline was established and enforced to ensure no change was made to the interface between user programs and the operating system. In short, the Service used its previously acquired system software skills to fulfill all that had been pledged in terms of maintaining compatibility. The resulting user

Cambridge Computing: The First 75 Years

interface became known informally as Phoenix, and over the following 25 years the name assumed official status.

Fair Shares for All

The second achievement was in the allocation and control of computer time and file storage, which for long had been an issue for shared mainframe systems. Allocating resources to users, whether big or small, in a manner that is both responsive and perceived as fair was a major challenge.

Those same users who had demanded compatibility also demanded an effective and democratic system of resource allocation. There had to be a committee, they said, composed of users and weighted towards larger users (who were, at least to them, the most important) to allocate computer time to faculties, departments and user groups. Having observed the inadequacies of this approach, which was deep-rooted in other institutions and more political than logical, the Service decided it could do better. Fortunately the issue was raised when the new computer was lightly loaded, and there would be room for manoeuvre before the political pressures would come to bear. To give them their due, the big users accepted this and left the Service to prove what they could do.

The task was to provide a mechanism to control resources in a fair manner and according to real rather than perceived need. The mechanism had to enable users, however big or small their requirements, to articulate their relative priorities. Every user had some work that to them was relatively important, while they were prepared to wait a bit longer for the rest. The challenge was to enable users to state which of their work was relatively more urgent, while ensuring that their overall use remained reasonable compared to that of other users. Similarly in the case of file space, users' requirements fluctuated with peaks and troughs, so that a large amount for a small time should be available if balanced by relatively small amounts over a longer period of time. To put it simply, it was desirable to give every user the incentive to delete or archive files

Below: Judy Bailey succeeded Eric Mutch as Superintendent of Computing Services in 1969. She became Deputy Director and took responsibility for all resource allocation to users. A 2008 obituary said: 'She knew them all personally providing a human interface to perceived hostile technology and was their knowledgeable friend and supporter.'

Left: John Larmouth developed Titan Fortran as a research student and was then one of two senior programmers who transferred to the Computing Service in 1970. He conceived and designed the 'shares' resource control system and resigned to become Director of the Computing Service at Salford University in 1976. This cartoon was presented to him on his resignation.

Chapter Six: Computing for All: Networking the University from EDSAC Users to Desktops and Laptops

Richard Stibbs, long-serving Head of User Support.

whenever they could. In these ways finite total resources could be made to go a great deal further.

There were two overriding concerns: to avoid the waste of resources, and to avoid politically motivated committees. This is how it was done. It was realised that both computer time and file storage are wasting assets, that is commodities that can neither be stored nor saved. Therefore it was appropriate to measure and control the rate of (or average) use rather than total use. In times of high demand resources are relatively costly, while at times of low demand (for example in the small hours) they are relatively cheap. So the system calculated and recorded use as a function of both resources used and demand, the amount being decayed over time. This established for each user a rate of working, and for a user that tried to exceed some preset level their work was not stopped but slowed down, meaning it was put further down the job queue. The formula for doing this was a complex function of time used, priority accorded by the user, and past pattern of use, as well as a record of the times of high and low demand.

To allow some to have a higher rate of working than others, each user had an allocation of 'shares'. Shares were a dimensionless quantity which simply meant that a user with twice the shares of another user was able to consume resources at twice the rate.

So the next part of the process was to determine the share allocation for each user. It could, of course, have been done by an allocation committee dividing shares among University departments and leaving it to the latter to sub-divide their allocation to groups and individuals. This was not done. Instead every new project was given a nominal allocation of shares, and the user told 'see how you get on and come back for more if you think you need it'. Requests for an increased allocation were briefly scrutinised to check that the user was being sensible, and an increase was usually granted there and then, again being told 'see how you get on and come back for more if necessary'. In this way resource allocation became a continuous bottom-up process rather that the periodic top-down approach by an allocation committee. All allocation decisions were small ones and errors in the system tended to cancel out.

Until it was shown to work in practice, everyone was sceptical whether the shares system would be satisfactory but, with a certain amount of fine tuning, it was. And there was a safety mechanism: users had right of appeal to the Computer Syndicate if they thought they had been unfairly treated. Not a single such appeal was lodged in the lifetime of Phoenix, a period of almost 20 years. As a tail piece, several years into the running of the mainframe service some of those who had initially doubted the Service and had called for a democratic allocation committee, stated that they were impressed with what had been achieved. It was, of course, a superb solution to a problem that today no longer exists, but it is still a testament to the Service's inherited skills.

A Multi-Service Organisation

The mainframe facility was in effect a central service covering the needs of research and teaching throughout the whole University. The number of users of the Titan had grown to around 1,000 by the time it was replaced, and in the following succession of IBM mainframes the number peaked at around 8,000 and was still about 5,000 when the mainframe service was eventually closed in the mid-1990s.

The mainframe service provided interactive facilities to users at terminals located around the University. From the beginning, using IBM equipment to provide remote connectivity was expensive and inflexible and, in the tradition of the past, it was natural to set about building a home-grown facility. An expanding collection of PDP 11 computers was assembled and duly programmed to control teletype terminals and remote job entry equipment. Being a programmed system, there was flexibility to add new facilities. Slowly, a growing number of other computers elsewhere in the University were connected, so that all terminals could access all connected systems. In this way the front-end became a switch, thus creating a network. Today it is accepted that a data network is the most important centralised service. At that time, research in the Computer Laboratory was developing high-speed local area networking technology, which in due course

THE GRANTA BACKBONE NETWORK

Towards the end of the 1980s, the Service was eager to obtain increased bandwidth and connectivity across the University. The advances provided by local area networking technology were needed over the wide area. By and large the average university is a campus located within a city, whereas the Cambridge 'campus' has a city within it. Single-campus organisations can easily lay their own cables from building to building, but Cambridge seemingly could not.

In those days, telecommunications regulations dictated that circuits across the University had to be provided commercially. Fortunately in the late 1980s the government was implementing a policy of telecommunications liberalisation. So a campaign was mounted: the University was persuaded that, unlike computers, underground ducting and cables were inherently low technology that would last for decades and that the costs could be written off over a long period. At the same time colleges had the foresight to accept that there would be a growing use of computers by undergraduates, and it became clear that they would become customers for a city-wide network. It also helped that the government was prepared to grant the University a special telecommunications licence.

By including colleges in the scheme, the need for ducting to cross third-party land was minimised, and it became practical to create the Granta Backbone Network (GBN) in 1992. The GBN is a system of copper and optical-fibre cables in ducting that links together almost every University and college site stretching from Girton College in the northwest to Addenbrookes Hospital in the southeast. It cost about £3.5 million to install and is the joint property of the University and 31 independent colleges. Its running costs are virtually nil when compared with the offerings of commercial providers. It can reasonably be claimed that this was at the time the first high-bandwidth university-wide network that covered a whole city – some 80 separate sites interconnected by almost 30km of underground ducting. In 1973 there were about 150 devices connected to the mainframe; today there are in excess of 130,000 devices connected to a broadband network, and Cambridge has bandwidth to burn.

provided the stimulus to migrate to higher bandwidths. In the shorter term the challenge was how to provide connectivity over a wide area in an economic manner. To this end a standardised device, known as a Packet Assembler/Disassembler (PAD) was developed in house, commercially manufactured and installed in considerable numbers not only in Cambridge but in universities around the country. For a time, the PAD solved local connectivity problems as well as providing a useful income stream.

A New Service Ethos and Another Review

In the mid-1980s personal computers became widely available and the Computing Service adapted to offer an advisory service to all University users. Continuing advances in microelectronics caused the Service to re-assess its role periodically in line with advances in technology. In the mainframe days, the Service had to manage the choice and purchase of a single system, to ensure it was efficiently operated and shared among the users and to manage resource allocation. Now, choice and purchase were in the hands of the user and efficient use of hardware was no longer an imperative. But there was a role to help and support: to negotiate discounts (of both hardware and software), to provide training and to manage connectivity. Above all was the realisation that those that had the funds had the right to buy what they wanted, and whether or not the Service agreed with their choice, the Service had the responsibility to provide support and assistance when asked. Service staff were all affected and had to learn new skills. Fortunately they did, while at the same time maintaining the tradition of doing it right and doing it well.

However, by the early 1990s, the mainframe had become a looming problem. The IBM 370/165 had been replaced in 1982 by a 3081D and in 1989 upgraded to a 3084Q, a four-processor behemoth, complete with an automated tape cartridge store which provided, for those days, almost unlimited online and offline archive storage. The mainframe, running Phoenix, was in a sense a victim of its own success. By this time, the advent of powerful workstations had enabled many departments to acquire their own systems, usually to support research

Chapter Six: Computing for All: Networking the University from EDSAC Users to Desktops and Laptops

From left to right: Chris Cheney joined the Laboratory as an electronics technician, eventually becoming Head of Communications and Networking. He was Project Manager for the development of the JNT PAD and the Granta Backbone Network. Roger Stratford established Institutional Liaison, becoming respected by heads of departments and other senior staff. Peter Crofts, first shift leader of the IBM mainframe, eventually became the Laboratory's Head of Operations. Steve Kearsey was Head of Applications Software, Deputy Director since 1994 and Acting Director in 2004.

and personal computer clusters for student teaching. The Service itself was also providing such facilities, either for general use or for specific networked functions. But many users were still dependent on the mainframe for a variety of purposes ranging from office-type functions to significant computation.

In 1993, the General Board decided it was time for a review of computing services. It had been almost 25 years since the previous review that had led to the re-organisation of the Laboratory in 1970; another was long overdue but in hindsight the delay was fortuitous since, in retrospect, the Service had been in some turmoil in the latter half of the 1980s. Computing and communication technology were advancing at a furious pace and the Service was absorbed in coping with the need for a change of ethos. The review chaired by Peter Swinnerton-Dyer, a former member of the Laboratory, took place just about the time the Service was beginning to understand future trends and what its role should be.

Swinnerton-Dyer reported that the era of large, central, general-purpose mainframes was over, and that the future would be high-performance distributed systems, optimised for a limited range of tasks and connected by a high-bandwidth network using the Granta Backbone Network. Following this new strategy, the last users were moved from the Phoenix mainframe service, which was closed in 1995, and transferred to a distributed environment of Unix-based servers for electronic mail and web services, IBM- and Macintosh-based teaching clusters sharing file store and applications, and a Central Unix Service (CUS) for researchers without their own equipment. The CUS was an interim solution and served 5,000 residual Phoenix users. It took until 2004, a further ten years, for this to dwindle to 2,000 users, whereupon CUS was retired. The secure-cartridge tape store of the IBM mainframe was replaced by a Unix-based system developed by the Service.

Phoenix had been used substantially for student teaching, and this was taken over by a Personal Workstation Facility (PWF), with 160 seats and a 32GB file store. In the next ten years the facility expanded to 1,600 seats, 2.6TB file store and 17,000 users. This expansion included the Managed Cluster Service (MCS), in which similar college- and department-owned clusters were managed on their behalf. Phoenix had also been the main e-mail system used by the University, and this was taken over in 1994 by Hermes, a dedicated Unix-based system. About two decades later, Hermes supports 21,000 users.

Over the years, the data network has expanded enormously in connectivity and bandwidth. The original 9.6Kb per second (Kbps) asynchronous lines of the 1970s were replaced by 10Mbps ethernet connections, which in turn gave way to much higher bandwidth. By 2002 there were 81 connections at 100Mbps and 43 at 1Gbps. In the same period the connection to the national JANET network increased from 10Mbps to 10Gbps. There was no doubt that the Granta Backbone Network had already justified its £3.5 million investment.

Distributed Strategies

Not only did computing become distributed but so did the making of computing strategy. In the late 1980s a small institutional liaison group had been formed whose function was not to assist individual users but to advise departments and colleges on their strategies. In due course senior staff became members of departmental IT strategy committees. The old model of resources being provided at the centre together with advice on how to use them was gradually being replaced by a cooperative model of common resources at the centre and dedicated resources in departments and colleges. This was particularly important in building bridges between the Service and the large departments such as Physics, Mathematics, Engineering and Clinical Medicine. The Service also developed close collaboration with the University Library, taking part in IT planning and supporting systems for major Library facilities.

Into a New Millennium

The academic side of the Computer Laboratory moved to a new building on the West Cambridge Site in 2001, which was the cue for the separation of the two sides, and the University Computing Service became a separate department in the University. This clearly marked the end of an era.

The mission of the Service is 'to maximise the productivity of teaching and research in the collegiate University'. In addition to ensuring that services are both fit for purpose and usable, there is a particular emphasis on the whole being greater than the sum of the parts. In general the Service plays a key role by supporting collaboration between active users who are provided, for example, with authentication services and network facilities.

The data network, which now includes wireless as well as fixed-line high-capacity bandwidth, remains the most valuable enterprise-wide asset supporting research. Data volumes have increased at an exponential rate largely due to increased high-energy physics data from the Large Hadron Collider at CERN in Geneva and widespread use of gene sequencing data from all over the world. Facilities have to be large, scalable, fast, robust and flexible. Flexibility is important because the Service cannot afford to constrain what is connected to the data network.

The development of systems in support of teaching and research requires both effective institution liaison and excellence in execution. New services are perceived and executed even though departments or colleges may not at first demand it. For example, the Streaming Media Service created in 2009 was an immediate success. Already there have been a very large number of viewings

Mike Sayers (left), Deputy Director from 1984 and Director from 1994 to 2002, and Ian Lewis, Director from 2003.

Chapter Six: Computing for All: Networking the University from EDSAC Users to Desktops and Laptops

of media content provided by upwards of 100 University institutions. By and large, current services aim to provide a high degree of autonomy to any department or college using them. One principle is to enable institutions to treat their data as their own data even though it may be stored centrally. For example, the University Training Booking System, introduced in 2010, unlike most systems of this type does not assume all training is provided by one central provider, and inherently supports the addition of new providers who can manage their own content and course bookings. There are now 12 training providers using the system, and approximately 8,000 members of the University attend training courses each year.

The new University wireless network known as Lapwing is unusual in that it provides a similar degree of flexibility to departments and colleges, who can add and manage their own students, staff and visitors. In 2011 the network supported 30,000 visitors, a number far larger than would have been supported had the design assumed purely central administration.

Recently a web content management system called Falcon was adopted to maximise productivity.

Departments are provided with their own 'instance' of a hosted web content management environment, with a high degree of control over the administration, structure and content, while the system itself is centrally managed. Common style templates are provided supporting an integrated look and feel across the wide range of content, and the Service manages the servers and the open-source content management software. So far, 80 departments and research groups have adopted it.

It has not been practical to describe all the achievements of the last four decades. For many years a maintenance service for computer hardware dealing mainly with IBM PCs and Apple Macintosh computers provided fast and low-cost servicing, although increased reliability has latterly reduced demand. A reprographics and photography service continues in much demand, and even provides a financially beneficial service photographing graduands receiving their degrees in the Senate House.

Just a few years ago the convergence of communications technologies enabled telephony and data networking to be merged over the Granta Backbone Network, resulting in what, at the time of installation, was arguably the largest installation of voice-over-IP (VOIP) technology in the world. At the same time, high-performance computing has become the domain of specific research groups who have pooled their funds to acquire an extremely powerful installation with over 1,150 processors. The Computing Service houses and supports this new kind of mainframe, which is far more powerful and has far fewer users. Just another example of the change of ethos over nearly 40 years.

Computing services in the University have come a long way in the last 75 years since the foundation of the Laboratory. The original remit to help researchers with their computations, from the development by Maurice Wilkes of some of the world's first computers, through to the microelectronic revolution, early systems have changed from being optimised and shared services to resources that can be proliferated, supported and developed. Since 1970 the University Computing Service has delivered a high degree of quality and professionalism. The inheritance from the pioneering days of a tradition of 'doing it right and doing it well' has been sustained with many firsts to its credit. It is set to continue to do so in the future.

Brian Westwood was appointed in 1969 to write the case for the IBM mainframe, and drafted all major policy documents until his retirement in 2003. He became an Assistant Director responsible for finance and administration and was appointed Deputy Director in 1988.

93

CHAPTER SEVEN

Spreading the Word
Teaching Computer Science and Technology

Peter Robinson

The original report of the General Board proposing the establishment of a Computing Laboratory in Cambridge noted that an assistant would be necessary to advise on the most efficient use of the machines and who might also give lectures on modern methods of computation. Maurice Wilkes enthusiastically fulfilled this role, and spreading the word of computing has always been a key part of the Laboratory's mission.

As soon as EDSAC had run its first program Wilkes organised a conference on High-Speed Automatic Calculating Machines in Cambridge at the end of June 1949. This was the first conference on computing outside the USA and attracted over 140 participants, roughly half from industry and government organisations, and half from academia including ten people from outside the UK. The meeting opened with a presentation about EDSAC and a demonstration of the machine in action. This was followed by two days of presentations reviewing projects around the world, reporting on relevant technologies and discussing the challenges of programming.

The final session was given over to a wide-ranging discussion of the challenges facing the discipline, which was seen to be 'at the beginning of a new and exciting adventure'. Some of the observations have faded with time, but many remain completely relevant today. Wilkes closed the meeting by remarking that, 'when a machine was finished, and a number of subroutines were in use, the order code could not be altered without causing a good deal of trouble. There would be almost as much capital sunk in the library of subroutines as the machine itself and builders of new machines in the future might wish to make use of the same order code as an existing machine in order that the subroutines could be taken over without modification.' Maintaining backward compatibility is not a new problem.

Formal teaching soon followed. Douglas Hartree had been giving advanced lectures on 'Numerical Analysis' in the Mathematical Tripos, and these were supplemented by a course on 'Automatic digital computing machines' presented by Wilkes and Renwick in October 1949. These were supplemented by a guild system where postgraduate

Report on the September 1949 conference in Mathematical Tables & Other Aids to Computation.

Chapter Seven: Spreading the Word: Teaching Computer Science and Technology

RECOLLECTIONS FROM DURWARD CRUICKSHANK

In September 1950 Durward Cruickshank was appointed Lecturer in Mathematical Chemistry in the University of Leeds. Professor E G Cox immediately sent him to the Cambridge Summer School. Cox had been a pioneer from 1937 onwards of X-ray structure analysis by Fourier methods with three-dimensional data. The Leeds Laboratory was strong in computing by punched-card methods and Cox was keen to exploit new ways for handling ever-larger crystallographic calculations.

'My recollection of the ten-day School is that there were some 20 to 24 participants of varying seniority. We were given the September 1950 issue of the Report on the preparation of programs for the EDSAC and the use of the library of subroutines. I still have my copy and also my manuscript notebook. It shows lectures on the following topics. To indicate the relative sizes, I show in parentheses the number of my pages on each topic:

    D R Hartree: Numerical Analysis (15 pages)
    S Gill: Programming (21)
    R A Brooker: Logical Design of the EDSAC (5)
    D J Wheeler: Subroutines (13)
    S Gill: Checking Routines (4).

'Evidently numerical analysis was considered a prerequisite to good programming. There were two external speakers:

J N Wilkinson: Programming for ACE (3)
T Kilburn: Programming for the Manchester Machine (6).

'The final General Discussion opened with a description by M V Wilkes of developments in the USA (3 pages). The participants by then had realised how splendid was the success of the Cambridge team in bringing EDSAC into working operation in 1949.

'I have lost my copies of the programming exercises we were given. By the end of the School some of the students were running their own problems on EDSAC. One Dutchman found that a certain 20-decimal number was factorisable. He was lucky. He got the first factor in 15 minutes. If the number had been prime, the run would have taken 12 hours.

'One student who made no attempt to do the exercises was B V Bowden, who had done his PhD in Rutherford's lab and was now computer salesman for Ferranti. Vivian's objective in the exercise periods was to chat individually to the participants about the computer Ferranti was building in Manchester. This was the commercial version of the first electronic stored-program computer, built and run by F C Williams and Tom Kilburn in 1948 using cathode-ray storage tubes.'

---

research students who were familiar with the EDSAC machine initiated their colleagues in its mysteries, frequently across Corn Exchange Street in the Bun Shop. Authorised users were also permitted to operate the machine by themselves through the night, or at least until it stopped working. Most of these students were based in other departments and Wilkes's liberal policy proved exceptionally wise as their supervisors were surprised to see the rapid progress that the students were making with their calculations. The value of the new instrument was apparent to all and Wilkes never had to resort to University politics to secure further funds.

Summer Schools

Wilkes knew that computing was going to be of wider interest than just solving problems for academics, and wanted to spread the word outside the University. In collaboration with the University's Board of Extra-mural Studies he established a series of Summer Schools on 'Programme design for automatic digital computing machines' which ran from 1950 to 1958. The course lasted ten days and involved a mixture of lectures on programming and practical work on EDSAC.

Students were drawn from industry and academia, with about 50 attending each year. Many pioneers of Computer Science had their first taste of the new subject at the Summer Schools. Wilkes was keen to look beyond the parochial Cambridge world of computing and invited guest lecturers from other leading laboratories. Alan Turing returned to Cambridge to talk about the work by Freddie Williams and Tom Kilburn in Max Newman's group at Manchester.

Clifford Robinson attended the Summer School in 1951. He had recently joined the English Electric Company as a mathematician designing electrical equipment. Two of his colleagues had attended the 1949 Conference and the company decided to produce its own computer. DEUCE was developed as a commercial version of the Automatic Calculating Engine (ACE) which had been built at the National Physical Laboratory (NPL). His son Peter was born a year later, and subsequently became Wilkes's successor as Professor of Computer Technology at the University of Cambridge.

Analysis and Automatic Computing should be instituted. The proposed course would last an academic year and would include theoretical and practical work in numerical analysis and in the programming of problems for electronic computing machines. It would also include instruction about the various types of electronic computing machine in existence and the principles of design on which they were based.

The proposal found favour with the University, and the first class started in October 1953, the world's first taught course in Computer Science. The course was divided into two more-or-less equal parts: numerical analysis, which drew on earlier experience with mechanical calculators, and the new topics of digital electronics and programming. The syllabus covered hardware, software and applications.

Wilkes, Wheeler and Gill edited the course notes into a book – *The preparation of programs for an electronic digital computer* – which was published in April 1951. This was the first book on Computer Science and became the indispensable reference work in the field.

Diploma in Numerical Analysis and Automatic Computing

It soon became apparent to the Faculty Board of Mathematics that there was growing demand for postgraduate instruction in numerical analysis and automatic computing, and that there was a danger that the application to scientific research of the machines being built would be hampered by the lack of graduates with suitable training if this demand was not met. They noted that the Summer School only lasted for ten days and dealt with programming rather than with the general theory of the numerical methods which were programmed. They accordingly proposed that a Diploma in Numerical

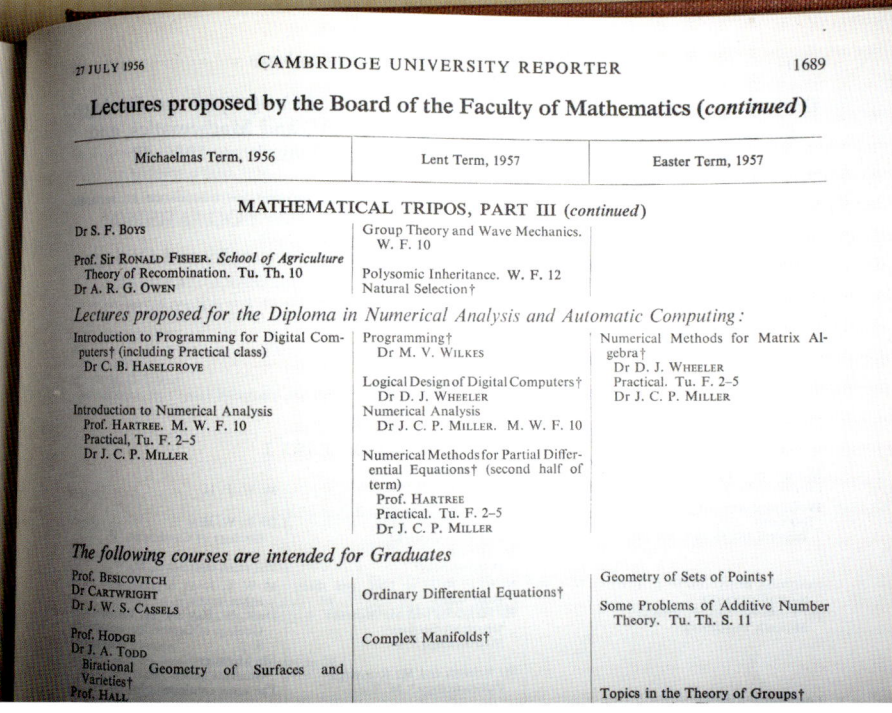

Lecture schedules for the Diploma.

Chapter Seven: Spreading the Word: Teaching Computer Science and Technology

RECOLLECTIONS FROM PETER WEGNER

Peter Wegner recalls: 'In the spring of 1953, I was completing my BSc degree in mathematics at Imperial College when Douglas Hartree gave a visiting lecture and persuaded me to come to Cambridge for the summer. I worked with him on a problem that involved collaboration with Rudolf Peierls in Birmingham and the two young physicists Jerry Brown and Sheila Brenner. This problem involved solving differential equations with Bessel function right-hand sides by the Runge–Kutta–Gill method. I was able to simplify the solution procedure by representing the Bessel functions by differential equations rather than tables, solving a larger set of differential equations without the need to resort to tables and interpolation. The idea of replacing laboriously computed tables by differential equations seemed counter-intuitive, but simplified and speeded up the solution process.

'One of my early assignments was writing a program for solving linear equations. I was fascinated by the ability to look at the memory content while the computation was progressing and watch successive data values being zeroed as a part of the elimination procedure. I was sloppy in providing test data for the equation-solving program and ran my first test with two identical rows, which should have caused the program to crash on division by zero. However, round off error came to my rescue and I watched the program divide by 2^{-35} and provide a solution of rather large numbers that, on back substitution, provided a satisfactory solution to several decimal places. Thus, I was able to successfully invert a singular matrix.

'Our first Diploma class in 1953 consisted of three students. The other two were Ernest Albasiny, who subsequently worked in the National Physical Laboratory on numerical analysis, and Stan Bootle, a colourful married student with a family of five children whose door was always open to my visits, and who later became quite a well-known radio personality.

'I still have my Diploma thesis, with over 100 yellowing pages that include chapters on the initial orders, the differential equation problem, and philosophical chapters on computation, which are dated but include a discussion of software complexity, systems with multiple interfaces, and other topics that later became important areas for technical analysis.

'Maurice Wilkes had a strong influence on my intellectual development. Recognising my inclination towards philosophy, he asked me to look into the work of Leibniz on early calculation, and I translated an article by Leibniz from German into English. I have greatly valued my continued contact with Maurice over the years, meeting with him several times a year during his years in Boston working for DEC.

'Cambridge was an exciting place in the 1950s. I organised a small philosophical study group with Amartya Sen, who later won the Noble Prize in Economics for his work on world hunger. I often went to tea at the Cavendish Laboratory, where they sold delicious cakes for two pence each, and attended the quantum theory lectures of the eminent Cambridge physicist Paul Dirac. In the evenings I often ate at the local ABC restaurant and remember having dinner there with Francis Crick on a couple of occasions. On one occasion, I was "progged" by a bulldog and two proctors for not wearing a gown after dark. I had to pay 13 shillings and 4 pence because I was a graduate student (the fine for undergraduates was six and eight pence). I lived in an attic in the vicarage at 45 Jesus Lane, right opposite the entrance to Jesus College.

'My short, one-year stay at the Maths Lab played a key role in my professional life whose importance I am only now beginning to appreciate. After Cambridge, I spent a short time in Manchester working with Brooker, and later became a part of the brain drain, working on time-sharing at MIT, returning to the London School of Economics to work on operations research, and then back to the USA to work on programming languages, semantics and software engineering.'

Right: Peter Wegner, Diploma Class of 1953.

Cambridge Computing: The First 75 Years

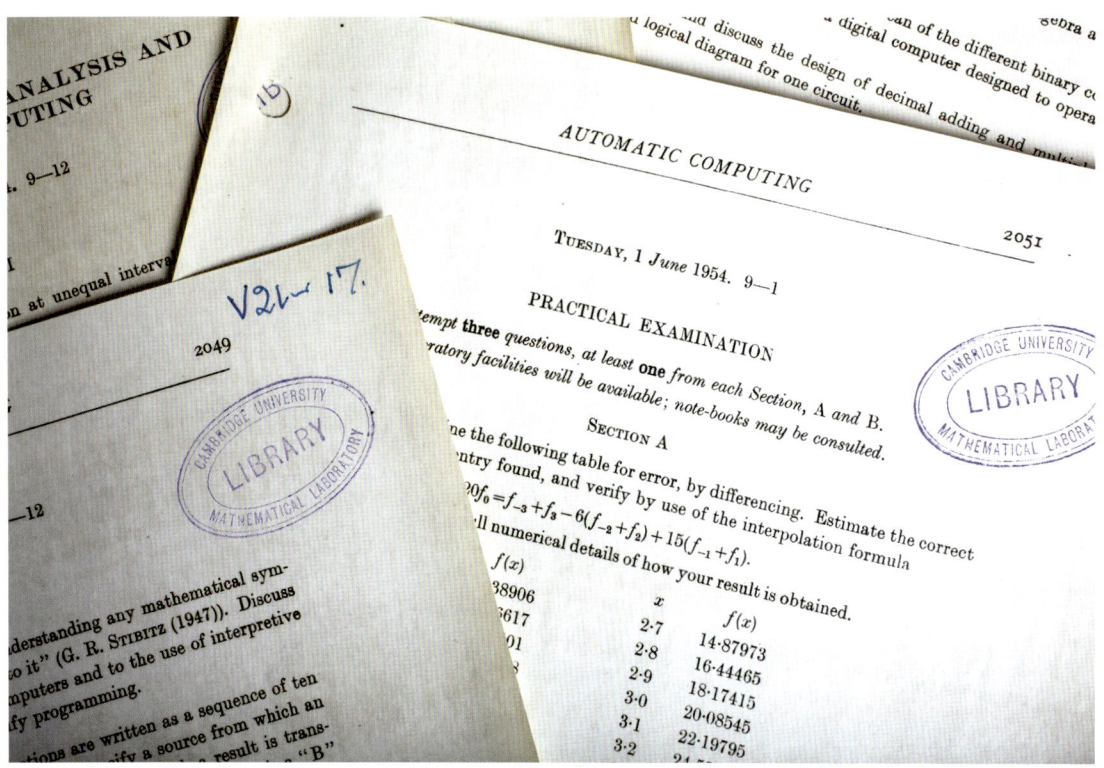

Opposite: Four members of staff in the Computer Laboratory have been awarded Pilkington Teaching Prizes by the University, recognising exceptional excellence in teaching. Neil Dodgson created interactive demonstrations of graphics algorithms and used excerpts from movies to make the underlying concepts memorable and comprehensible; Peter Robinson introduced group practical projects into the course to give students a taste of working as a team against tight deadlines; Larry Paulson teaches the initial programming course that has to engage students with very different levels of previous experience; and Simon Moore has taken an innovative approach to developing studio-based teaching of practical skills, and designed new hardware to support practical work.

Left: Questions from the first Diploma examinations: Numerical Analysis, Automatic Computing, and Practical.

The course combined lectures in the morning with practical work including use of the EDSAC machine in the afternoons. Students also undertook a substantial practical project through the year and wrote it up in a dissertation. The projects often involved the use of the new computer to solve problems suggested by academic staff and research students in other scientific disciplines.

The course was examined in two papers lasting three hours each, together with a four-hour session solving practical problems. Apart from changes in technology, the questions would not be out of place today.

Three students took the course in its first year. Ernest Albasiny continued to a career in numerical analysis at NPL. Stanley Bootle worked for IBM and Sperry-Univac before becoming a freelance consultant and writer of books, articles and songs (as Stan Kelly-Bootle). Peter Wegner joined the faculty of Brown University in Rhode Island, where he continues to contribute to the theory and practice of programming.

Numbers on the course grew steadily and exceeded 40 by the 1980s. Interest then faded as undergraduate Computer Science courses became more widespread, and the Diploma course was finally withdrawn in 2008.

Computer Science Tripos

Many other universities introduced taught courses in Computer Science, including undergraduate courses through the 1950s and 1960s, and Cambridge finally introduced a one-year course to be taken after two years studying a cognate subject such as Mathematics,

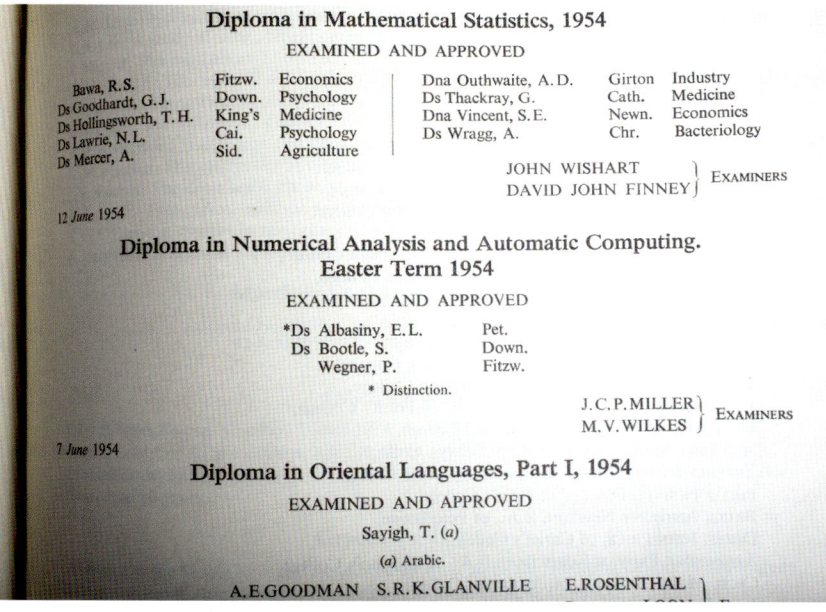

Class list from the first Diploma course.

Cambridge Computing: The First 75 Years

Below: Andrew Birrell was one of the first cohort of students taking the one-year Computer Science Tripos in 1971. He stayed in the Computer Laboratory to work for a PhD and then enjoyed a career in research with Xerox, DEC and Microsoft in California.

Engineering or Natural Sciences. This was given as a final-year option in the Natural Sciences Tripos in 1970, and as a fully fledged, independent Computer Science Tripos with 34 students in 1971.

The taught course was the same as the Diploma, although the examination had extended to four three-hour papers. The old Diploma practical examination was absorbed as part of one of the written papers and supplemented by a series of assessed exercises for the Tripos and a more substantial project written up as a dissertation for the Diploma.

The 1970s saw rapid growth in the subject, and the Tripos was extended to two years in 1978, to be taken after one year studying a cognate subject. The preliminary year continued to match the taught part of the Diploma, while the final year introduced more advanced topics and introduced a substantial practical project.

Computer Science finally became a full three-year subject admitting its own students in 1989, and a fourth year leading to the MEng degree was added in 2011.

About 100 students are admitted to the course each year. The first year covers the foundations of the subject and students also spend a quarter of their time taking Further Mathematics, Social Psychology, or an experimental subject from Part IA of the Natural Sciences Tripos. The second year presents core Computer Science and the third year moves on to advanced topics. A small number of students stay on to take the fourth year, which is intended as preparation for research.

Meredydd Luff was one of the final cohort of students taking the one-year Computer Science Tripos and Diploma course in 2007. He then stayed in the Computer Laboratory to work for a PhD before joining Google in California.

Chapter Seven: Spreading the Word: Teaching Computer Science and Technology

The Laboratory organises an annual fair for its industrial supporters in the William Gates Building. About 50 companies compete to recruit the Laboratory's graduates and there is usually a waiting list of other companies who would welcome the opportunity to attract students.

Employers compete fiercely to recruit graduates from the course, and there is always a waiting list for companies wanting a stall at the Laboratory's job fair each autumn. Opportunities cover the entire spectrum from local start-ups to large technology companies, with a steady stream going into the city and consultancy. Many continue with postgraduate study.

Master's Courses

The explosive growth of computing in the 1980s fuelled demand for graduates with specialised skills in particular areas. The Computer Laboratory introduced a one-year MPhil course in Computer Speech and Language Processing jointly with the Department of Engineering in 1985. This combined expertise in signal and speech processing in Engineering with language processing and information retrieval in the Computer Laboratory, and drew a regular class of 20 students each year.

A second MPhil course, in Advanced Computer Science, started in 2009, and subsumed the existing course

Andrew Moore lecturing to students in the Computer Laboratory.

101

Cambridge Computing: The First 75 Years

a year later. Both serve as preparation for research and have proved extremely popular with students from both Cambridge and around the world.

Service Teaching

Until the late 1960s the principal extra-departmental teaching consisted of students from other departments sitting in on selected Diploma lectures. A major development was the introduction of lectures recorded on videotape by David Hartley in 1968. Other notable milestones include the introduction of courses for Arts students, and the incredible persistence but eventual demise of Fortran.

There has been a long-term trend away from teaching programming to the teaching of applications. Almost everyone now uses some kind of wordprocessor and even mathematicians have appreciated that spreadsheets are not just tools for accountants. The Computing Service took over most service teaching in the 1980s and the Natural Scientists finally assumed responsibility for teaching Matlab to their undergraduates in 2010–11.

The Future

The Laboratory remains committed to ensuring that its students are fully informed about the current state of the art, and are thoroughly equipped to meet the challenges of the future. The Lab will continue to ensure that they

Frank King coordinated extra-departmental teaching, combining lectures recorded on videotape (**above**) with practical sessions (**below**) using computer terminals.

Chapter Seven: Spreading the Word: Teaching Computer Science and Technology

have a proper training in both principles and practice – for example in system theory, design and engineering – to contribute as computer science and technology professionals to all areas of employment where computing has or acquires a role.

Innovation in teaching continues. The early lectures on videotape in the late 1960s have now been replaced with online material and various lecturers have been experimenting with more sophisticated systems for computer-assisted learning across the whole curriculum from electronics through programming to mathematics. Most of the teaching material is already openly published online and is already being used outside Cambridge. The Computer Laboratory expects this contribution to global education to grow in the years to come.

Pioneering research is reflected in teaching that continues to look forward, so that graduates will meet the emerging technical, economic and social challenges that global-scale information and communications technologies will bring.

Open Days for school leavers who might be interested in studying Computer Science are popular in early July each year.

103

CHAPTER EIGHT

The Computer Laboratory, 1980–2012
The 'Needham Years' and the Modern Era

New Leadership and a New Ethos

Roger Needham became Head of Department on 1 October 1980 after serving an apprenticeship of almost 20 years from research student to University Reader in Computer Systems. One year later he was belatedly promoted to Professor of Computer Systems, which reinforced his position within the Department and gave him credibility beyond Cambridge. During his time at the Computer Laboratory he had not only made a name as a computer scientist of the highest order but had also personally led many important projects and become Wilkes's right-hand man and close confidante. He therefore assumed his new responsibilities with a clear understanding of the Laboratory's historic achievements over the 35-year reign of Maurice Wilkes, and he must have been very conscious that he needed to formulate his own vision for the future of the Computer Laboratory. He inherited a very successful laboratory in an academic discipline that was growing in importance across the world, but he needed to introduce new research topics, to appoint more academic staff and to find more space on a site that was overcrowded. At the start of his tenure in 1980 the teaching and research staff numbered just ten. There were ten postdoctoral research fellows and 43 students studying for a PhD. Fortunately he took over in a national climate of generous government support for tertiary education and university research. Later in life he described his first ten years as Head of Department as 'halcyon days – an expanding Laboratory and no external interference'.

In his last decade at the Computer Laboratory Wilkes had become a somewhat remote figure to most of its members. He worked from his office for much of the day and did not join the staff and students who frequented the popular tearoom. Needham on the other hand was a constant presence in the Laboratory, happy to join in discussions in the tearoom, in the corridors, in his office and occasionally in the local pub. Many of his colleagues recall that conversations with him required that one had to sit still and follow his constant movement around his office as he talked. A staff member remarked that, after Wilkes's departure, 'the Head of Department's office became a much less forbidding place'. Needham was very approachable and invariably helpful both on research issues and on administrative matters. He brought an informal and modern style of management to the Computer Laboratory and changed its ethos.

Expansion and Needham's Growing Influence

In the early years of Wilkes's reign the subject of computer science had advanced steadily, concentrated mainly on developing better mainframe computers. Progress had been slow at first but accelerated following the development of integrated circuits. In Needham's time there was an explosive growth of the subject, fuelled by dramatic improvements in the performance of processing chips and semiconductor memories. The computer became inexpensive, compact, easy-to-use and ubiquitous across the world.

In 1981, a ten-year research programme including aspects of computing ranging from artificial intelligence to societal benefits of computers was announced in Japan, 'The Fifth Generation Computer Project'. The UK Department of Trade and Industry sent a working party, chaired by John Alvey, to Japan on a fact-finding mission. Needham was the only academic member appointed to this delegation. The Alvey committee made recommendations to the government for a UK-wide programme of research

Roger Needham was Head of the Computer Laboratory, Pro-Vice-Chancellor of Cambridge University and Managing Director of Microsoft Research, Cambridge.

and development, the Alvey Programme. It was designed to create multi-partner research projects within the UK and Needham's position of leadership in this programme gave him a great deal of influence nationally as well as within the University.

Needham had been a frequent visitor to the USA since 1958 and had long-standing contacts in Xerox PARC and the Systems Research Centre of the Digital Equipment Corporation. He visited one or other of these organisations almost every summer for approximately two months and returned with fresh ideas for research and sometimes with donations of equipment for the Laboratory. Students and staff active in the Laboratory in the 1980s and early 1990s benefited a great deal from Needham's American connections.

Needham's influence continued to grow and in 1986 he became a member of the University Grants Committee, which allocates funds for research to universities in the UK. A few years later he was appointed a member of the Wass Syndicate which was charged with reforming the administrative structure of Cambridge University. It proposed that there should be a Pro-Vice-Chancellor to assist the Vice-Chancellor, and Needham was chosen as the first Pro-Vice-Chancellor of Cambridge University. At the same time, in 1996, Alec Broers, later Lord Broers, was appointed Vice-Chancellor.

Under Needham's leadership the Computer Laboratory continued to acquire more space on the New Museum site. As other departments moved off the site the Computer Laboratory was extended from Corn Exchange Street at one end to Free School Lane at the other. The new sections had to be connected to each other via bridges across roads and passages.

In 1983 there was a large increase in the number of academic staff, with five new posts allocated to the Computer Laboratory in recognition of its achievements; Andy Hopper and Peter Robinson were among those who were appointed to Lectureships. In the ten years from 1980 to 1990 no less than 19 new academic appointments were made by Needham, and a number of new areas of research were started by the newly appointed staff. By 1990 the established teaching and research staff numbers had risen from ten to 27. There were 30 postdoctoral research fellows and 92 students working towards PhDs.

Major Research Projects

Needham initiated a number of new research areas in the Laboratory. One of the most significant was theoretical research in computing following the appointment of Mike Gordon to a University Lectureship. He started work in the Laboratory on the formal verification of hardware designs. Gordon's appointment brought to the Laboratory the theoretical element that had been absent in Wilkes's time.

UNIVERSE

Needham launched a major, multi-partner, £3 million collaborative project which was jointly funded by the Science Research Council, the Department of Trade and Industry and two industrial companies. It involved three universities (Cambridge, Loughborough and University College, London), three industrial companies (BT, GEC and Logica) and the Science Research Council's Rutherford and Appleton Laboratory (RAL). This project was a significant departure from the Laboratory's normal practice of carrying out research projects entirely within its own resources. The project, called UNIVERSE, an acronym of UNIV-Expanded Ring and Satellite Experiment was based on the interconnection of several Cambridge Digital Rings at different sites in the UK working with a version of the Cambridge Distributed System. Its purpose was to demonstrate the feasibility of linking a number of local area networks (LANs) through a satellite.

Cambridge Digital Rings were located in each of the collaborating partners' laboratories and linked by a high-bandwidth communication link. The network was given a single name space and the system could transmit speech, images and video at slow scan speeds between the participating laboratories. The satellite used for the communications link was the European Space Agency's Orbital Test Satellite, with a bandwidth of 2Mb per second. The project was demonstrated successfully at an important telecommunications conference and was concluded in 1983 when the satellite was no longer available. UNIVERSE made it possible to test the scaling of LAN protocols over wider areas, as well as efficient network management, security aspects and encryption techniques. The project also gave Roger Needham national visibility and recognition. In the course of the project he became a significant figure within organisations concerned with the direction of future national research. A number of research staff and students, including Ian Leslie, Andrew Herbert and David Tennenhouse, worked with Roger Needham on this project.

Unison

Needham was able to launch a follow-on project, Unison, which ran almost to the end of the 1980s. The national telephone network was becoming digital and it used the new 'isdn' digital phone links in place of the satellite link. The project objectives were to investigate the use of LANs in intersite office work using e-mail, document transfer and interactive conferences. It also explored multimedia information transfer using text, graphics and voice. The Cambridge Fast Ring which had been developed by Andy Hopper and his team was used as the LAN at each site. The fast ring used short packets compared with the frames of the ethernet systems, which made it possible for multimedia information to be transmitted in real time with very little delay. The partners were Cambridge and Loughborough universities, two industrial companies, Acorn Computers and Logica, and RAL was the coordinating body. The project, valued at £2.6 million, continued to bring resources into the Computer Laboratory and was concluded in 1989. It pioneered what is now called 'flow aggregation', where a number of separately dialed connections between sites are seamlessly combined to form a channel with greater throughput.

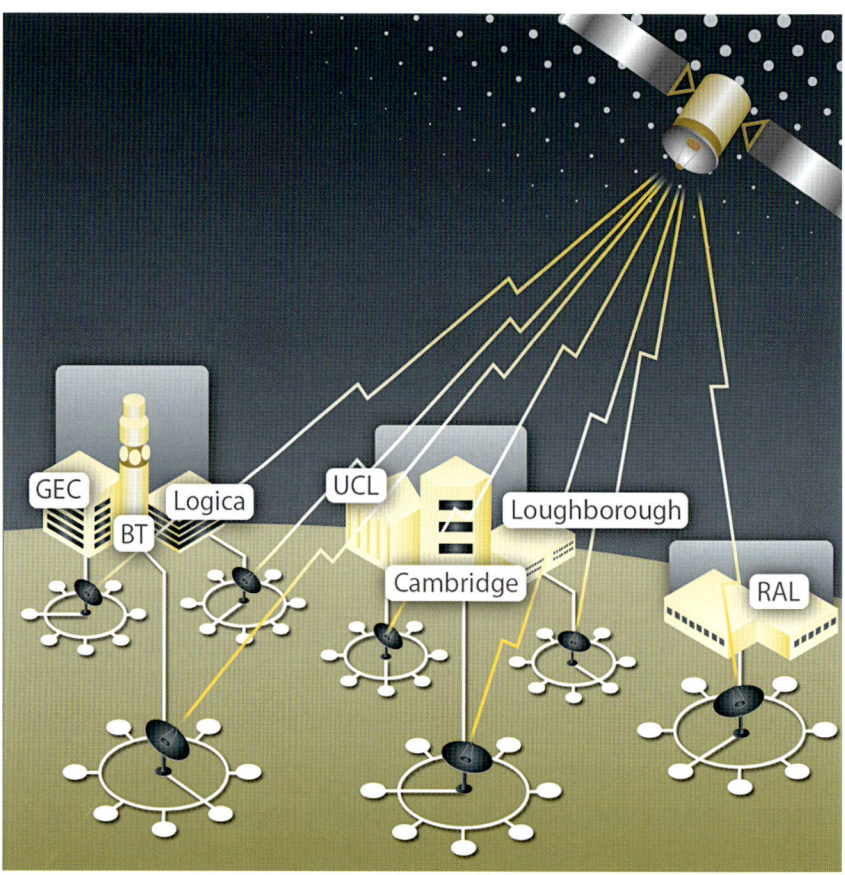

Personal Research Contributions

Within Cambridge Needham was heavily involved in managing and contributing to the major projects underway in the Laboratory, namely Titan, CAP and the Cambridge Model Distributed System. It was during his regular visits to Xerox PARC and the Digital Equipment Corporation that he was able to work on his personal research interests. He is widely recognised today for his contributions to designing cryptographic protocols for authentication and security in personal computing systems. He began working on this subject in the 1970s with Michael Schroeder at Xerox PARC. They described the now well-known Needham–Schroeder authentication protocol in a joint paper in 1978. This protocol was the first sound solution to the then urgent need for mutual authentication between two parties communicating over an insecure network, and is now recognised as the standard solution. As such it is the basis for virtually all subsequently developed mechanisms for secure Internet communication. While carrying out this work

Project Universe was a multi-partner collaborative project designed to explore communication between research centres using a satellite linking Cambridge Digital Rings installed at the partners' sites.

Chapter Eight: The Computer Laboratory, 1980–2012: The 'Needham Years' and the Modern Era

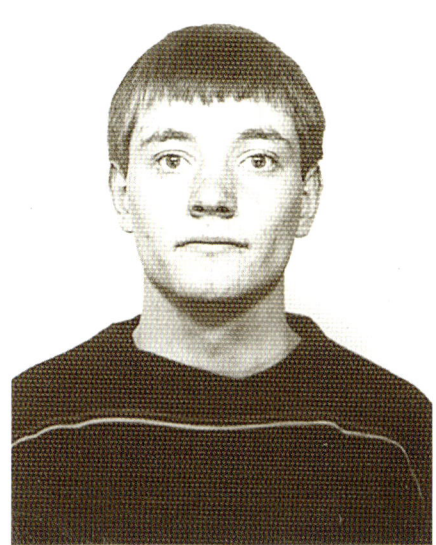

After graduating from University College, London, Mike Burrows moved to Churchill College, Cambridge, as a PhD student in the Computer Laboratory, where he was supervised by David Wheeler. He was at the Laboratory from 1984 to 1988, working on data compression – particularly on the approach which is now well known as the Burrows–Wheeler Transform (BWT). He then went to work at the Digital Equipment Corporation's Systems Research Centre in the USA. While he was there he worked with Needham, who was making one of his annual visits to DEC, and with Martin Abadi on authentication. The software they created is now well known as the BAN Logic. Burrows also worked with Karen Spärck Jones on search engines while he was creating the AltaVista Search Engine. After DEC was sold to Compaq, Burrows went on to join Google. The photograph was taken c.1984 while Burrows was a student at Churchill College.

Needham gave the name 'nonce' to the security number introduced during a conversation between two parties over the Internet, enabling the recipient to check that the conversation is a 'fresh' one. Needham always enjoyed using the English language to its fullest extent and 'nonce' merely means a word that is invented to be used just once! The security number was updated for the next conversation.

By 1985 the use of personal computers had increased significantly, and Needham decided to return to the subject of authentication for large networks. He worked for three months at DEC with his former student at Cambridge Michael Burrows, and with DEC mathematician Martin Abadi, whose expertise was formal logic. The three scientists devised the formal logic solution to the problem of authentication, now known as the BAN logic after the initial letters of the surnames of the authors. By 1994 Needham had begun to address the question of failure in security as a consequence of the deliberate or inadvertent human actions rather than formal protection methodology. He expanded on this theme during his Clifford Patterson lecture to the Royal Society in 2002 by suggesting that 'humans involved in managing security are fallible, lazy and uncomprehending', therefore the challenging problems for security are with people, rather than with electronic or mathematical protection techniques.

Progress of the Computer Laboratory

In 1987 the Computer Laboratory celebrated its 50th anniversary. Some of the many outstanding research results reported on this occasion were: verification of the VIPER chip by Gordon and Cohn; extensive research on authentication and security led by Needham; work on the theorem proving program 'Isabelle' led by Larry Paulson; middleware research led by Jean Bacon and Ken Moody; Project Unison, led by Ian Leslie; and iris recognition initiated by John Daugman, which received worldwide recognition and the British Computer Society (BCS) award in 1997. Throughout the Laboratory there was increasing emphasis on multimedia projects. In 1996 the Hitachi SR2201 parallel processing machine was installed in the Laboratory and used by a number of science departments. It came to the Laboratory through Needham's connection with the company as a consultant to its Advanced Research Laboratory in Japan.

Michael Schroeder (on the left) and Roger Needham relaxing during a break while teaching a course on distributed computing in Portugal, 1992.

ROGER NEEDHAM (1935–2003)

Roger Needham studied Philosophy in his final year as an undergraduate at Cambridge University after two years of Mathematics; he came into contact with the Cambridge Language Research Unit (CLRU), led by the idiosyncratic Margaret Masterman, and thereby became interested in the Unit's research into automatic language translation. At the same time he was attracted to the newly emerging field of computing and registered for the 'Diploma in Numerical Analysis and Automatic Computing' offered by the Mathematical Laboratory. He now combined his interest in machine translation with computing and worked at the CLRU for five years while simultaneously pursuing a PhD project in the Mathematical Laboratory. CLRU members were using the collection of synonyms in 'the thesaurus' for purposes of translation, information processing and document retrieval.

Needham's research centred on automatic classification and its applications and he developed a 'theory of clumps' which defined a class and applied it *inter alia* to document index terms, lexical data and prehistoric pots. He obtained his PhD in 1961 and joined the staff of the Mathematical Laboratory as a Senior Assistant in Research in 1963. He was promoted to Assistant Director of Research a year later, at a time when the Laboratory was engaged in the Titan project, and he played a major part in ensuring its success. From then on he became a key member of the Mathematical Laboratory and later of the Computer Laboratory. He was elected a Fellow of Wolfson College in 1966, where there is now a room named in his honour. His wife Karen Spärck Jones was also a Fellow, and she too has a room named after her, in recognition of her distinction in natural language processing research.

Roger Needham and Karen Spärck Jones at their wedding in 1958.

When Needham was dying his former students and colleagues came from far and wide and held a symposium in his presence. The proceedings were published as *Computer Systems: Papers for Roger Needham*, and the occasion vividly demonstrated the high regard and deep affection with which he was held by all who worked with him.

In 1999, four years after Needham had given up the headship of the Department, the 50th anniversary of the commissioning of EDSAC was celebrated with a two-day event, EDSAC 99 (15–16 April). The vast expansion of research, academic staff numbers and research student numbers is reflected in the list of research topics reported at the celebration. These included: Self-Timed Logic (Simon Moore and Peter Robinson), Autostereo 3D display (Neil Dodgson and Stewart Lang), Next-generation Workstations (Ian Pratt and Austin Donnelly), Warren Home Network (David Greaves and Daniel Gordon), the Nemesis Operating System (Steven Hand and Paul Menage), The Active House (Jean Bacon, Andrew McNeill and Alexis Hombrecher), Network Control and Management (Ian Leslie and Richard Mortier), Proving Protocols Correct (Larry Paulson and Gianpaolo Bella), Xisabelle – Supporting Proof (Katherine Eastaughffe), Floating Point Verification (John Harrison and Myra van Inwegen), Modelling Interactive Systems (Philippa Gardner), Natural Language Processing (Steve Pulman),

Chapter Eight: The Computer Laboratory, 1980–2012: The 'Needham Years' and the Modern Era

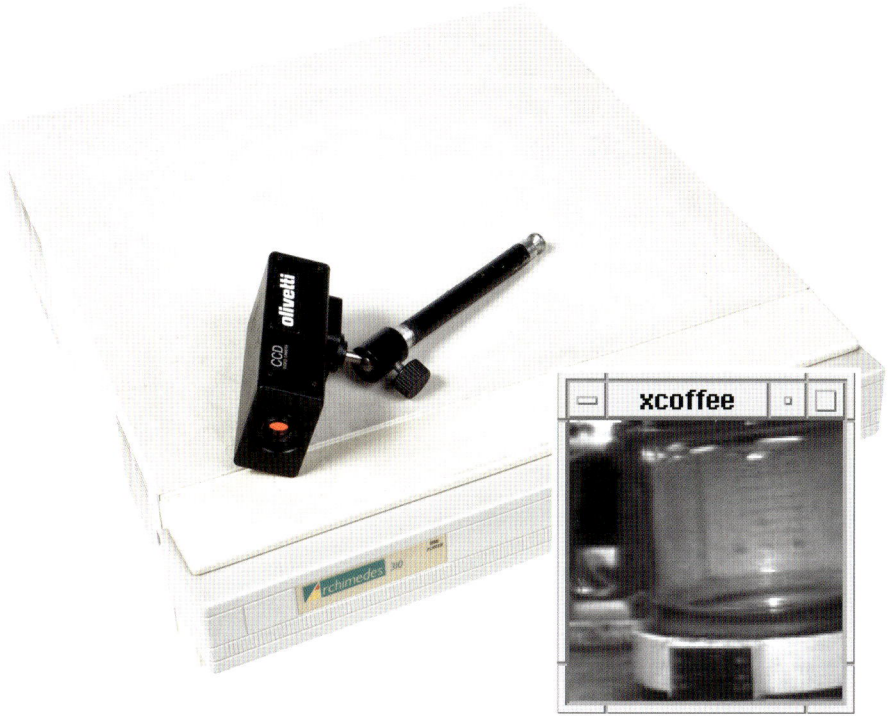

The world's first 'webcam' was installed in the Computer Laboratory to monitor the state of the coffee machine.

Iris Recognition (John Daugman), Modelling and Animation (Neil Dodgson and Peter Robinson) and Video User Interface (Peter Robinson and Richard Watts).

There were other lectures by many who had contributed to the research in the Computer Laboratory, including Professor Sir Maurice Wilkes, who gave a lecture called 'EDSAC 1 – getting it all going', and David Wheeler, who talked about EDSAC 2. More details about this important, landmark occasion can be found in the booklet prepared by the Department which is available on its website.

One of the more unusual outcomes of the work in the Computer Laboratory on multimedia systems was the world's first 'webcam'. A lashed-up camera watched a coffee pot shared by a group of people and placed a live image displaying the status of the coffee pot on the desktops of all group members. It alerted people at some distance when a freshly brewed pot was available and unnecessary journeys were thus avoided. In 1993 it was obvious that web browsers could be used to display the image and the camera was connected to the Internet. The picture of the coffee pot became visible to Internet users and gained in popularity at an amazing rate. The story of the coffee pot was featured in the *Washington Post*, the *Times* and the *Guardian*. When the Computer Laboratory moved from its site in the centre of Cambridge to the new William Gates Building the camera was finally switched off, generating renewed interest in the story.

From 'Computers' to Computer Scientists

After the end of the Second World War there was a shortage of women available to work as 'computers' and Wilkes bemoaned the fact that he had been unable to fill all of the six positions the University had allocated to the Mathematical Laboratory. Later, following the commissioning of EDSAC, a number of women were employed in the Laboratory in non-academic positions working as assistants and machine operators. The first woman to carry out scientific work on computing was Beatrice Helen Worsley (1922–72), who was present when EDSAC came to life and wrote a compiler for the Ferranti computer. She was a registered PhD student at Cambridge University and received her degree in 1952, which probably makes her the first woman ever to gain a doctorate in computing anywhere in the world. She worked in the Mathematical Laboratory for a short while before returning to Canada, where she worked as a computer scientist for 20 years at Toronto University.

Another woman, Charlotte Fischer, was one of Hartree's PhD students who used EDSAC for her research. She described her experiences working late into the night and noticing that errors crept in when the room got hotter and the mercury delay line memory started misbehaving! She went on to write that it was usually necessary to run a program repeatedly until two, or better still three, results from EDSAC were identical.

These pioneering women research students were followed by a number of women scientists who used computers for research, including Joyce Blackler, who used EDSAC's derivative, sometimes described as EDSAC 1.5, for her PhD research project in Astrophysics.

women@CL

women@CL is a network designed to provide support for women in computing research in the Computer Laboratory. Founded in 2003 by Ursula Martin and Mateja Jamnik and now directed by Jamnik, it organises local, national and international meetings and seminars with women speakers, provides peer-to-peer mentoring

109

Cambridge Computing: The First 75 Years

JEAN BACON

The first woman to take up an academic position at the Cambridge University Computer Laboratory, Jean Bacon was appointed to a University Lectureship in 1985. She applied for the position on noticing an advertisement in the *Guardian* newspaper seeking to fill a vacancy for a Lectureship in the Computer Laboratory. At this point in her career she was working as a Principal Lecturer at the Hatfield Polytechnic (now Hertfordshire University). There is a story, possibly apocryphal, that she was the first woman ever to apply for an academic post in the Computer Laboratory, but was also the only woman in the list of candidates.

After her appointment she started the Opera Research Group at the Computer Laboratory, working with Ken Moody. This group worked on the design and deployment of open, large-scale, widely distributed, multi-domain systems, based on secure, asynchronous middleware. From the early 1990s she pioneered asynchronous, event-based middleware, now widely recognised as the most appropriate paradigm for global and pervasive computing. Her research on expressing and enforcing security policy in middleware included Role-Based Access Control and Information Flow Control. Applications for this work included electronic health record systems, personal healthcare management and transport monitoring.

She also taught a number of undergraduate courses, introducing *inter alia* concurrent systems, and participated in the academic management of the Laboratory. She was elected to a teaching Fellowship at Jesus College, Cambridge, in 1997 and appointed Director of Studies in Computer Science. She was the first woman to hold such a position in any of the constituent colleges of Cambridge University. In 1999 she became the first woman to be a Reader in the Computer Laboratory, taking the title Reader in Distributed Systems, and in 2003 became Professor of Distributed Systems, following the precedent of Karen Spärck Jones, who was promoted in 1999. These promotions created landmarks for women in computing at Cambridge. Bacon is a Fellow of the IEEE and the BCS and has supervised 36 PhD students in her career. Today there are several women in academic positions at the Computer Laboratory, but it still seeks to increase the number of women in senior academic positions.

Above: Women academics at the Computer Laboratory. From left to right: Simone Teufel, Jean Bacon, Ann Copestake, Mateja Jamnik and Cecilia Mascolo.

Left: Jean Bacon, the first woman to be appointed to a University Lectureship at the Computer Laboratory, in 1985.

The closure of ORL was marked with a 'goodbye' party attended by ORL staff and members of the Computer Laboratory.

and organises social events. Its principal goals are to increase the recruitment and retention of women in computing research, to encourage women to take leadership roles in their careers in computing and to take part in entrepreneurial ventures.

THE OLIVETTI RESEARCH LABORATORY IN CAMBRIDGE, 1986–2002

The Olivetti Research Laboratory (ORL) was founded in 1986 by Hermann Hauser and Andy Hopper in the aftermath of the acquisition of Acorn Computers by the Italian company Olivetti SpA. As part of the agreement between Olivetti and Acorn, Hauser was appointed Vice-President for Research and placed in charge of all existing Olivetti SpA research laboratories, and also given the remit to establish new laboratories. He approached Andy Hopper, Co-Director of Acorn Computers, to start and direct an ORL in Cambridge. Hopper was then a University Lecturer in the Computer Laboratory, and with his support Hauser planned to forge strong links between his nascent laboratory and Cambridge University. Hopper and Hauser approached Roger Needham and sought his support. Needham consulted his senior colleagues, David Wheeler and Neil Wiseman, and all three agreed to establish a close link between ORL and the Computer Laboratory.

Initially the arrangement was informal and based on mutual trust, with no contractual documentation, but it was stipulated that there would be an annual review of progress. (A formal agreement was eventually signed between ORL and the University in the late 1990s.) Hauser then approached Maurice Wilkes, who had recently returned to Cambridge after spending six years in the USA. Wilkes was appointed staff adviser to ORL and Hopper was appointed Managing Director. ORL started operations at 4A Market Hill, the original home of Acorn Computers, but in 1987 ORL acquired new premises in part of the old Addenbrookes Hospital site after successful negotiations between Wilkes and the University's Department of Estate Management. At its peak ORL had as many as 60 employees. Initially it was sponsored entirely by Olivetti SpA, later by Olivetti and Digital Equipment Corporation and still later by Oracle and Olivetti until eventually, in 1999, ORL was bought by AT&T and closed down in 2002, when the American company went through a period of financial restructuring.

Structure and Modus Operandi

ORL carried out research projects on behalf of Olivetti but was free to choose its own directions and priorities, and local management was authorised to make all strategic and operational decisions. The first ORL employee was Alan Jones, rapidly followed by others who wished to carry out research projects in an environment resembling that of a university research laboratory but with a pervading culture of entrepreneurship. The essential requirement was to undertake novel and exciting research following the model that Wilkes had created in the Computer Laboratory, but if the outcome of the research showed some potential for successful commercial exploitation a business model was associated with it by Andy Hopper. Projects were designed to make an impact in a period between three to ten years after their commencement. ORL philosophy discouraged development work linked to current trends in computer research and encouraged research on real working systems, whether software or hardware. There was an emphasis on creating innovations that disrupted established technologies. At an appropriate stage the Director, Andy Hopper, could be approached to identify sources of funding for a commercial venture. These funds could come from venture fund managers, business angels or large corporations. It was stressed that there was a global marketplace for all commercially successful research projects in computing science and technology.

The management structure was informal and staff members were allowed a great deal of freedom in choosing their projects. The policy of empowering talented people 'to do their own thing' was retained throughout the life of the Laboratory and research workers could use 20 per cent of their time to explore their own ideas. The ORL management believed that by giving staff some 'free time' barriers to innovation would be removed. Projects which showed commercial promise were supported by additional funding and extra personnel, and individuals who succeeded were given strong personal recognition by the management.

Sponsors were offered 'first option' to exploit projects which had the potential to succeed commercially. The offer was on a 'use it or lose it' basis but 'lose it' did not preclude the sponsoring organisation from sharing in the venture and gaining from any successful outcome. This ORL policy

Active Badges of different generations worn by members of the Olivetti Research Laboratory and the Computer Laboratory. The Kalumpit was a badge for equipment and the base station for the location system is in the middle of the picture. The badge transmitted a coded signal at infa-red frequencies every ten seconds which was detected by sensors distributed around the building. The badge holder was located by signals from the sensors. The project was led by Andy Hopper, and the team comprised Roy Want, Andy Harter, Tom Blackie, Mark Choping, Damian Gilmurray and Frazer Bennett. There were 200 badge holders in the Computer Laboratory.

Chapter Eight: The Computer Laboratory, 1980–2012: The 'Needham Years' and the Modern Era

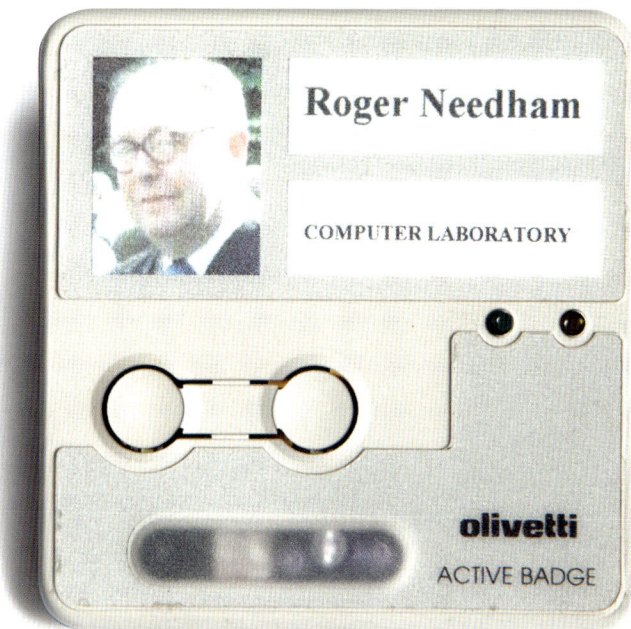

Roger Needham supported the ORL–Computer Laboratory link and participated enthusiastically in collaborative projects.

ensured that commercialisation was not prevented, impeded or delayed by slow and cautious reactions from ORL's corporate sponsors. There was strong support for ORL from Olivetti's headquarters in Italy and management at the highest level recognised that ORL was enhancing the image of the parent Italian company.

Spin-out companies comprised the core project team and the business venture was assisted with seed funding and some initial customers were identified. Help was provided for the preparation of a business plan and intellectual property was assigned to the venture, which was legally separated from ORL, thus making it easier to transfer the business to a corporate buyer at a suitable stage. Seventeen companies were spun out of ORL either directly or indirectly.

What Did ORL Achieve?

Within the first five years a number of groups were established in ORL around projects that were innovative and had the potential to disrupt existing technologies. Virata was founded in 1998 and gained 40 per cent of the worldwide market for digital subscriber line (DSL) chips. After a very successful period the company merged with Globespan who transferred the company to the USA and the Cambridge site was closed in 2005. An extraordinary outcome was that former employees started or became key employees in more than a dozen business ventures including Adventiq, Cambridge Silicon Radio, Camrivox, Green Custard, Broadcom and SaleOrigin. Another company, VNC, became a successful open source software business, and its product became a worldwide standard for remote control of computers. Its successor company, RealVNC, was awarded two Queen's Awards for innovation and for export success in 2011. The Active Badge project pioneered location-sensing technology in ORL and led to the foundation of another spin-out, Ubisense, which also gained two Queen's Awards in 2012.

ORL's sponsors could potentially receive a return many times greater than their original investment, and many employees who decided to spin out companies became personally wealthy. When ORL was closed down almost all on-going projects were taken up by the teams working on the projects, and a number of spin-out companies were formed. Most of these companies have since performed well and some have also created subsidiary businesses. The overall success rate of companies formed through ORL has been extraordinarily high.

The Relationship Between ORL and the Cambridge University Computer Laboratory

Throughout the period during which Needham was Head of the Computer Laboratory there was a harmonious relationship between ORL and the University. Unfortunately this very close liaison was lost when Robin Milner became Head of the Department and Hopper was appointed to a Chair in the Engineering Department of Cambridge University. ORL's proximity to the Computer Laboratory and its working practices were attractive to talented people in the University who relished the possibility of a real-world impact from their research and the prospect of making substantial personal financial gain.

ORL also had a symbiotic relationship with the academic members of the Computer Laboratory and funded a number of PhD students. In 16 years, 55 PhD students had a link with ORL and many were funded by ORL. The Laboratory also sponsored University research projects and offered employment to new graduates. Hopper continued with his full quota of teaching in the Computer Laboratory while directing ORL. Annual donations were sent to the Computer Laboratory to be used at Needham's

NEIL WISEMAN (1934–95)

Wilkes and Wheeler were the dominant academics in the Mathematical Laboratory in its early years and there were no appointments to senior positions until 1961, when Neil Wiseman was appointed Chief Engineer, becoming a full-time employee after almost ten years of occasional contact. Wiseman brought a strong academic background in electrical engineering (BSc in Engineering, Queen Mary College, London University, 1957 and MS in Electrical Engineering, University of Illinois at Urbana-Champaign, 1959) and a great deal of practical experience gained while working in the electronics industry. Following the arrival in the Computer Laboratory of the DEC PDP 7 minicomputer with a type 340 vector display in 1965, Wiseman designed a high-speed data link between the minicomputer and Titan, the Laboratory's mainframe computer, which was arguably the first distributed system anywhere in the world. The DEC-Titan computing system became an invaluable research facility for the two Computer-Aided Design (CAD) activities running in parallel in the Laboratory. One, led by Charles Lang, concentrated on mechanical design, while the other, led by Wiseman, concentrated on electronic circuits. Wiseman's project was known as the Rainbow Integrated Design System. It combined electronic circuit design, interactive computer graphics, data structures and the control of change in large bodies of data.

In devising his research projects Wiseman was often ahead of his time with ideas and research objectives. Using the PDP 7 he started work on screen editors for text, anticipating word processing on computers and the disappearance of the typewriter. His foresight led him next to attaching a television camera to the PDP 7 computer, thus anticipating multimedia computing, which became one of the main areas of research in the Computer Laboratory. A more quirky invention was his personal portable tape recorder, which anticipated the Walkman!

Nine years after his appointment he had published a number of significant papers, supervised several research students registered for PhDs and had gained sufficient academic credibility to be promoted to a University Lectureship. Following a change in the University's regulations in 1966, he was able to obtain a doctorate himself by submitting his published work.

The success of his work on the use of the computer in design led to his secondment to the Cambridge University Press (CUP) to help with computer-aided typesetting and book production for the printing works. It is not known where this proposal first arose but it is possible that CUP approached Maurice Wilkes, and that he nominated Wiseman to work on the project. His initial experiences at CUP were not without serious problems, mainly because of the strong unionisation

Left: The optical device designed by David Kindersley for letter spacing.

Below: Neil Wiseman (left) and Kindersley collaborated on projects designed to use computer graphics for lettering and letter spacing and started a company, Logos, to commercialise their research.

of printing activities and strictly regulated working practices. Objections were raised to his proposals and informal method of working, but Wiseman had the personality to overcome and to circumvent difficulties, and stayed at CUP until the project was successfully completed.

He returned to the Computer Laboratory in 1973, and from then until his untimely death he had 22 years as a highly productive research scientist and was a very popular supervisor of research students. He started a new Rainbow Project using the newly acquired PDP 11 computer and a Vector General display, and attracted a number of able students to work alongside him. Wilkes was heard to mutter 'far too many students are opting to work with Wiseman', but nevertheless he strongly supported the Rainbow Project.

In the mid-1970s Wiseman started a collaborative project with David Kindersley, the well-known letter-cutter and type-designer (alphabetician). He was an expert on the aesthetics, science and technology of lettering and believed that letter spacing was the key to producing the most expressive and harmonious lettering. He invented and designed an optical letter spacing machine which was built by Cambridge Consultants. Wiseman persuaded Kindersley to explore computer-aided methods for creating typefaces and controlling letter spacing. They worked together in the Computer Laboratory with the Rainbow CAD system on Saturdays to avoid conflict with the needs of the students. In 1977 they founded a commercial company, Logos, and obtained funding from an investor. They tried to develop computer-aided systems for sale but did not have the time to bring their inventions to fruition. The venture failed and the company was closed down soon after its foundation. They then started another company, Fendragon, in partnership but again the venture was short lived.

In 1985 Wiseman's pioneering work on the Rainbow Display was recognised with the BCS Technical Award, and in 1986 he was promoted to Reader in Computer Graphics. He continued his research with undiminished vigour, supervising no fewer than 40 research students. After Wilkes's retirement he worked closely with Needham, who consulted him frequently on matters of policy. He died prematurely in 1995 but work on interaction and graphics continued, led by his former research student and later academic colleague, Peter Robinson.

discretion. Although publication was not the first priority in ORL, more than 100 technical papers were published jointly with members of the Computer Laboratory. The Active Badge System was used in the Computer Laboratory daily by 200 users. Pandora, an experimental distributed multimedia system, supported digital video and audio on a workstation. Nineteen workstations were deployed between the Computer Laboratory and ORL and used regularly for videoconferencing and video mail.

In conclusion it can justifiably be claimed that the collaboration between ORL and the Computer Laboratory created a highly original and successful model for interaction between a university laboratory and an industrial laboratory. ORL provided a middle ground between spin-offs straight out of a university, always a high-risk strategy, and commercial developments within a large corporation, which can often be constrained by cumbersome company rules and regulations.

Karen Spärck Jones: Natural Language Processing and Information Retrieval
Early Career
Karen Spärck Jones was a member of the Cambridge University Computer Laboratory for most of her working life and made highly significant contributions in natural language processing and information retrieval. She graduated from Girton College with a degree in History and then read Moral Sciences (later Philosophy) for a year. In that year she met her future husband Roger Needham, who was also reading Philosophy. He introduced her to the Cambridge Language Research Unit (CLRU), an independent unit with no official status within the University which was maintained mainly by grants garnered from defence establishments in the USA. CLRU was situated on a plot of land close to the private residence of Margaret Masterman and her husband Professor Richard Braithwaite in Millington Road. This sleepy private road on the outskirts of Cambridge went nowhere and was lit eerily with gas lamps, as it is to this day.

CLRU was housed in a small brick building bearing a sign that described it as Adie's Museum. It had carvings of Far Eastern gods on the wooden doors and inside there were artefacts from Adie's collection. Adie was a Cambridge academic who specialised in teaching Indian Languages in the 1950s. He had travelled widely in Asia and collected artefacts which were displayed in the house which he owned and let to the CLRU. When he died the house was held in trust for many years until the CLRU ceased to exist.

CLRU shared the house with the Epiphany Philosophers, a small religious community which did not exist for very long in Cambridge. The building was surrounded by an apple orchard which was sadly neglected but produced large quantities of windfalls which lay rotting around the trees. In this unusual environment some extremely talented young people gathered together to work on a wide diversity of intellectual topics, including machine translation and computational linguistics. They included Michael Halliday, who was to become an influential linguistic theorist; Roger Needham, later Head of the Cambridge University Computer Laboratory; Margaret Boden, later Professor of Cognitive Science at Sussex University; Richard (Dick) Richens, a pioneer of machine translation well known for his work on the interlingua in machine translation of natural languages and Director of the Bureau for Plant Breeding and Genetics; Yorick Wilks, who later became Professor of Artificial Intelligence at Sheffield University; Martin Kay, who went on to the Chair of Linguistics at Stanford University, and Ted Bastin, the physicist and cricket enthusiast in whose company the author visited the CLRU on one or two occasions. Karen Spärck Jones was obviously in good company in this group of remarkable intellectuals led by Margaret Braithwaite!

Spärck Jones carried out the research for her PhD at the CLRU in close association with Margaret Masterman but was formally supervised by Professor Braithwaite to satisfy the regulation which required that all students must be supervised by an accredited member of the University. Her PhD dissertation, *Synonymy and Semantic Classification* was completed in 1964 and published in 1986, by which time it was recognised as a pioneering piece of work, decades ahead of its time and of great relevance to natural language research. She also worked closely with Roger Needham at the CLRU and some of her earliest work in collaboration with him was on the automatic construction of thesauri.

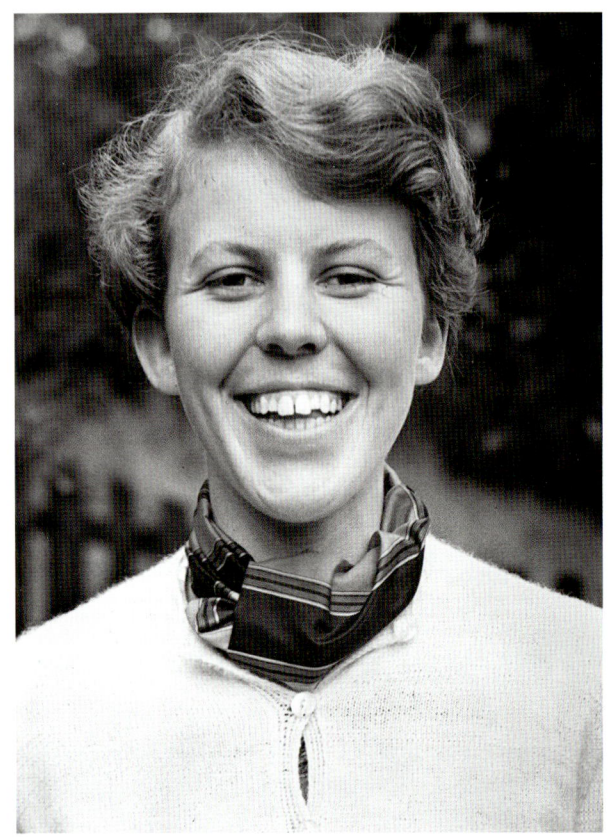

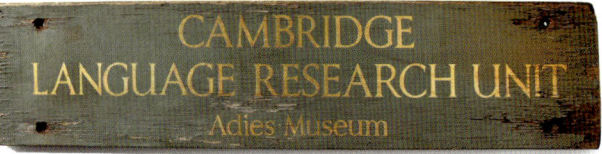

Below left: Karen Spärck Jones as a student at Cambridge University.

Below: This derelict house was the home of the CLRU in Millington Road, Cambridge. The sign on the house for Adie's Museum was rescued from a skip when the building was demolished.

Chapter Eight: The Computer Laboratory, 1980–2012: The 'Needham Years' and the Modern Era

Right: Karen Spärck Jones in later life as Professor of Computers and Information and Fellow of the British Academy in conversation with Professor Quentin Skinner, Pro-Vice-Chancellor of Cambridge University.

Inset: The Lovelace Medal awarded to Karen Spärck Jones in 2007.

Major Research Contributions

In the 1960s Spärck Jones began to work on Information Retrieval (IR), a research area for which funding was more easily available than for natural language processing. She focused on statistical approaches to information retrieval and made the innovative contribution of term weighting. Her most notable contribution was made by inventing the concept of Inverse Document Frequency (IDF), where she noted that terms occurring in many documents are not the best to use for purposes of indexing. Her derivation, the tf*idf formula, is used for information retrieval in almost all search engines today. She developed her ideas on information retrieval further with her student Stephen Robertson, and together they made important contributions to IR. Her work in this area is used today by millions of people all over the world as they search the Web. She and Stephen Robertson summarised the work in a technical report which was both self-contained and accessible. It was published in 1994 as *Simple Proven Approaches to Text Retrieval*.

This report was made available by Roger Needham to his former student Michael Burrows, who was working for the Digital Equipment Corporation (DEC) in the USA. Roger was a long-standing consultant at DEC and had come to know that Burrows was developing a search engine, AltaVista. Burrows immediately saw the value of Spärck Jones's research and incorporated some of her ideas in his work, thanking her in an e-mail. In December 1995 he wrote and invited her to assist him and to take up a week's paid consultancy in California. Spärck Jones agreed and collaborated with Burrows to develop AltaVista search engine. Michael Burrows went on to work for Google and is widely considered the leading computer scientist in search engine development for the Internet.

Spärck Jones continued to work on computational linguistics and gathered a small number of talented research workers around her in the Natural Language and Information Processing Group (NLIP) at the Computer Laboratory. For more than three decades Spärck Jones's link with the Computer Laboratory was always tenuous and based on short-term contracts of employment but outside Cambridge University her work was widely recognised and she became a significant national figure when she was appointed adviser to the Alvey programme, which had been set up in response to the Japanese 'fifth-generation' initiative in computing research.

In the 1980s she played a major part in helping to establish the Stanford Research Institute International's Cambridge Computer Science Research Centre. The interaction with SRI International began with the transfer of a Research Fellow from California to Cambridge for a short period and developed into an SRI Cambridge Laboratory, which began to operate independently in 1986 and continued until 2001. SRI and the Computer Laboratory collaborated extensively in research on natural language processing.

Teaching and Research Supervision

In 1985 the MPhil course in Computer Speech and Language Processing was started by the Computer Laboratory in collaboration with the Cambridge University Engineering Department. Spärck Jones played a full part in the teaching and organisation of this course. In 2001 the MPhil changed to Computer Speech, Text and Internet Technology, and in 2010 it was merged with the MPhil in Advanced Computer Science. By most accounts she was not the best of teachers on the MPhil course but it was a different matter when she supervised her PhD students. She was commendably diligent and particularly careful and demanding when work reached the stage where it was ready for publication. She was also a powerful advocate for more women in computing and served as a role model for many young women coming into a subject dominated by men. Her legacy in the Computer Laboratory is the well-established NLIP research group.

'Recognition at Last'
By the 1980s, Spärck Jones was internationally recognised to be among the most prominent computer scientists in natural language processing and information retrieval, but she still did not hold a formal position in the Computer Laboratory. This anomaly was corrected in 1988, when she was appointed Assistant Director of Research at the Computer Laboratory, a relatively lowly position, but nevertheless it made her, as Roger Needham remarked, 'an honest woman' at long last. By 1994 she was promoted to Reader in Computers and Information, a title implying equivalence to Associate Professor at an American university. In 1995 she was elected a Fellow of the British Academy, a well-deserved accolade for a long and distinguished research career, and in 1999 she was finally promoted to a personal Chair and became Professor of Computers and Information. She served as President of the Association for Computational Linguistics and towards the end of her career she received a clutch of national and international awards, which included the Ada Lovelace Medal in 2007 and the medal of the ACM Special Interest Group in Information Retrieval. She died in 2007, a hugely respected figure in the world of natural language processing and information retrieval. There is an excellent obituary by John Tait who was among the large number of research students supervised by her. Tait went on to become Professor of Intelligent Systems at Sunderland University.

The Modern Era – Milner, Leslie and Hopper

Needham served as Head of Department for 16 years and before him Wilkes had reigned for 35 years. In more recent times Heads of Department have had a more limited tenure, and in the last ten years there have been no fewer than three Heads of Department.

Robin Milner served as Head of Department from 1996 to 1999.

Robin Milner
In 1994 Robin Milner was appointed to the Laboratory's first established Chair. It is surprising to reflect that not one endowed Chair had been established in the Computer Laboratory for 50 years despite its outstanding success both nationally and internationally. Milner came to Cambridge with an established reputation of being one of the finest theoreticians working in computer science. In 1991 he had been awarded the ACM Turing Prize and his pioneering research work was recognised throughout the world. In 1996 Milner succeeded Needham as Head of Department at a very difficult time. He remained in position for only three years and it is believed that the administrative responsibilities of the Head of Department did not sit easily with him. During his tenure the Department stagnated, research income remained static and only one appointment was made to an academic position. The Computer Laboratory on its site in the centre of Cambridge was overcrowded and it was difficult to initiate new research projects because staff and equipment simply could not be accommodated in the Laboratory. In fairness to him a good deal of his time and energy were taken up with the early planning, design and construction of the new home on the West Cambridge site. He resigned from his position as Head of Department just as construction of the William Gates building started, but continued to work in the Laboratory until his formal retirement from University office.

Chapter Eight: The Computer Laboratory, 1980–2012: The 'Needham Years' and the Modern Era

Below: Ian Leslie, Robert Sansom Professor of Computer Science and Head of the Computer Laboratory, was in charge of the transfer of the Computer Laboratory from the centre of Cambridge to the William Gates Building and went on to become Pro-Vice-Chancellor for research in 2004.

Ian Leslie

Milner was succeeded by Ian Leslie, who was promoted from a Lectureship to the Robert Sansom Chair of Computer Science. Leslie remained in post for five years before resigning to take the position of Pro-Vice-Chancellor for Research at the central offices of Cambridge University in 2009. At the beginning of his tenure as Head of Department he spent much of his time leading the Department through the political and practical problems arising from the move from central Cambridge to the new site in West Cambridge. He did not follow the culture of secrecy about the move in the time of his predecessor but gave full details of all plans and encouraged discussion in the Department. As a result almost all individuals who had doubts accepted that a great deal would be gained from moving into a purpose-built laboratory.

He also encouraged research groups to raise more grant income, and over his five-year tenure he succeeded in increasing the annual income from research contracts from £2 million to £4 million. In his tenure the pace of appointments to academic positions increased very significantly and 14 appointments were made. He was of course fortunate that there was no lack of space in the new William Gates Building to accommodate new staff members and their projects. The Department was awarded a 5* rating in the 2001 Research Assessment Exercise. Leslie also served on the University Council and on some of its important sub-committees during his tenure as Head of Department.

The William Gates building was opened in 2001, most appropriately, by Professor Sir Maurice Wilkes. At long last the Computer Laboratory had a home that was appropriate to its needs.

Leslie was responsible for overseeing the formal separation of teaching and research in the Computer Laboratory from the University Computing Service. This move was begun by Roger Needham before his departure from the Computer Laboratory. Many academics in the

Right: from left to right: Ian Leslie, Head of the Computer Laboratory in 2001, with three former heads, Robin Milner, Roger Needham and Maurice Wilkes, at the opening of the William Gates Building.

Cambridge Computing: The First 75 Years

Chapter Eight: The Computer Laboratory, 1980–2012: The 'Needham Years' and the Modern Era

University had believed that this separation was long overdue and should have been achieved many years earlier, when Wilkes first made his proposals to the University for a nominal separation. Leslie was succeeded as Head of Department by Professor Andy Hopper in 2004.

Andy Hopper

Andy Hopper was born in Poland in 1953 and became a British citizen in 1964. He was an undergraduate at the University of Wales, Swansea, from 1971 to 1974 and moved to the Computer Laboratory in 1974 to work towards a PhD under the supervision of David Wheeler. His thesis, entitled *Local Area Computer Communication Networks*, was completed in 1977. He then worked for two years as a research assistant and from 1979 to 1983 as an Assistant Lecturer at the Computer Laboratory. In 1983 he was promoted to the position of University Lecturer. Three years later he became one of the founders of the Olivetti Research Laboratory (ORL) in Cambridge while simultaneously holding his University Lectureship in the Computer Laboratory. He was appointed the Managing Director of ORL and promoted to Vice-President. In 1992 he was promoted to Reader in Computer Technology at the Computer Laboratory and from 1997 to 2004 he was Professor of Communications at the Engineering Department at Cambridge University. He returned to the Computer Laboratory in 2004 as Professor of Computer Technology and Head of Department and was elected to the Council of the University in 2011. From 1981 to 2011 he was a Fellow of Corpus Christi College, Cambridge, and in October 2011 he was elected Honorary Fellow of Trinity Hall, Cambridge. He combines his academic employment with a parallel career in industry and has co-founded a number of spin-out and start-up companies, three of which were floated on the stock market. He also works as a consultant for multinational companies. He is Chairman of RealVNC, which was awarded two Queen's Awards in 2011, and Chairman of Ubisense plc, which was awarded two Queen's Awards in 2012.

He was elected a Fellow of the Royal Academy of Engineering in 1996 and a Fellow of the Royal Society in 2006. He is President of the Institution of Engineering and Technology and was appointed CBE in 2007 'for services to the computer industry'. He has won numerous prizes and medals and holds a number of positions on advisory boards of industrial companies and academic institutions.

In his research career he has been widely recognised for his contribution to the Cambridge Digital Ring project, the Active Badge project and to digital technology as a whole. His current research interests include computer networking, pervasive and sensor-driven computing and using computers to ensure the sustainability of the planet.

After more than 20 years at the Cambridge University Computer Laboratory, Hopper accepted the Chair of Communications Engineering at the Cambridge University Engineering Department in 1997. He built up an extensive research activity in the Department and continued to direct ORL in parallel. Following the resignation of Leslie in 2004 he returned to the Computer Laboratory as Professor of Computer Technology and Head of Department, taking the same title that Wilkes had taken when he was promoted *ad hominem* in 1985. The expansion and diversification of research activities has continued in this period, with 11 new appointments having been made thus far. The Computer Laboratory has been awarded the top grade of 5* in all government-initiated Research Assessment Exercises. These assessments are designed to evaluate and compare the quality of research in University departments across the UK. Furthermore in 2008, within Cambridge University, the Computer Laboratory was placed equal first in ranking scores with the Engineering and Materials Science Departments of Cambridge University.

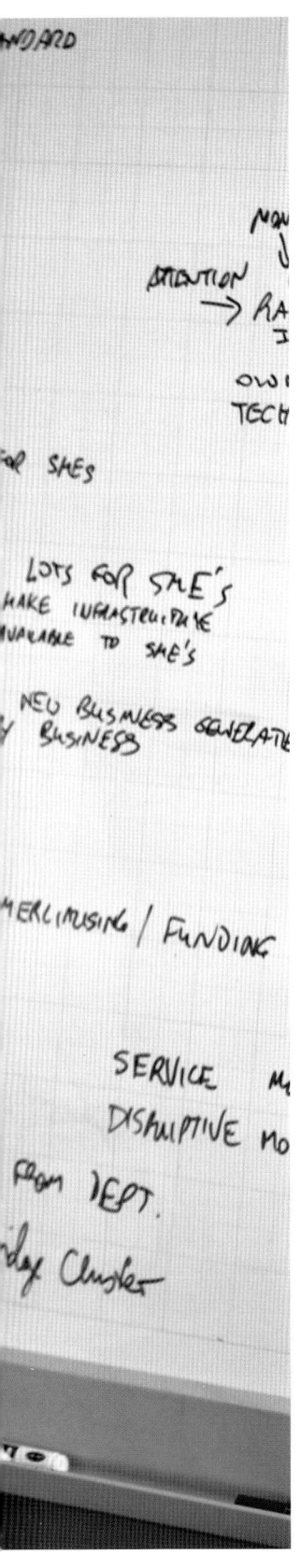

Andy Hopper became Head of Department in 2004 and leads the research of the Digital Technology Group.

CHAPTER NINE

Entrepreneurs, Spinning Out, Making Money and Linking with Industry

Entrepreneurs

Over the past 40 years the Computer Laboratory has been the source of a phenomenally large number of start-up companies – nearly 200 at the last count. This is an extraordinary and unusual story which is unlikely to have been repeated in any other academic department in the University of Cambridge nor, perhaps, in any other university in the UK.

Records show that only one business enterprise, Media Dynamics Ltd arose from the Laboratory in the 1960s. During the next decade, the number increased to six and included Shape Data Ltd and Acorn Computers Ltd, both remarkably successful start-ups. From 1980 to 1990 the pace accelerated, with 22 new businesses started, including Olivetti Research Ltd and Sophos plc. The pace continued to increase in the 1990s with 66 new companies emerging, including Virata Ltd, Bango and Sintefex Audio, and by 2012 more than 100 start-ups had been added to the list, including the hugely successful games company Jagex Ltd, RealVNC Ltd and blinkx. The vast majority of the companies are based on software products or consultancy services; hardware-based companies are few in number. The evidence clearly shows that software-based companies are easier to start, easier to manage and easier to bring to profitability and eventually to capital gain. Their key advantage is that products are normally sold worldwide and there is no limitation on the size of the available market. Hardware-based companies are often constrained by difficulties in raising the necessary investment, by the small size of the market in the UK and by the length of time required to bring them to profitability.

Historical evidence on a nationwide basis shows that a large proportion of businesses started in the UK fail within a few years. A few become moderately successful and profitable but fail to grow. To investors, such businesses are 'living-dead' companies because of their failure to provide a large capital return. A very small number of companies are spectacularly successful and make their founders and investors extremely wealthy. Data for the Computer Laboratory indicate that a disproportionately large number of companies which have been set up by computer science graduates become dramatically successful compared with the national average. The publicity given to these highly successful companies both locally and internationally attracts more budding entrepreneurs.

Early Days

The very first entrepreneurs were members of the academic staff of the Computer Laboratory. Charles Lang had worked in the Computer Laboratory on Computer-Aided Design for ten years before starting Shape Data Ltd. In the 1970s academics owned the benefit of their research within the University, and it was implicitly assumed that those who created a commercially viable idea had the absolute right to exploit it. Only if the work was funded by an outside body was there any restriction on exploitation. The only University directive was that the letterhead of the University Department should not be used by staff for any consultancy correspondence in case a liability might fall on the University. The phrase 'intellectual property rights' was virtually unknown in Cambridge at that time.

Throughout the whole of Wilkes's tenure as Head of Department and some of Needham's, members of the Computer Laboratory were allowed to spin out companies and interact with industry without any restrictions. Early in its history the Computer Laboratory had collaborated

Opposite: Two boards placed in the entrance foyer of the William Gates Building. The board on the right lists companies started by graduates of the Computer Laboratory, known as 'Hall of Fame Companies'. The companies that have won a 'Hall of Fame Award' and companies that have been recognised as 'Company of the Year' are listed on the board on the left.

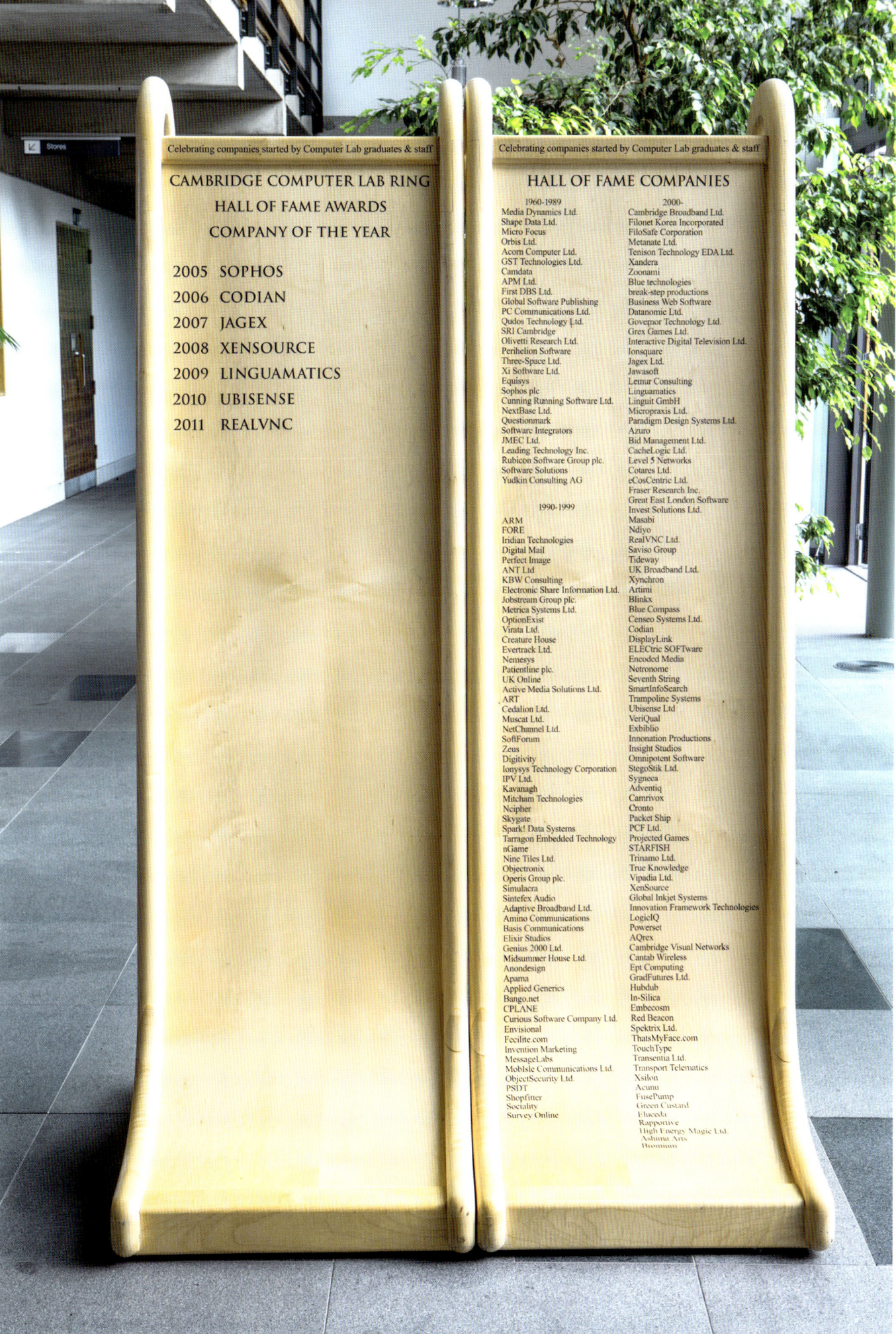

with the Lyons Catering Company, and this had led to the foundation of LEO Computers Ltd. Wilkes and Needham had themselves acted as paid consultants for commercial companies and encouraged other staff members to do so also. Needham spent several weeks in the year working as a paid consultant for Xerox PARC in the USA and brought fresh ideas, new expertise and sometimes modern equipment back to Cambridge. Needham and Wilkes asserted that 'there would not be a Computer Laboratory without a thriving computer industry', and valued their connections with industry.

When Andy Hopper, then a University Lecturer, was appointed Managing Director of the Olivetti Research Laboratory there was no objection to his holding two appointments simultaneously, and Needham quietly suppressed a few murmurs of dissent from members of the Computer Laboratory. Close interaction was established between the Cambridge University Computer Laboratory and the commercially owned ORL. In the beginning there was no formal agreement between the two parties and there is some doubt that there was even an exchange of letters setting out the terms and conditions of the collaboration. In the event there were no problems, and the collaboration with ORL was of great benefit to both parties. It changed the culture of interaction between an academic department and an industrial company because, in this instance, the industrial laboratory was virtually embedded within the Computer Laboratory. ORL was eventually closed down in 2002 but in the decade that followed the number of entrepreneurs continued to increase. The Computer Laboratory Graduate Association, the Ring, founded in 2001, also encouraged a culture of entrepreneurship among Computer Laboratory graduates.

Case Studies

The history of entrepreneurship linked to the Computer Laboratory is best illustrated with case studies of some of the companies started by alumni. The accounts that follow have been chosen to illustrate the wide variety of companies that have been set up. They reflect the changing international environment which embraced the high-tech and dot com boom periods (1995–2000) and the local 'Cambridge Phenomenon', which describes the exceptionally high rate of growth of high-tech companies in and around Cambridge compared with other cities in the UK. Some companies are based on a fresh idea, some on an incremental but meaningful advance on current practice and a few on 'disruptive' innovations which have created an entirely new market. It has only been possible to describe a few companies in this chapter and many interesting and successful companies have had to be omitted due to lack of space.

Two of the four co-founders of Shape Data – Charles Lang (Computer Science PhD, 1975, Emmanuel College) and Ian Braid (Diploma in Computer Science, 1969, Darwin College). The other founders were Alan Grayer (Computer Science PhD, 1977, Christ's College) and Peter Veenman (Delft University, MSc, 1964).

Case Study 1
Shape Data Ltd, Founded 1974

This company was the first to be spun out of the Computer Laboratory. It was founded by Charles Lang, Ian Braid, Alan Grayer and Peter Veenman, all members of the Computer Laboratory. They started the company partly because they could sense that there was commercial value in their research and partly because funding for CAD research from the Science Research Council was becoming uncertain. All of the founders believed that the team had achieved worthwhile research results which would bring substantial benefits to the design and manufacturing industry of the future, and they had the foresight to recognise that computers would play an increasingly important role in the engineering industry.

The word 'entrepreneur' was barely known in 1974, and infrastructure for supporting a start-up company was non-existent. These early entrepreneurs funded the whole

Chapter Nine: Entrepreneurs, Spinning Out, Making Money and Linking with Industry

enterprise from sales and were aware of only one or two other companies that had already emerged from University departments. Very few senior academics held the view that publicly funded University research should not be commercialised without a direct return to the University. Wilkes was totally supportive towards Charles Lang and his colleagues. He ensured that the link between the CAD Group and the fledgling company remained strong as long as it was needed. The success of the Laboratory's Titan operating system and the outstanding work of the CAD Group led directly to the foundation by the government of the CAD Centre in 1968. A number of other commercial companies also grew out of the CAD Group's research, notably NC Graphics, which was eventually sold in 2007.

Shape Data developed the first commercial 3D modeller, Romulus, which was licensed to companies building CAD/CAM systems. The company was sold to the Evans & Sutherland Computer Corporation of Salt Lake City in 1981.

Case Study 2

The Rise and Fall of Acorn Computers Ltd, Founded 1978, and the Rise and Rise of ARM, Founded 1990

Hermann Hauser and Christopher Curry founded first Cambridge Processor Unit Ltd and then a second company, Acorn Computers Ltd, in 1978 and merged them, adopting the more memorable name, Acorn Computers Ltd. In 1979, Andy Hopper, then a Lecturer in Computer Science, sold his company Orbis to Acorn in exchange for Acorn shares, and he was appointed to the Board of Directors of the company. His appointment created a valuable link between Acorn and the Cambridge University Computer Laboratory. The first Acorn product was the Acorn System 1 computer, which was designed by the remarkably talented Sophie Wilson. Other products followed, including the Atom, the BBC Micro (originally the Proton), the Electron and the Archimedes.

The BBC Micro transformed the fortunes of the company. In 1980 the BBC launched a national computer literacy campaign and needed a computer to sell in support

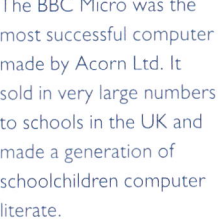
The BBC Micro was the most successful computer made by Acorn Ltd. It sold in very large numbers to schools in the UK and made a generation of schoolchildren computer literate.

of its television series. The BBC's management explored proposals from six potential suppliers but eventually chose the computer offered by Acorn. Behind Acorn's success against strong competition from larger rivals is an interesting story. After the initial meeting with the BBC, Herman Hauser enthusiastically promised to demonstrate a prototype within a week, although he was fully aware that he did not have a computer to demonstrate! He then persuaded Sophie Wilson and another talented employee, Steve Furber, that the project could be completed in five days, ordered the parts immediately and assembled a 'team of all talents', including members of the Computer Laboratory, to build a prototype. The prototype worked and the BBC's representatives, returning to Acorn a week after the first meeting, were very impressed but totally unaware that the machine had been completed only a few hours before the demonstration. They duly awarded the contract to Acorn.

After the computer's adoption by the BBC, Acorn had a piece of good fortune when the BBC Micro was chosen for use in schools. The Department of Education and Science had launched an initiative to introduce computing concepts in schools and were prepared to pay half the cost of the BBC Micro or any other computer purchased by a school. Over a period of four years the computer was a phenomenal success and Acorn profits rose from a few thousand pounds in 1979 to nearly £9 million with a turnover of just under £100 million in 1983. The company moved from its original premises at 4A Market Hill into new, purpose-built headquarters on the outskirts of Cambridge in 1982. It was floated on the stock market and with an initial market capitalisation of £135 million reached a peak of almost £200 million.

Warren East and Hermann Hauser seen outside the ARM Holdings headquarters in Cambridge. The company arose out of the pioneering work on the RISC processor at Acorn Computers Ltd, co-founded by Hauser. ARM was co-founded by Robin Saxby (now Sir Robin Saxby) in 1990, and under his leadership it became the predominant semiconductor design company worldwide. East took over as CEO in 2001 and under his leadership ARM has continued its spectacular growth. He expects 10 billion chips to be manufactured to ARM designs in 2012.

In the early 1980s, there was a great deal of bespoke chip design work in the Cambridge Laboratory, and Andy Hopper and his colleagues were aware that chips were being designed by research workers in the USA, particularly at the University of California, Berkeley, aimed at novel computer architectures and brought these developments to the attention of Acorn's management. At the same time, Acorn engineers picked up the details of the RISC project which was underway at Berkeley and Sophie Wilson and Steve Furber started the Acorn RISC Machine (ARM) project in 1983. They designed integrated circuits for a RISC computer and VLSI Technology manufactured silicon chips to their designs, which were named ARM 1.

Unfortunately the home computer market collapsed dramatically in 1984 and Acorn was badly affected because it had extended its production base to meet anticipated demand which did not materialise. It also had a number of expensive development projects underway which were not yet in a position to generate revenue. In 1985, under immense pressure from creditors, the company avoided bankruptcy by persuading Olivetti to take a 49 per cent stake for £12 million, a dramatic reduction in the capital value of the company, and a few months later Olivetti took majority control of Acorn. The company remained extant for some years but its glory days were well and truly over. Despite its failure as a computer manufacturer, the Acorn RISC machine became the basis of collaboration between Acorn and Apple Computers in the US, which eventually led to the formation of Advanced RISC Machines Ltd (ARM Ltd) in November 1990 by Robin Saxby (now Sir Robin Saxby) and a group of colleagues, including many technical experts from Acorn. The rest is a history of the unprecedented success of ARM, which is now the most successful company founded in Cambridge with a connection to the Computer Laboratory.

ARM Holdings, Founded 1990
The basic principle of RISC architecture is to use a set of simplified instructions instead of the complex instruction set which slows down the operation of conventional machines. The RISC chip designed in Acorn by Sophie Wilson and Steve Furber not only operated at an incredibly high speed compared with conventional designs but the simplicity of the design also ensured that its power consumption was very low, making it particularly appropriate for mobile computing and mobile telephones. The Acorn RISC chip had anticipated the revolution that was to come some 20 years later! Apple became interested in using RISC chips and agreed to collaborate with Acorn in the development of chips for its hand-held Newton Computer system. Very soon afterwards companies in the UK and Japan decided to purchase ARM products and the company began to grow.

ARM's business model was to license microprocessor designs as intellectual property, mainly to manufacturers of mobile telephones, and the company captured a phenomenal 95 per cent share of this immense market. Successful designs were manufactured by independent silicon foundries, usually based in the USA and the Far East. Using this strategy ARM avoided the enormous costs and risks associated with setting up and operating a chip manufacturing facility.

The company needed large numbers of very bright, computer-literate designers, and there was no shortage of such talent in the Cambridge area. It also made a large number of acquisitions of high-tech companies to expand and diversify its business. By 1998 ARM was successful enough to be floated on the Stock Exchange in London and the NASDAQ in the USA. In 2001 Saxby retired and Warren East was appointed CEO. Under his management the company continued to advance at a remarkable rate. Today billions of chips designed by ARM are sold to major clients across the world. The success of Apple products that use ARM chips, such as the iPad and the iPhone, has been reflected in the very rapid growth of ARM Holdings. Very recently Microsoft announced that it will no longer run its new software, Windows 8, exclusively on Intel chips but will also enable it to run on ARM chips. This decision by Microsoft gives ARM another opportunity to expand its sales. In 2012 it is expected that 10 billion chips will be based on ARM designs.

Case Study 3
Sintefex Audio, Founded 1997
This company was co-founded by Mike Kemp, who studied Computer Science at Cambridge University for

Cambridge Computing: The First 75 Years

a year following two years of Mathematics. He started a PhD under Neil Wiseman's supervision in the Computer Laboratory but left without completing it in order to follow his passion for recording music and to devote his time to the company he had set up with Gary Lucas, Spaceward Studios. He used his knowledge of computing to build a mixing desk and designed computer graphics equipment for television. From this work arose an offshoot of the original company, Spaceward Microsystems, which developed high-quality graphics for the television industry. Unfortunately the project ran into problems over disputes concerning the ownership of intellectual property rights and had to be terminated. Kemp returned to working on audio and set up Studio Audio and Video Ltd, where he developed a computer-aided audio editing system. In 1994, together with some of his colleagues, he moved to the Algarve region of Portugal to set up Sintefex Audio, leaving behind a research and development laboratory in Cambridge under the direction of Simon Widdowson, another Cambridge graduate. Kemp created a breakthrough by inventing a process called 'Dynamic Convolution' which is able to generate 'analogue-sounding' music out of a 'clean-sounding' digital system. The technology has advantages over true analogue machines and has now been licensed into several successful commercial products.

Today the company is dedicated to research, development and consultancy in digital audio technology and works for other companies, in partnership, to generate novel features in their products. Innovations are licensed to enable Sintefex to share in the commercial success of the product. Software is designed in Portugal and hardware in Cambridge. The unique Dynamic Convolution together with Kemp's experience in studio work, through which he implements innovative technical solutions in areas related to the arts, keeps Sintefex ahead of its competitors. Mike Kemp's unusual journey in entrepreneurship is an example of the wide range of possibilities that can arise for entrepreneurs graduating in Computer Science.

Case Study 4
Bango, Founded 1999
This company, based in Cambridge, was co-founded by Ray Anderson, who read Computer Science at Cambridge University. Anderson developed a business model based on his belief that there would be a merger of the Internet and the increasingly ubiquitous mobile phone. Bango streamlines the process of collecting payments from mobile phone users on behalf of content retailers, service providers and app stores. Its strategy is to take advantage

Left: Mike Kemp (Computer Science, 1974, Emmanuel College), founder of Sintefex, working in his office in the Algarve, Portugal.

Below: Ray Anderson (Computer Science, 1980, Pembroke College), founder of Bango.

Chapter Nine: Entrepreneurs, Spinning Out, Making Money and Linking with Industry

of the ability of the modern mobile phone to allow users to 'browse and buy' in a manner familiar to the Internet user, and to benefit from the billing systems in place for mobile operators to charge for phone calls and other services.

Anderson claims that he first started to devise a model for his company when he was shown graphs illustrating the simultaneous exponential growth in the use of the Internet and mobile phones. The graphs followed such closely similar trends that he could sense huge implications if the two technologies could be brought together. His ideas were vindicated in early 1999 during a trip to Japan, when he saw that Internet-connected mobile phones were becoming available. He decided to enter the market as quickly as possible by setting up a small company. Today most of the world's major app stores and many smaller content providers use Bango products to collect payments for their sales of apps and content. The company has recently signed agreements with Amazon, Microsoft and Facebook. Bango was floated on the London Stock Market (as AIM) in June 2005.

Before founding Bango, Anderson had first founded Torch Computers, delivering the world's first computer with an integrated modem, and then IXI, which created the industry standard graphical user interface for Unix workstations. Like many other entrepreneurs from the Computer Laboratory, Anderson is not only an entrepreneur but also an innovator, an inventor and more recently a 'business angel' investing in many growing companies in the UK. He was named 'Technology Entrepreneur of the Year' in 2006 and named Business Person of the Year in 2012. His company has also been recognised with a large number of awards since 2004. Bango won the Ring's Hall of Fame Product of the Year award in 2012.

Case Study 5
RealVNC, Founded 2002
This company was founded by Andy Harter, Andy Hopper, Tristan Richardson, James Weatherall and Lily Bacon in 2002. It was based on a piece of clever software, Virtual Network Computer (VNC), which enabled a nominated computer to take over the screen, keyboard and mouse of another computer. It was released in 1998 as a non-commercial, open-source venture and created a market for software which could provide remote support, helpdesk and troubleshooting services to customers. In

Below right: Andy Harter (BA Fitzwilliam College, PhD Corpus Christi College), founder and CEO of RealVNC.

other applications users can use the software to connect to the same desktop, which is invaluable for exchanging information, collaborative working, distance learning and sales demonstrations.

RealVNC is a commercial company pioneering what is now a popular business model. When it was founded there were already more than 100 million users of the open source version of software supplied by VNC. The product was well known and well liked. A business opportunity arose when the new company, RealVNC, offered to support companies with large-scale deployments for a fee. The offer was taken up by many users of the original open source software. The business grew rapidly and even cashed in on its large established base of users by selling mouse pads and T-shirts with the VNC logo to its hundred million strong fan club!

Commercial-grade versions of the software were developed with new features and sales grew even more rapidly. Another business strategy was to license the software, which is now found in Intel chips, Google products, consumer appliances and in the automotive industry. The business was profitable from the outset and expanded without requiring any external funding, reinvesting profits to create new products and markets. The company is owned entirely by the founders and its phenomenal success was recognised when it was awarded two Queen's Awards in 2011, one for innovation and the other for international trade. RealVNC is an excellent example of commercial success based on technical innovation coupled with novel sales and marketing tactics which entirely disrupt traditional methods. Its success will no doubt encourage new marketing techniques for sales of software.

Case Study 6
Sophos plc, Founded 1985
This company was founded by Jan Hruska, who graduated from Downing College in 1978, and Peter Lammer, whom he met while they were working on their doctorates at Oxford University. Sophos was their second attempt at founding a company. Their first company, Executive Computers Ltd, failed, but they had remained undeterred because they felt that they had learned a valuable lesson. They realised that the reason for the failure of the venture was their reliance on a hardware product for which they did not have the financial resources to bring to the marketplace.

Jan Hruska (Engineering, 1977, Computer Science, 1978, Downing College), founder of Sophos plc.

Sophos started by selling a number of software modules written in the computer language C and designed to provide data security to corporate computer users. Their first products were implementations of Data Encryption Standard (DES) and RSA encryption. In 1987 computer viruses first appeared on the scene and they rapidly diverted Sophos to developing antivirus products. The timing of the change of direction was perfect, and the company has now become a world leader in information technology security for business, education, government organisations and service providers. It has more than 1,600 employees worldwide. In May 2010 Hruska and Lammer sold a majority stake to Apax Partners in a transaction which valued Sophos at $830 million. They retained a minority shareholding and became non-executive directors. The company remains highly profitable.

These committed entrepreneurs succeeded by concentrating on software rather than hardware and by anticipating the worldwide problem of computer viruses. Their expertise and experience enabled them to be perfectly placed to develop commercial products to deal with the problem.

Chapter Nine: Entrepreneurs, Spinning Out, Making Money and Linking with Industry

Case Study 7
Jagex, Founded 2001

This company was founded only 12 years ago by Andrew Gower and his brother Paul immediately after Andrew had graduated from Fitzwilliam College in 2000 with a degree in Computer Science. Their passion from boyhood days had been computer games, and they knew precisely which games they had enjoyed most and consequently which games might sell. Within a decade Jagex has become the largest independent developer and publisher of online games. The company's well-known browser-based multiplayer online game Runescape became immensely successful shortly after its launch. Jagex was awarded the Industry Legend Prize in 2010 and again in the following year, and the company also won the Queen's Award for Innovation in 2011.

Gower acquired a great deal of skill in writing games software at an early age, and working with his brothers created games for the Atari ST. He became skilful in writing software using the computer language C, assembler and Java. While he was still an undergraduate at Cambridge University, he developed a version of the popular game 'multi-user dungeons', and launched a version on the Internet soon after graduating. The game was offered free to players but he hoped to make money by advertising. Unfortunately he could not afford the cost of the servers in the post dot com bubble period, when advertising revenue dried up. After unsuccessfully asking players for donations he created a membership system offering premium items to members for a small fee. This proved successful and he and his co-founders managed to attract 2,000 subscribers in the first hour and 5,000, the break-even figure, in just one week! They then reinvested the proceeds into improving the site. The more attractive the site became the faster membership grew. What a success story!

In 2010 Andrew and Paul Gower featured in the *Sunday Times* Rich List. They had amassed a fortune of £138 million and received the accolade of being the wealthiest game entrepreneurs in the UK. This example is a case of entrepreneurs starting young with very few responsibilities and taking a flexible attitude towards their business model. It is also an example of a company which survived and grew in strength during and after the years of the dot com bubble. In 2010 Andrew and Paul Gower resigned from the board of Jagex and moved on to other ventures. Mark Gerhard, the then Chief Technology Officer of the company, became the CEO. Jagex now has approximately 500 employees, mainly in the Cambridge area.

Case Study 8
blinkx, Founded 2004

This company was founded by Suranga Chandratillake after he left his position as CTO for Autonomy in the USA, with Autonomy retaining an equity share in blinkx as part of the spin-out deal. Chandratillake developed an Internet search engine for audio and video content which claims to be the largest and the most advanced multimedia search engine on the Internet, having indexed more than 35 million hours of content from the publicly accessible Internet and responsible today for powering video search at popular sites such as MSN, Ask.com and AOL.

Chandratillake claims the idea came to him when he found 3,000 e-mails on his computer on returning to work from a few months leave. Finding that it took him a week to organise the messages he became convinced that technology was needed to deal with unstructured information overload not only in corporations but also in the lives of other consumers. He decided that the available methods were very limited in performance and founded blinkx to overcome the problems he had identified. His

Suranga Chandratillake (Computer Science, 2000, King's College) founded blinkx.

company's technology is based on the novel concept of using speech recognition and visual analysis in order to infer more detailed metadata with which to index and later search for video content. A further part of his business plan was to exploit this additional metadata to aid in the automatic targeting of advertising placed within Internet video content as it is being watched.

In the fiscal year 2012, revenue was $114.4 million and profit was $12.7 million, with business opportunities expanding daily. Recently blinkx has acquired existing businesses to expand its opportunities in the market which is believed to be worth several billion dollars. The company is an example of an entrepreneur starting in corporate employment and establishing a track record before spinning out an independent business.

Case Study 9
Camrivox, Founded 2005, and Green Custard, Founded 2009
Camrivox was a spin-out from Conexant Systems which had acquired Virata Ltd which itself had spun out from Olivetti Research Ltd, thus making Camrivox a third-generation start-up with a link to the Computer Laboratory. Founded by Jonathan Custance and James Green, Camrivox developed user-friendly Voice over Internet Protocol (VoIP) products for consumers who were finding it difficult to use existing products. Their system was demonstrated in May 2005 and, encouraged by the response, they decided to go into production. They needed to raise external finance to start manufacturing hardware, but acquiring funding for a hardware business is difficult in the UK. They were helped by a successful local entrepreneur, Charles Cotton, who advised them on fundraising. They entered and won the Running the Gauntlet competition, thereby gaining an investment of £1 million. In 2007 the company introduced a business IP phone product and pivoted their business to focus on Unified Communications software by integrating their telephone with the computer (CTI). They made their software compatible with competitors' phones, increasing their market, and reducing the need to manufacture their own hardware. The company now concentrates on providing services to small and medium-size enterprises (SMEs), and is compatible with virtually all business phone systems, integrating them with leading Customer Relationship Management (CRM) systems. A few years ago, recognising the direction in which the software industry was heading, the two entrepreneurs founded another company, Green Custard, which offers consultancy on web services and mobile apps. They have a client base from small start-ups to large blue-chip companies, and advise on matters such as fundraising, patents, system design and implementation. These two entrepreneurs have demonstrated how important it is to keep abreast of rapidly changing technologies and capitalise on new opportunities.

James Green (Computer Science, 1996, Fitzwilliam College) on the left and Jonathan Custance (Computer Science, 1995, St John's College), founders of Camrivox in 2005 and Green Custard in 2009.

Case Study 10
The Raspberry Pi Foundation, Founded as a Charity in 2008
This foundation was established following concern that the number of applicants to read Computer Science had dropped by some 60 per cent since 2000, perhaps because children were no longer exposed to programming tasks in school. Lessons in school were judged to be irrelevant, trivial and inappropriate for producing computer scientists of the future. A campaign was launched to press the government to ensure that today's schoolchildren would be equipped with more sophisticated computer-related skills than just training in word processing, spreadsheets and web browsing. Three decades ago the BBC Micro produced by Acorn Computers had introduced basic concepts of computing to a very large number of schools in the UK, and today the

Ian Pratt (Computer Science, BA 1992, PhD 1997, King's College), co-founder of XenSource.

Raspberry Pi Foundation is hoping that its 'ultra-small, staggeringly cheap computer will again excite and engage children'. The charity was founded in 2008 by trustees Eben Upton, Alan Mycroft, Robert Mullins and the entrepreneur Jack Lang (all present or former members of the Computer Laboratory), among others. Their intention was to encourage schools to teach computer science and electronics. The tiny machine is based on an ARM processor chip and plugs into a domestic TV set as its output; a keyboard is connected to input the data. It is no bigger than a credit card and sells for the incredibly low figure of $25 for the basic version and $35 for a more advanced model. The Raspberry Pi can be used to play high-definition video and Xbox-quality graphics. At the beginning of 2012 the first ten Raspberry Pi modules were auctioned on eBay and a sum of £16,000 was raised to fund development, with further donations and funding from Cambridge Angels. From the middle of 2012 Raspberry Pi has been available to children across the world to learn programming skills.

Case Study 11
XenSource, Founded 2004

This company arose from research in the Computer Laboratory led by Ian Pratt, Senior Lecturer, and three of his colleagues. The team created the Xen hypervisor, software to enable multiple operating systems to be run on the same physical machine, enabling more efficient use of computing resources. Following Xen's release in 2003 as open source software, a developer community formed around the project and the software became the most widely deployed hypervisor in the cloud. XenSource began as a consultancy service advising banks and other businesses on deploying Xen. It became clear that there was a significant business opportunity in building and supporting an 'enterprise-ready' version of Xen. The open source business model made seeking funding in Europe challenging, but reaction in the USA was more positive, resulting in the creation of XenSource Inc.

Ivo Hadley (age eight) and Jem Bennett (age six) enjoying their first experience with the Raspberry Pi.

Xen's success was based on its position of neutrality and freedom from control of any CPU hardware or operating vendors, and they therefore maintained their position of independence by turning down funding from any single vendor. The project was developed on two sites, one in Cambridge and the other in California, and initial difficulties in working on two remote sites were gradually resolved. From the second quarter of 2006 the business expanded and then doubled in each subsequent quarter. Their original intention had been to work towards an initial public offering (IPO) for the company but they unexpectedly received an attractive offer from Citrix, giving them the opportunity to achieve critical mass especially in reselling and marketing. They decided that by working with Citrix they would be able to compete with established companies in the same field, and XenSource was sold to Citrix in 2007 for $500 million. Ian Pratt became Vice-President for Advanced Products, but left in 2011 to form a new company. Like many other successful entrepreneurs with links to the Computer Laboratory he obviously enjoys starting up new businesses.

Case Study 12
Rapportive, Founded 2010
After graduating from Cambridge with an outstanding performance in the Computer Science examinations Martin Kleppmann decided to become a composer. His first composition was a success but in 2007 he changed direction, decided to become an entrepreneur and founded a company, Ept Computing, located in the St John's Innovation Centre in Cambridge. The company's product 'Go Test It' was acquired by Red Gate. He then went into partnership with two other Computer Laboratory graduates, Sam Stokes and Rahul Vohra, and the three entrepreneurs went on to found Rapportive. They recruited Conrad Irwin and Lee Mallabone, also from Cambridge, who became key members of the team that built up Rapportive. The company creates software to extend Google Mail (Gmail) with information from social websites, allowing users to learn more about their contacts while emailing them. It automatically

The team that built Rapportive. Left to right: Conrad Irwin (Computer Science, 2010, Corpus Christi College), Sam Stokes (Computer Science, 2005, Robinson College), Rahul Vohra (Computer Science, 2005, Christ's College), Martin Kleppmann (Computer Science, 2006, Corpus Christi College) and Lee Mallabone (Computer Systems and Software Engineering, 2001, University of York). Before their acquisition by LinkedIn, their San Francisco office overlooked the Bay Bridge (in the background).

Chapter Nine: Entrepreneurs, Spinning Out, Making Money and Linking with Industry

enables someone replying to an e-mail to view their correspondent's 'tweets', LinkedIn contact information and blogs, thus providing a full picture of the person at the other end of the e-mail correspondence. Rapportive's software is designed to make all interactions 'socially brilliant not just effective'. Rapportive's 'accidental' launch was an exciting moment for the founders. While they were trying to present their product to prospective investors it was discovered by the press looking for a story on the 'next thing on the web'. The publicity for the product caused

user numbers to grow from five to 10,000 in 24 hours! After this phenomenal response investors queued up to support Rapportive and the company was well and truly launched. Very soon afterwards the company established a good working relationship with LinkedIn, who acquired it in 2012. The agreement between the two companies allowed Rapportive to continue its service to Gmail users. Rapportive is an interesting example of the persistence of the true entrepreneur and the advantage of forming links with like-minded individuals.

The Cambridge Computer Lab Ring: Encouraging a Culture of Entrepreneurship

In 2001, Ian Leslie, Head of the Computer Laboratory, decided to set up a graduate association for members of the Computer Laboratory and invited Stephen Allott to take responsibility for this proposal. Allott had been President of Micromuse, a successful ICT company which had been floated on the NASDAQ. He decided to spend a little time as a visitor in the Computer Laboratory, where he had built up connections while he was at Micromuse. Allott brought an imaginative and novel approach to the task by creating an association which was named the Cambridge Computer Lab Ring. He decided that the mission of the Ring should be to benefit Computer Science graduates in their careers, throughout their lifetime, from graduation to retirement, and he built into his design a mechanism for giving alumni from different generations easy access to each other. The benefits of membership of the Ring would be social, professional and technical. The Ring was launched in October 2002 as a not-for-profit, independent members association. An alumni magazine, *The Ring*, was launched in September 2002. The first issue stated that the name of the graduate association and its magazine had been derived from the 10Mb Cambridge Digital Ring project which had been initiated by Maurice Wilkes in 1970, and he had also suggested the inspired name. It was expected that the Ring would enable networking among former members of the Computer Laboratory, established entrepreneurs and industry professionals, and would also help to establish relationships between individuals, form connections between Laboratory graduates and introduce budding entrepreneurs to their peers, potential recruits and occasionally to venture capital providers.

Membership categories and fees ranged from free annual membership for recent graduates to a lifetime membership for £800. Benefits included a copy of the magazine every three months, access to the Computer Laboratory's library and seminar series, career advice, mentoring and a helpline.

The Ring was an instant success. Approximately two years after its formation it had nearly 300 members, including more than 100 paying members, and interest in its services appeared to be increasing. Ten years later membership had risen to almost 1,000. The magazine had changed character from an informal production stapled together into a glossy, professional production. Its calendar of events had grown from year to year and an annual dinner with a speech from a distinguished computer scientist had become a feature. The first speaker was Andy Hopper in 2003, and the late Professor Sir Maurice Wilkes was guest speaker in 2004.

The Ring introduced novel inducements to encourage entrepreneurship, such as a Company of the Year Award and a Product of the Year Award which are listed in the Hall of Fame. Two impressive wooden boards at the entrance to the Computer Laboratory list award winners. The Ring's success came to the attention of the

Stephen Allott created the Ring, and Jan Samols manages the Graduate Association and edits *The Ring*.

Chapter Nine: Entrepreneurs, Spinning Out, Making Money and Linking with Industry

Andrew Herbert (BSc Leeds, PhD Cambridge, 1978, University Lecturer, 1980) in front of the Roger Needham Building of Microsoft Research, Cambridge. He succeeded Roger Needham as Managing Director of Microsoft Research in 2003 and became Chairman of Microsoft Research, EMEA, in 2010.

government and was commended as an excellent model for creating new business ventures. The association has almost certainly had a great deal of success in creating entrepreneurs and successful corporate employees among graduates of the Computer Laboratory, but it is difficult to measure this success with quantitative data. An example of how the Ring assists people is the case of Robert Folkes, who returned to England after 20 years in Australia and had no contacts at all in this country. Through Ring contacts he was introduced to Psymetrics Ltd, an energy management company and he helped it to commercialise its 'smart' energy technology. The company became a world leader with this technology and agreed a lucrative trade sale in 2011. In 2012 the Computer Laboratory decided to absorb the Ring into its own management structure. The purpose of this realignment was to enhance the presence of the Ring and accelerate its growth. The annual subscription was removed and in the reorganised structure all Computer Laboratory graduates will automatically become members of the Ring.

Microsoft Comes to Cambridge

During the tenure of Sir Alec Broers as Vice-Chancellor of Cambridge University, extremely fruitful contacts were established with the Microsoft Corporation. A munificent donation of $210 million from the Bill and Melinda Gates Foundation in October 2000 enabled the University to establish a large number of postgraduate scholarships for the brightest graduates from across the world to enable them to come to Cambridge to study for PhDs. Nearly 100 Gates scholarships are awarded each year. A few years earlier, Microsoft, under the guidance of Nathan Myhrvold, its Chief Technology Officer, had decided to establish a research laboratory in Europe to complement the laboratory in Redmond, California, and having spent a year at Cambridge University as a postdoctoral scientist, he decided that Cambridge would be a good location. He and his colleagues, including notably Rick Rashid, had come to know that Needham, then Head of the Computer Laboratory, was considering leaving academia and might become interested in the position of Director of the Microsoft Laboratory in Europe. Microsoft's management grasped this opportunity to recruit one of the most eminent computer scientists in Europe and acted with urgency. They

met Needham in December 1996 at San Francisco airport – a curious place to have a meeting, but it was entirely successful and by April 1997 a formal announcement was made that a Microsoft Research Laboratory would be established in Cambridge with Needham as its Founding Director. Needham was given the remit to recruit the best people he could find and encourage them to initiate research projects in areas where they had real expertise. He was asked to be a 'risk taker' in the selection of projects because Microsoft did not expect that every project started in the Laboratory would be successful.

At the same time there were separate negotiations between Cambridge University and the Bill and Melinda Gates charitable foundation concerning the possibility of a donation to Cambridge University to build a new Computer Laboratory. The University and the Department were acutely aware that this was a pressing need. The subject of Computer Science was growing across the world with ever increasing rapidity and the buildings in the New Museums Site were overcrowded and had not been fit for purpose for many years. A donation of £10 million was secured from the foundation to meet half the cost of a new building on University land in West Cambridge.

The initial plan was to embed the Microsoft Laboratory within the new Computer Laboratory with both laboratories in the same building but there was considerable opposition to this proposal within the Department. Some academic staff did not wish to move from the central Cambridge site that was conveniently

137

close to their colleges. They felt that they would lose their daily lunchtime contact with their peers in other subjects, which is so much a feature of Cambridge academic life. Others feared that Microsoft's higher salaries and much greater resources might divert their talented students and junior staff away from academic research activities into employment with Microsoft. Another concern was that intellectual property created within the University might be transferred to Microsoft without due recognition for the creators of the ideas within the University. Other objections were that the very best PhD students would be recruited by Microsoft and would not stay in their research group on postdoctoral appointments. Needham reminded his colleagues that there was before them a once-in-a-lifetime opportunity to acquire a purpose-designed building for the Computer Laboratory. The existing Computer Laboratory was overcrowded and ill designed to serve as laboratory for a modern and rapidly expanding academic discipline. He also promised that financial and intellectual benefits would flow from Microsoft's close interaction with the Computer Laboratory. At this time he was Pro-Vice-Chancellor of Cambridge University and extremely influential. He combined this role, somewhat controversially, with the position of Director of the Microsoft Laboratory for two years. The Head of the Computer Laboratory, Professor Robin Milner, supported Needham, but many senior staff members remained unconvinced.

The powerful combination of the Vice-Chancellor, the Pro-Vice-Chancellor and the Head of Department won the argument for moving the Computer Laboratory to West Cambridge, but not before making the substantial concession that the Microsoft Laboratory would not be embedded in the Computer Laboratory's building but located in a separate building. In 1999 Robin Milner resigned from his position as Head of Department and Professor Ian Leslie was appointed in his place. Construction began in 1999 and the new Computer Laboratory was completed in 2001 at a cost of £20 million and named the William Gates Building after the father of Bill Gates. It was opened, most appropriately, by Professor Sir Maurice Wilkes who, more than 50 years earlier, had walked through the green door of the Mathematical Laboratory and started the subject of Computer Science in Cambridge. In 1998 Roger Needham's period of tenure as Pro-Vice-Chancellor came to an end,

but he remained Managing Director of Microsoft Research Cambridge until he died prematurely in March 2003. His former student Andrew Herbert was appointed in his place. The building which housed Microsoft Research Cambridge was named the Roger Needham Building in his honour.

Cambridge Enterprise (2001–10)

Cambridge Enterprise occupied a corridor in the William Gates building which was used to host start-up companies for short periods. Basic facilities such as communications, Internet access and common areas were provided. A modest rent was charged and companies were expected to leave the premises as soon as they had become viable commercially or decided that the venture was not viable. The arrangement was terminated when the Computer Laboratory needed more space for its own research activities.

The Intel Laboratory (2003–6)

In 2003 Intel announced that it was setting up a small laboratory in Cambridge within the Computer Laboratory. It was planned that Intel research staff and University academics would collaborate on open research projects on computing and communications. The research would be focused on developing networking systems and software technologies to enable new types of distributed systems to be created. The idea was the brainchild of David Tennenhouse, Intel Vice-President and former member of the Computer Laboratory. The first Managing Director was Derek McAuley. The venture was short lived, and three years after the laboratory was opened it was abruptly closed down as part of a major reorganisation within Intel.

The Marconi Laboratory (2000–2)

In 2000 a multi-million pound deal was signed between Cambridge University and the Marconi Company. It was proposed that a new building, the Marconi Communications Research Centre, would be constructed on the West Cambridge site at a cost of £12 million and an additional £18 million would be donated to the University for research purposes. The new laboratory's remit was to develop technology for the Internet and data transmission that would create a communications revolution in the UK. The project was announced with a great deal of fanfare but two years later Marconi collapsed spectacularly and the

Chapter Nine: Entrepreneurs, Spinning Out, Making Money and Linking with Industry

Jack Lang, Emmanuel College 1965–69, Diploma in Computer Science 1969, University Demonstrator in the Computer Laboratory 1973–76, Affiliated Lecturer and Founder of the Computer Laboratory Supporters Club.

project was never implemented. Both these ventures were rather unfortunate episodes in the history of the Computer Laboratory and reflect the need for long-term planning and long-term contractual commitments from industrial partners before collaborations are agreed by the University.

The Computer Laboratory Supporters Club

The Supporters Club was founded in 1980 by Jack Lang, Demonstrator in the Computer Laboratory from 1973 to 1976, to create a link between industry and the Computer Laboratory. The central aim of the club was to develop a forum through which companies could engage with the Laboratory and recruit graduates. The club offers a range of opportunities to companies. Representatives are able to attend an annual recruitment fair held in the Computer Laboratory, and they can contact students to offer them short-term internships and graduate positions. Members of companies are able to act as clients for design projects carried out as part of the qualification for the Computer Science degree. The projects are designed to offer mutual benefits to the company and the student. The long-established weekly seminar series held in the Computer Laboratory during the academic term is open to company representatives. Supporters Club members are invited to an annual dinner with the academic staff and postgraduate students of the Computer Laboratory. The Club can also assist companies with arranging events for students. Lang teaches courses in Business Studies, E-commerce and organises Business Studies seminars with outside speakers.

Membership of the Supporters Club is gained by giving a donation to the Computer Laboratory. The amount is expected to be around £300 for a start-up company and up to £5,000 for a well-established and successful business. Today there are approximately 70 members, including well-known names such as the online retailer Ocado, Google, Microsoft Research, ARM and Morgan Stanley. A full list of members can be found at http://www.cl.cam.ac.uk/supporters-club/members.html.

Right: Group of research students and academic staff. From left to right: Robert Mullins, Agata Brajdic, Robert Harle, Gareth Bailey, Alastair Beresford and Sam Staton.

Overleaf: The home of the Computer Laboratory is the impressive William Gates Building completed in 2001.

CHAPTER TEN

The Computer Laboratory on its 75th Birthday
A Centre of Research Excellence

The Computer Laboratory in its 75th year was a centre of excellence in computing research, covering a wide range of modern, exciting and challenging topics. The research group contributions which follow describe briefly the strength and diversity of the Laboratory's research programme and the descriptions demonstrate that the groups are interlinked and inter-dependent, with many individuals crossing boundaries to work in disparate areas. This cross-fertilization is a consequence of the organic growth of research in the Computer Laboratory. The groups also have extensive collaborations with other research centres in the UK and across the world.

The quality of research in the Laboratory since its foundation is further demonstrated by the awards received for outstanding projects and the personal recognition received by academic staff and students. A number of prestigious British Computer Society (BCS) awards have been gained for highly original projects. Former heads of the Computer Laboratory Maurice Wilkes and Robin Milner were both holders of the 'Nobel Prize for Computing', the ACM Turing Prize. More than half a dozen members of the Laboratory have been elected to Fellowships of the Royal Society and the Royal Academy of Engineering and, uniquely, Karen Spärck Jones was elected a Fellow of the British Academy. Several graduate students have received the accolade of 'Distinguished Dissertation' for their PhD work. More than two-thirds of the academic staff members are Professors or Readers – a remarkably high proportion reflecting the quality of the research in the Laboratory.

The Research Groups
Systems Research Group
The Systems Research Group (SRG) comprises ten academics and approximately 50 PhD students. The SRG's research topics include building, measuring and characterising complete systems; defining the hardware–software interfaces for operating systems and networks; multi-scale computing (from large distributed systems down to small handheld devices); and modelling and optimising systems for performance and power consumption.

Networks and Operating Systems
Research into novel operating systems stretches back to the Cambridge CAP computer and the Cambridge Distributed System projects in the 1970s. More recently the group developed the Xen virtual machine monitor. This work was the basis of the world's first public Cloud Service, which was deployed by Amazon. Some of the key people responsible for Xen returned to work in the Computer

Members of the Systems Group, from left to right: Cecilia Mascolo, Steven Hand, Ian Leslie, Jean Bacon, Jon Crowcroft, Anil Madhavapeddy and David Greaves.

Laboratory on a follow-up project called 'Mirage'. The software is written in OCaml, providing strong type safety. It also allows extreme code specialisation, which leads to a much smaller footprint and attack surface for cloud applications. Steven Hand and Anil Madhavapeddy are the main contributors to this project.

The group has built novel programmable gigabit ethernet interfaces for networking research. It collaborates with companies such as Endace on high-performance (10Gbps) measurements. It also collaborates with Stanford University on teaching and research on the NetFPGA platform and recently developed its own OpenFlow controller integrated with the Mirage project.

Network Analysis

There is activity in the group on anomaly detection and repair, specifically in designing the Vigilante self-certifying alert and patching system. The project, led by Andrew Moore and Jon Crowcroft, saw deployment of the system into Microsoft's Azure Cloud Service.

The group is also working on theoretical rigour in networking. Richard Gibbens has contributed to the development of Dynamic Alternative Routing for telephone networks and to later advancements in resource pooling in general. Tim Griffin works on applying algebraic specification of policy routing systems. He and a number of PhD students have built tools that allow fixed, mobile and content routing implementation of protocols that are correct by design.

Sensor Networks

The group is also active in designing and deploying sensor systems that allow the federation of multiple-sensor networks. This allows a number of stakeholders to run multiple applications while retaining isolation and privacy which, as sensors proliferate into buildings, streets and vehicles, is not just desirable but essential. The SRG is part of the collaboration with architects and civil engineers to study how sensors can help in the monitoring of structures and infrastructure. Much of today's sensing is performed by smartphones, and the group is pioneering techniques that use sensors to monitor human activities efficiently and accurately. In this context the group has activities across a range of mobile, wireless and social systems.

Ian Leslie's current interests are in the use of information systems to reduce energy demands based on providing sensor platforms which both facilitate the understanding of how and why energy is used by individuals and how the same outcomes might be achieved with less energy use.

Social Networks

The SRG is interested in the new interdisciplinary study which includes mathematical techniques for analysing graphs (of the Internet and the web, of people's encounters in real spaces and of the social graph in the online world). These data can be used to understand human travel, building use, transport, energy and epidemics with fine temporal and spatial granularity. Cecilia Mascolo is developing complex techniques and metrics to model and predict how these networks evolve. Applications range from the ability to recommend and suggest items, places and activities to the optimisation of underlying system performance.

Middleware

Jean Bacon leads the research on middleware. Early middlewares provided message passing for system integration or RPC (Remote Procedure Call) for distributed programming. For large-scale, widely distributed systems the asynchronous, event-based paradigm supports many applications including environmental and personal monitoring. Composite events specify conditions that trigger actions. Publish/subscribe middleware, such as Hermes, multicast messages (representing events) from publishers to subscribers who have expressed interest in the data.

A new programming language for data centres, CIEL, an improvement on Google's MapReduce system has been developed. Eiko Yoneki has developed the Crackle system for efficient processing of large-scale graph-structured data analysis which is a requirement in network science.

Collectively, the group believes that there could be a total loss of privacy unless trust and access control in the database society is achieved. The theme of the group's research across many projects is the design of better tools and techniques for anonymity and the control of disclosure of personal data.

Computer Architecture Group

The Computer Architecture Group's main concern is the building of computer systems, including both hardware and software. Given this broad remit, there is much collaboration with other groups in the Computer Laboratory in order to take advantage of their collective expertise in systems, security, compilation and verification.

Efficient Many Core Processors

Advances in hardware technology force us to develop power-efficient and highly parallel computer systems. Building upon experience garnered from designing on-chip networks, Robert Mullins is exploring a broad range of massively parallel single-chip architectures that place the network at the heart of the design. This project spans computer architecture and compiler techniques, using simple cores that are more deeply interconnected to each other than in traditional designs, sharing some similarities to Field Programmable Gate Arrays (FPGAs). The network is free to carry both instructions and data between cores, allowing individual cores to be exploited in a variety of interesting ways.

Communication Centric Computer Design

Current electronic technology trends favour transistors over wires. Alan Mycroft (Programming Languages), David Greaves (Systems), Robert Mullins and Simon Moore (Computer Architecture) are investigating how to design computers for a time when communication rather than computation is treated as the primary design constraint.

Daniel Greenfield, a PhD student in this field who was supervised by Simon Moore, received the UK Distinguished Dissertation Award for his work 'Communication Locality in Computation: Software, Chip Multiprocessors and Brains'.

Biologically Inspired Massively Parallel Architectures

This multi-institution project is investigating computing systems with more than a million processor cores. Simon Moore leads the Cambridge team in collaboration with Steve Furber (Manchester), David Allterton (Sheffield) and Andrew Brown (Southampton). There are two threads of work: a one million ARM processor machine under development at Manchester and an FPGA-based machine in Cambridge with software infrastructure written by the

Members of the Computer Architecture Group. Alex Bradbury, Robert Mullins, Daniel Bates, Robert Norton, Theo Markettos, Timothy Jones, Simon Moore, Steven Marsh, Niall Murphy, Milos Puzovic, David Greaves, Alan Mujumdar, Jonathan Woodruff, Ali Mustafa Zaidi, Greg Chadwick, Muhammad Shahbaz, Andrew Moore and Andreas Koltes.

Southampton and Sheffield teams. The objective is to build massively parallel and yet power-efficient and affordable computers for scientific computing. The focus of current applications is on massively parallel neural simulation.

Rethinking the Hardware–Software Interface for Security

This large DARPA-funded project (codenamed CTSRD) spans security (Robert Watson and Ross Anderson) and computer architecture (Simon Moore). The latter revisits capability-based protection mechanisms which can be used to enforce the principle of least privilege. Many of these core concepts have been known for over 40 years and yet nobody has, so far, built a computer that can efficiently support these mechanisms. Pioneering attempts include the Cambridge CAP computer in the 1970s and the Intel iAPX 432 in the 1980s. Using modern processor architecture techniques these systems can be prototyped rapidly and can run real OS and application codes.

Resilient Cloud Computing

Incorporating the capability processor ideas from the CTSRD project, another DARPA-funded project is underway. Its mission is to explore robust and secure massively parallel and massively connected ('cloud') computer systems. As with CTSRD, this project spans several research groups: security (Robert Watson), systems (Steven Hand and Andrew Moore) and computer architecture (Simon Moore).

HELIX – Automatic Parallelisation

With multicore processors now at the heart of devices across the computing spectrum, it is important for applications to take advantage of the available hardware parallelism to achieve high performance. The HELIX project, run by Timothy Jones in collaboration with colleagues at Harvard University, aims to achieve this by automatically extracting loop-level parallelism during compilation and runtime, even for programs that have been designed and implemented with sequential semantics. The research is exploring new compilation, runtime and architectural schemes for extracting parallelism and reducing the cost of communication between cores within the same chip, thereby aiming to scale performance with the number of cores.

Security Group

The Computer Laboratory has a long history of key contributions in the field of computer security and today it is home to some of the world's leading computer security researchers. The group makes core contributions in cryptographic protocol design, CPU and operating system security, anonymity research, and malware analysis, but also does foundational cross-disciplinary work in security economics, cybercrime measurement, security psychology, human factors, and domestic and international policy.

Security Economics and Cybercrime

Humans are increasingly dependent on global-scale systems with billions of users and millions of competing companies. Incentives in such a system are important yet complex: if Alice guards a system while Bob pays the cost of fraud, failure is likely. Ross Anderson is a pioneer in the field of 'security economics', which applies game theory and microeconomic analysis to system design, with a global impact. The group's reports have influenced EU policy on cybercrime and Internet resilience. A former research student is now responsible for White House cyber security policy, and Anderson's 2009 'Database State' report was adopted by the Lib Dems and (in part) by the Conservatives. Richard Clayton and Ross Anderson study the economics of cybercrime by collecting spam, phishing, malware and other online abuse data, providing neutral cost estimates to deflate scaremongering vendors.

Anonymity

Steven Murdoch is a chief maintainer of Tor, a non-profit anonymous communication system. Tor allows human rights workers, businesses and journalists in countries like Iran and China to surf the Internet despite government censorship. Keeping communications open is a constant technical and social arms race, but is key to improving privacy for millions of users worldwide.

Hardware and Signal Security

Under Markus Kuhn and Sergei Skorobogatov, the group has become a world leader in hardware and signal security. Kuhn has pioneered open standards for emission security, a previously classified topic, and advised the Dutch government on electronic voting machine security.

Cambridge Computing: The First 75 Years

Members of the Security Group in the Hardware and Signal Security Laboratory. From left to right: Omar Choudary, Wei Ming Khoo, Rubin Xu, Dongting Yu, Laurent Simon, Sergei Skorobogatov, Markus Kuhn and Frank Stajano.

He also created new security protocols for authenticating radio receiver location for radio-frequency identification and satellite navigation systems, and new image and video forensic reconstruction techniques. Skorobogatov develops attack and defence technologies, and evaluates devices for the semiconductor industry. He pioneered techniques to extract secrets from semiconductor devices using optical methods, and novel power analyses to detect chip design changes, a critical supply chain problem.

Payment Systems and Secure APIs
The group has analysed the security problems of real systems, including vehicle monitors, electricity meters and medical records. Anderson and Murdoch studied the failure modes of banking systems, including 'chip and PIN'. They discovered numerous vulnerabilities, leading to technical improvements and helping fraud victims receive refunds. Anderson regularly speaks at central banking events, including Federal Reserve conferences.

Anderson extended protocol analysis to application programming interfaces (APIs) in work that forced the redesign of most commercial cryptographic processors. Complex systems are increasingly composed of variably secure components, which must be composed effectively using protocols and APIs for enforcement and proof – mobile phone CPUs are subject to malware, for example, whereas SIM cards are not.

Usability
The means and ease with which we interact with computers is in constant flux, and in continual need of reassessment. Frank Stajano has won a European grant to explore successors to passwords. One candidate is collaborative authentication, wherein your laptop believes it is in your possession if it can sense that your phone, watch, belt buckle and shoe pedometer are close by. Stajano and Anderson are also interested in online deception, and how the depersonalisation of transactions encourages deceptive, unpleasant or criminal behaviour, and reduces punitive actions towards offenders. While social networks start to put the humanity back into computing, they are limited by business models. Other ways of re-humanising socio-technical systems, such as physical interaction with everyday objects as part of the security protocols, hold further promise.

Opposite: The Programming, Logic and Semantics Group. Front: Sam Staton, Bjarki Holm, Peter Sewell, Mark Batty, William Denman, Mike Gordon, Marcelo Fiore, Andrew Pitts, Matko Botincan, Kathryn Gray and Mike Dodds. Middle: Scott Owens, Anthony Fox and Susmit Sarkar. Back: Tomas Petricek, Zongyan Huang, Marco Ferreira Devesas Campos, James Bridge, Magnus Myreen, Thomas Tuerk, Dominic Orchard, Kayvan Memarian and Robin Morisset.

Above: Members of the Security Group displaying modern versions of memory-protected computers designed and built in the Computer Laboratory, with the original CAP computer in the background. Standing: Jonathan Woodruff, Richard Clayton, Jonathan Anderson, Michael Roe, Ross Anderson, David Chisnall and Robert Watson. Kneeling: Khilan Gudka, Robert Norton and Simon Moore.

Capability Systems

The group's largest project explores software compartmentalisation with an aim of mitigating inevitable vulnerabilities. Robert Watson's Google-funded Capsicum project blends concepts from capability systems (such as the CAP computer) with contemporary systems in a 'hybrid capability system model', and has been used to implement robust sandboxing or compartmentalisation for security purposes for Google's Chrome web browser. The DARPA-funded CTSRD project, operated jointly with Robert Watson, Simon Moore, Ross Anderson, and Peter Neumann at SRI, transposes these ideas into hardware to support granular compartmentalisation. The CHERI CPU prototype implements intra-address space protection under the open source FreeBSD operating system, motivating contributions in architecture, compiler, operating system and application security.

Resilient Switching

Watson's DARPA-funded MRC2 project extends our network security interests into data-centre computing. Jointly with Simon Moore, Steven Hand, Andrew Moore and Peter Neumann, MRC2 improves scalability, security, resilience and energy use by decomposing monolithic switches into many trustworthy high-dimensionality 'switchlets', converging CPU interconnects and networking.

Programming, Logic and Semantics (PLS) Group

The Programming, Logic and Semantics (PLS) Group's work is centred on the study of programming languages, logic and mathematical models, addressing hardware, software and networks. It covers a wide range of applied and theoretical work including: rigorous semantics of multiprocessors and networks; programming language design, compilers and program analysis; the development of interactive theorem provers and automatic proof procedures; abstract models of computation; and the study of finite model theory and computational complexity.

The group today has absorbed smaller research groups including the Automated Reasoning Group, the Cambridge Programming Research Group and the Theory and Semantics Group.

Program Language Design

Alan Mycroft is interested in programming languages, type systems, program analysis and compilation, especially those techniques that bridge the theory–systems divide. A recurring theme in his work is type-like systems to control and optimise data transfer on multi-core processors both for software engineering and to avoid breaking the 'shared-memory' illusion of caches. Sam Staton, who is interested in the foundations of programming languages, is currently working on a new kind of algebraic theory for reasoning concerned with computer programs. Whereas traditional algebra has operations like addition and multiplication, the operations in Sam's algebra are computational effects such as memory access operations.

Computer Systems Analysis

Timothy Griffin is exploring firm mathematical foundations for the Internet's (organically evolved) routing protocols and applying this theory in the development of a high-level language for their design and specification. To manage the complexity of this task, he is using interactive theorem provers to construct a verified implementation of the language. Peter Sewell combines mathematically

rigorous modelling and experimental testing to clarify the behaviour of multiprocessors (x86, ARM, IBM POWER) and programming languages (C/C++), and to prove the correctness of compilers and concurrent algorithms. The wider goal is to put mainstream computation on a more solid foundation.

Interactive Theorem Provers

The use of higher-order logic for modelling hardware and software was pioneered by Mike Gordon. He has contributed to the development of theorem-proving tools (such as the HOL system) and their application to mechanically proving the correctness of computer systems, including microprocessors. Larry Paulson is best known for Isabelle, a widely used, interactive theorem prover for higher-order logic and other formalisms. He is responsible for the original design and much of the implementation of the program, and his most noteworthy application is to the formal verification of cryptographic protocols. More recently, he has introduced MetiTarski, an automatic theorem prover for the real numbers, including nonlinear arithmetic and transcendental functions.

Theoretical Foundations

The study of symmetry occurs in many branches of mathematics and computer science. Andrew Pitts has developed the theory of nominal sets, which extends the reach of computation theory from finite data structures and algorithms to ones that are infinite, but become finite when quotiented by their symmetries. A core insight in Glynn Winskel's current ERC project is the increased expressivity behavioural symmetry brings to event structures, to the types, processes and applications they can support. Through the key elements of events, causality and symmetry there is a clear, if challenging, way forward to next-generation semantics. Anuj Dawar is engaged in a project to characterise those properties of finite data structures that are feasibly computable and invariant under natural symmetries. Such a characterisation would shed light on the fundamental question of what is feasibly computable. His current work investigates the power of linear algebra in classifying feasible and symmetry-invariant properties.

Category theory provides a powerful mathematical language for building and relating emerging models for computation. Marcelo Fiore has applied it extensively to study varieties of computational languages. In 2012 his 2002 article 'Semantic Analysis of Normalisation by Evaluation for Typed Lambda Calculus' won the 'Ten-year most influential' PPDP (Principles and Practice of Declarative Programming) paper award.

Digital Technology Group

The group's research ranges from system design, analysis and implementation of the physical level to the development of novel devices and applications. The research covers mobile devices and sensors, energy efficiency, wireless communication, systems measurement, performance analysis and management of data and computation. The emphasis is on physical realisation and testing in real-world environments.

Computing on the Move

The trend towards smaller and lighter computing machinery has added a new dimension to computing mobility. Highly personalised devices accompany us wherever we go, fostering an interest in our 'location'. With GPS powering a new swathe of exciting applications, 'indoor GPS' is an attractive new prospect that could revolutionise navigation and control within buildings. The DTG has continued the indoor location work pioneered by ORL, with Robert Harle leading research into the use of sensors built into smartphones to provide accurate location without need for a specialised infrastructure.

Andrew Rice has pioneered Device Analyzer, a piece of smartphone monitoring software installed on volunteers' phones that logs their usage anonymously as a means towards improving functionality. Today almost 10,000 users around the world are donating information about how they use their phones by using Rice's app. The challenge now is to sift through the data, interpreting and modelling what people do with smartphones. The results will enable Rice's team to optimise the design of the next generation of devices and to establish what the Application Programming Interfaces (APIs) and semantics used to control them should be.

This research is dependent on volunteer-provided data and, with smartphones now so personal to users, privacy is a key issue. Alastair Beresford is finding means of collecting such information in the age of distributed

Chapter Ten: The Computer Laboratory on its 75th Birthday: A Centre of Research Excellence

Members of the Digital Technology Group with some of their research gadgets on display. Back row, left to right: Bogdan Roman, Sam Aaron and Andy Hopper. Front row, left to right: Alastair Beresford, Ian Wassell, Ripduman Sohan, Robert Harle, Andrew Rice and Sherif Akoush.

computing. He plans to use the cloud for reliable storage that can be used by smartphone apps, with neither the app developer nor the cloud storage owner able to see sensitive data. Algorithms that can do tasks like these will be crucial in the future, as more of the devices we encounter become connected and able to exchange information about us.

Making Sense of the World

The mobility push has been accompanied by advances in technology which enables computing machinery to sense aspects of the world around us. Using wireless networking technologies, small sensing nodes can share data and build a model of their surroundings. These so-called Wireless Sensor Networks (WSNs) are cost-effective and easy to deploy, and their full potential has yet to be realised. The DTG is taking an application-led approach to exploring this exciting area.

Ian Wassell and Frank Stajano are looking at the use of WSNs for physical infrastructure monitoring, tracking the progression of cracks in the Humber Bridge and London Underground tunnels. This application's requirement of long-term monitoring with ultra-low power consumption has motivated research into how radio signals propagate between nodes with minimum power expenditure. The added need to minimise the data transmitted has resulted in novel research into 'compressive sensing', which exploits the sparsity inherent in real signals to sample at rates lower than the theoretical (Nyquist) requirement.

At the other end of the WSN spectrum, Robert Harle has been attaching nodes to the shoes of athletes. For this application, battery lifetime is less important than providing reliable, single-hop networking that can exchange high-rate data to identify the sensors and processing techniques that help sportspeople optimise their training and avoid injury.

Double-Checking the Answers

Modern science is characterised by the need to analyse large datasets while ensuring that results are trustworthy. A 'provenance chain', which describes where the original (raw) data come from, along with all of the stages of processing and how conclusions were reached, is mandatory. Ripduman Sohan is researching how to add support for provenance at the operating system level, allowing users to archive, export and restore the entire computational workflow resulting in the creation or change of *any* file on a system.

Computing for the Future of the Planet

Andy Hopper has continued to pursue projects within the framework he developed in the mid-2000s, which describes how computing intersects with sustainability. Projects show how surplus renewable energy can be used to power computation (green computing), and how the energy and carbon footprints of large-scale manufacturing operations can be reduced by using sensor information (computing for green). Another research direction is engineering computing systems which provide complete assurance for use in situations where the digital infrastructure is critical and must never fail, or where modelling is used to inform major policy decisions, for example in predicting climate change.

Graphics and Interaction Group

The Graphics and Interaction Group investigates a diverse range of issues, all broadly related to the computer–

Cambridge Computing: The First 75 Years

human interface. The group collaborates with researchers in many disciplines, including mathematics, engineering, psychology and the performing arts. Among the group's research interests are the following large projects.

Emotionally Intelligent Interfaces

Rapid advances in technology coupled with users' expectation of computers mean that socially and emotionally adept technologies are becoming a necessity. Peter Robinson leads a team investigating the inference of people's mental states from facial expressions, vocal nuances, body posture, gesture and physiological signals. These are important channels for the communication of emotional and social displays and combine to communicate feelings, show empathy, and acknowledge the actions of other people. The team also considers the expression of emotions by robots and cartoon avatars.

The team's research has considered how emotional information can be used within a wider context to make useful inferences about a user's mental state within a natural computing environment in a way that increases usability. They draw inspiration from emotion theories on the role of facial expressions in inferring mental states, using an emotion inference system that is demonstrably as accurate as the top six per cent of human subjects tested. Applications include detecting cognitive overload in command and control operators, online teaching systems and interventions for children with autism spectrum conditions.

Tabletop Displays

The original tabletop display, the Digital Desk, was developed in the group in the early 1990s, in collaboration with Xerox. This led to the idea of augmented reality, where everyday objects acquire computational properties as an alternative to entering the synthetic worlds of virtual reality. The group has continued to experiment with such displays, investigating how one would interact with local and remote collaborators using large, high-resolution, tabletop displays.

Above: Each set of blocks follows a curved path representing a particular degree of Bézier curve: blue is linear, green is quadratic, red is cubic. The blocks are spaced evenly in parametric space, reflecting the group's work on B-splines and subdivision.

Left: Members of the Graphics and Interaction Group demonstrating the wide range of research equipment in the Laboratory. From left to right: Ntombi Banda, Christian Richardt, Lech Świrski, Zhen Bai, Tadas Baltrušaitis (at back), Andra Adams (at back), Ian Davies, Marwa Mahmoud and Peter Robinson.

Chapter Ten: The Computer Laboratory on its 75th Birthday: A Centre of Research Excellence

Subdivision Surfaces and NURBS

Subdivision surfaces and non-uniform rational B-splines (NURBS) are two alternative mechanisms for representing three-dimensional shapes, both of them having been developed in the 1970s. NURBS went on to become the industry standard in Computer-Aided Design (CAD) and subdivision was adopted in computer animation in the late 1990s, owing to the ease of design it allows – indeed it is still the standard tool in the field today. The CAD industry, however, has not yet adopted subdivision, as it is not fully compatible with their existing NURBS paradigm, and because it produces artefacts in the surface that are unnoticeable on a movie screen but that are critical when machining parts in the real world. Neil Dodgson and Malcolm Sabin lead a team that, over the last decade, has successfully addressed these problems of compatibility and artefacts.

The team's most significant recent result is in creating a subdivision method that is a true super-set of NURBS, reconciling the two approaches. The group continues this research with the aim of producing a solution that will benefit both CAD and animation industries.

3D TV

In the 1990s, the group developed a prototype 3D TV that required no glasses. More recently, researchers under Neil Dodgson have investigated the editing of stereoscopic video, important for movie post-production and gaze-based interaction with stereoscopic displays. The future for 3D TV is unclear: a glasses-free solution is needed, but no current technology makes it possible to bring a practical realisation to a wide home market.

Crucible and Interdisciplinary Design

Crucible is a research network that originated, under Alan Blackwell's leadership, in 2001. It has since become the largest organisation in the world dedicated to promoting rigorous research collaboration between technologists and researchers in the arts, humanities and social sciences. This collaboration focuses on design as a meeting point for widely differing research disciplines. Crucible activities include setting up research programmes, training researchers, influencing policy bodies and identifying suitable funding sources for research in interdisciplinary design.

Artificial Intelligence Group

The work of the Artificial Intelligence (AI) Group is multi-disciplinary, spanning genomics, bio-informatics, computational learning theory, computer vision, and diagrammatic reasoning. A unifying theme is to understand the problems involved in multi-scale pattern recognition, seeking powerful (often statistical) algorithms for modelling and solving them and learning from data. Work by members of the AI Group involves theoretical aspects such as modelling human problem solving, and has applications ranging from disease

A prototype 3D TV and 3D camera: a joint project between the Computer Laboratory and the Department of Engineering in the early 1990s, demonstrated by Professor Neil Dodgson who is currently Deputy Head of the Computer Laboratory.

modelling and pharmacological drug design to algorithms for automatic visual recognition of passengers at airports, thereby replacing passports. Looking forward, the AI Group hopes to continue to find new synergies among ideas based in statistics, mechanised reasoning, cognitive science, biology and engineering, and to develop practical applications.

Computer Vision and Statistical Pattern Recognition
One outgrowth of work in computer vision is iris recognition by a rapid automated method, allowing personal identity to be determined with very high confidence. Utilising remote mathematical analysis of the random patterns visible in the iris based on John Daugman's algorithms, this method forms the basis of all publicly deployed iris recognition systems worldwide. The government of India is currently using these algorithms to log the iris patterns of all 1.2 billion citizens in a national entitlements and benefits ID system called UIDAI. The goal is to improve social inclusion and fair access to welfare, and to reduce corruption; its slogan is: 'To give the poor an identity.' With 200 million persons enrolled already and another million enrolled daily, some 400 trillion iris comparisons are performed every day using these algorithms.

Automated Reasoning: Proof and Induction from Diagrams
Increasing our understanding of how people solve problems is one of the theoretical aspects of AI studied by Mateja Jamnik. Jamnik models this type of reasoning computationally to enable machines to reason in a manner similar to humans. In particular, she investigates and mechanises some of the 'informal' reasoning methods that people employ (such as the diagrams in proofs of mathematical theorems), and then integrates them with classical formal techniques. Offering new insights into both human and automated reasoning, Jamnik's work

Below left: The Artificial Intelligence Group tries out a new chess algorithm, and reaches the same final position as the famous match between IBM Deep Blue and world champion Gary Kasparov. Qd5: Mateja Jamnik, Re1: Pietro Lió, Nf2: Sean Holden, Kh2: John Daugman.

152

Chapter Ten: The Computer Laboratory on its 75th Birthday: A Centre of Research Excellence

overturned a widespread concern about diagrams being misleading and not suitable as a formal tool, and inspired others to apply human methods in new application areas.

Bio-informatics, Genomics and Epidemiology

Today multi-scale and complex biomedical data are gathered and analysed in a rather simple way that completely misses the opportunity to uncover combinations of predictive disease profiles. We are able to observe what happens at almost all scales, from the whole organism down to the molecular level, but putting things together in order to obtain real understanding is much more difficult and less developed. To address this issue, the work of Pietro Lió focuses on the development of novel computational disease modelling frameworks that integrate multilevel molecular information with clinical research results in order to obtain new diagnostic markers of diseases and therapies. The future is one in which computers will assist our health in a more effective and comprehensive way than they do today.

Machine Learning and Bayesian Inference

Machine learning is a sub-discipline within AI in which software is produced that improves its performance on the basis of its interaction with the world. Sean Holden works on both the theory and application of machine learning techniques, with notable success to date particularly in the field of drug design, where the software concerned uses existing knowledge of the properties of a collection of chemical structures in order to recognise new structures likely to have related properties. The aim is to extend this knowledge into more complex areas involving the chemistry of the cell, with further applications in medicine.

Natural Language and Information Processing Group

The Natural Language and Information Processing (NLIP) Group undertakes a range of research projects into computational models of human languages. Some of these are outlined here.

Analysing Scientific Texts

A series of projects over the last ten years have built systems for the automatic extraction of information from the text of scientific papers. The overall goal is to make it easier for scientists to analyse the vast amount of literature produced each year, especially in subjects such as biomedicine and chemistry. The CRAB project led by Anna Korhonen, for example, is concerned with automatically classifying scientific abstracts to build up a profile of the cancer risk from particular chemicals. Similarly the FUSE project, led in Cambridge by Simone Teufel, analyses the rhetorical structure of text and the way in which papers cite one another, in order to discover the emergence of novel ideas.

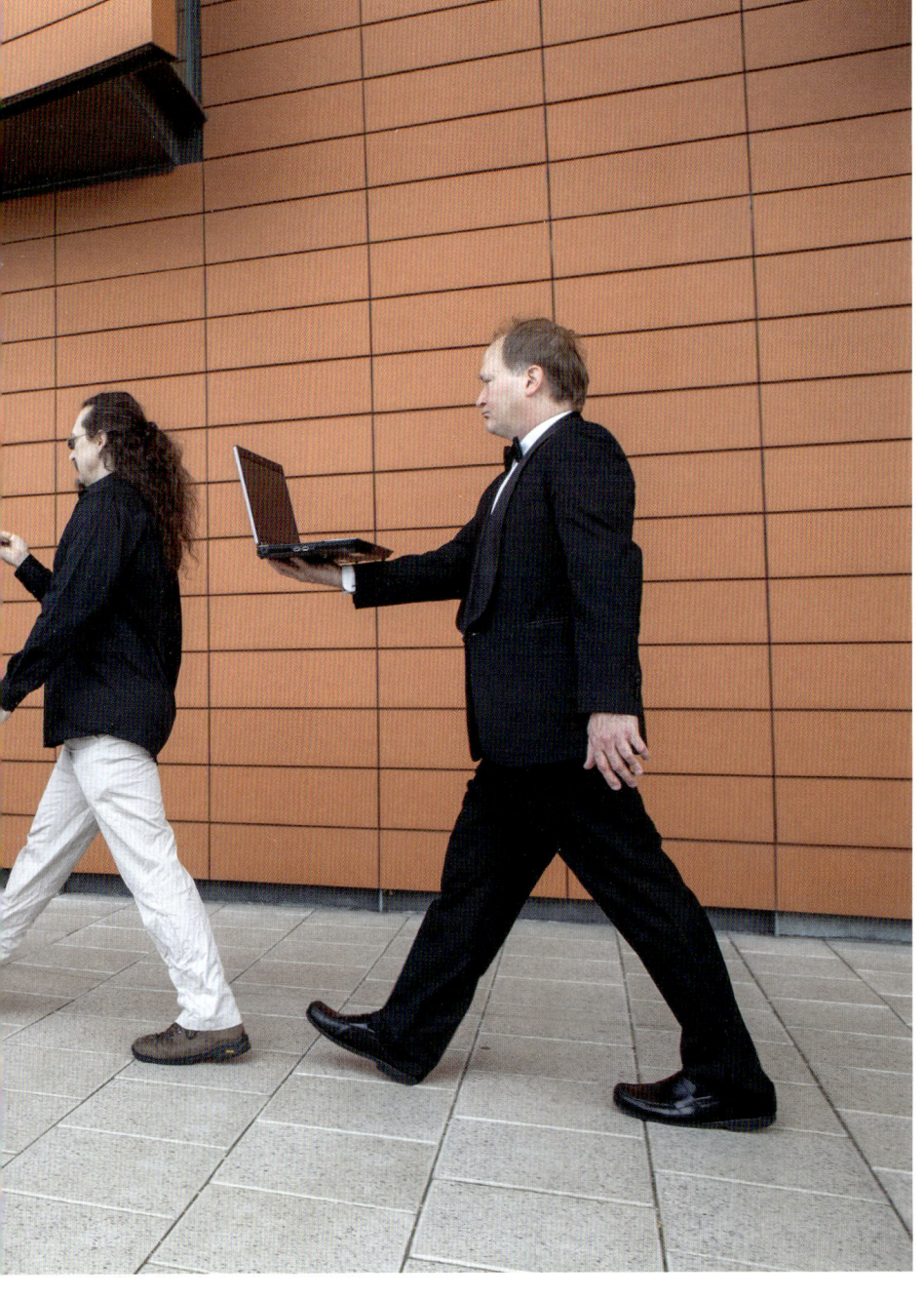

Below: AI Group on a day trip to make AI better, declares; 'All we are saying is give PCs a chance.'

Cambridge Computing: The First 75 Years

The Natural Language and Information Processing Group. From left to right: Dain Kaplan, Anna Korhonen, Diarmuid Ó Séaghdha, Laura Rimell, Marek Rei, Ann Copestake (Professor and Deputy Head of the Computer Laboratory), Stephen Clark, Frannie Chang, Helen Yannakoudakis, Ekaterina Kochmar, Wenduan Xu, Awais Athar and James Jardine.

Learner English

A very different application area is the development of technology to enhance the teaching and assessment of English for speakers of other languages (ESOL). For several years, the NLIP group has been part of the English Profile programme, in collaboration with and funded by Cambridge ESOL (part of Cambridge Assessment). Researchers in the group, led by Ted Briscoe, have worked on systems for the identification of a learner's level of English and of their native language, the automatic grading of short essays and the detection and correction of learner errors.

Development of Language Processing Theory and Technology

Underlying the group's development of applications is a broad range of research on theoretical approaches to computational modelling of language and on basic technology for language processing. Parsing (the analysis of the structure of language) has been a particular long-term research focus. The RASP system, co-developed by Ted Briscoe, is now distributed by a spin-out company, ILexIR. Ann Copestake is one of the originators of the DELPH-IN technology, which has been used for the development of tools for the analysis and generation of a very wide range of languages. The C&C tools, co-developed by Stephen Clark, include a highly efficient wide-coverage statistical parser which has been widely used in language processing research. More recently, as part of the EU SPACEBOOK project, Clark is leading work on semantic parsing for human–machine dialogues.

The Computer Laboratory Today and in the Future

The Growth of the Laboratory, 1937–2012

Wilkes followed Lennard-Jones through the iconic green door 75 years ago. He was then the solitary staff member. Today in the Computer Laboratory there are 16 Professors, seven Readers, ten University Senior Lecturers and four University Lecturers. There are approximately

Margaret Levitt, Secretary of the Computer Laboratory, is responsible for all administrative and operational functions in the William Gates Building, and is also Secretary to the Faculty Board of Computer Science & Technology. Debbie Peterson (seated) and Helen Scarborough are in Reception.

Chapter Ten: The Computer Laboratory on its 75th Birthday: A Centre of Research Excellence

40 Senior Research Associates and Research Associates, eight Research Assistants, and over 100 research students. There are 90 visitors to the Laboratory in various categories ranging from distinguished professors to short-term summer interns. Supporting the academic activity there are five Computer Officers. On the administrative side, under the Secretary of the Department there are a number of administrators looking after teaching, human resources, finance, outreach, reception, building maintenance and services such as the library and workshop.

Moving Forward

A decade ago the Computer Laboratory moved from an overcrowded site in the centre of Cambridge into the purpose-built William Gates Building on J J Thomson Avenue. This created an unprecedented opportunity for the Laboratory to expand and diversify its research activities, and the Head of Department, Professor Andy Hopper, is confident that in the years to come many more academic appointments will be made. Not only will existing research programmes be strengthened but new ones will be started, giving a fresh impetus to the Laboratory's research profile.

Hopper asserts that the challenge for the Computer Laboratory in the future will be to support and advance on a wide front the digital infrastructure that pervades the planet today. Digital computation and communication have changed society and brought enormous benefits in commerce, government, education and health, and he expects the Computer Laboratory's research programme will continue to address all aspects of computing that could bring real benefits to society. At the same time computing research must ensure that society's dependence on the digital infrastructure is protected by robust systems. He warns that there have been far too many recent examples of system failure in the digital infrastructure and frequent breaches in security, with unfortunate consequences for individuals and organisations. Future computing research must endeavour to create systems that will minimise the risks from system failures and eliminate altogether the risk of failure in highly critical applications such as health, safety and security.

This theme is echoed in the future plans for Systems Research Group 'as computing and communications services become ever more critical to the everyday functioning of modern society. It behoves us to invent

The Support Staff members of the Computer Laboratory are responsible for assisting the academic staff in their teaching, research and administrative duties. From left to right (seated): Cynthia Curtis, Caroline Matthews, Megan Samons, Jiang He, Dinah Pounds, Nick Batterham, Ian Burton-Palmer and Martin McDonnell. From left to right (standing): Lise Gough, Carol Nightingale, Kate Cisek, Tanya Hall, Louis Massuard and Nicholas Cutler.

Cambridge Computing: The First 75 Years

> **OUTREACH ACTIVITIES**
>
> The Computer Laboratory is privileged to be based in the modern William Gates Building, with its outstanding facilities for holding functions and events. The building is regularly used for internal and external outreach activities:
>
> - An annual two-day event designed to attract bright young people to take up computer science
> - An annual Industrial Supporters Fair
> - The Annual Wheeler Lecture
> - Open Wednesday Seminars
> - The Ring AGM
> - Women@CL Events
> - Local Academic Conferences
> - Meetings of Professional Associations

An undergraduate laboratory class in progress at the Computer Laboratory.

and develop research tools and techniques that permit the creation of services that, to all intents and purposes, never fail. The old "five nines" availability mantra is simply not good enough for the future.' Systems research must absorb the very latest research results from other disciplines of computer science, including formal verification theory and type safe programming languages. Systems research must also explore design patterns taken from the world of highly optimised tolerant systems as seen in biology and other natural large-scale efficient and resilient natural phenomena. These approaches are best evaluated in real-world settings, which is in itself a systems challenge requiring access to constellations of millions of processors!

Computer security and privacy have become matters of great concern in today's digital world. Research in these areas is no longer a niche activity but in the mainstream, with hundreds of academic publications annually and almost daily news coverage. The Laboratory's Security Group works in cryptographic protocol design, technology and privacy tensions, weak security engineering, economics and human factors, and cyclic infrastructure dependencies, and the group's interests will continue to evolve in the future into ubiquitous networking, financially and politically motivated adversaries.

Proliferating technology has exposed new vulnerabilities within the digital world and rendered existing solutions inadequate. In security economics and psychology, the group will study the burgeoning activities of online criminal groups and develop effective policies to control their criminality. Security research in the future will investigate fundamental new technologies: clean-slate processors able to mitigate security flaws, new location system security models, human-friendly authentication systems, and new approaches to online anonymity. The subject will continue its transition from art to science and engineering, tenets which have been pioneered at the Computer Laboratory.

The long-term aim of the Computer Architecture Group is to maintain its ability to prototype future computer systems, removing the boundaries in commercial computer systems which tend to blinker research work in

The Computer Officers, seen here in a server room, are responsible for maintaining and extending the infrastructure supporting the research, teaching and administration of the Computer Laboratory. Some are also involved in research and teaching. From the back, left to right in all cases: Graham Titmus, Robin Fairbairns (standing), Martyn Johnson, Piete Brooks (kneeling), Chris Hadley (standing), Jiang He and Brian Jones (kneeling).

applied computer science. To be effective this research requires a dedicated team of people with a range of skills, a long-term commitment to build reusable infrastructures and substantial funding.

Another objective is to deliver ever more computing power without consuming more electrical power. Current trends in manufacturing microelectronics favour transistors over interconnecting wires, which lead to greater power consumption in moving data around in proportion to the computation achieved. Predictions from the group's current research work leads to the conclusion that efficient communication will become the dominant factor in delivering power-efficient computer systems in the future.

The Digital Technology Group expects that, in the future, personal devices will be able to monitor health and wellbeing. Carefully engineered new sensors and new data analysis techniques to derive context from the data will be needed, together with a reliable computing infrastructure. In another area the goal is to enhance the battery life of mobile devices by monitoring real-world usage and providing support for writing and recognising efficient applications. Another aim is to capture personal privacy requirements and trade-offs in order to develop the technical mechanisms to deliver non-invasive connected services to users. Work is planned in the area of data provenance and reproducible computation, creating systems which will archive, record and replay complex computational workflows in general-purpose computing environments. In another area, research is planned on the application of advanced signal processing concepts, for example compressive sensing, combined with advanced materials technology, such as graphene, to enable low-cost, low-power wireless sensor networks.

The long-term goal of the Natural Language and Information Group's work is to build systems that can capture more of the meaning of natural language. Mohan Ganesalingam is developing a system for the analysis of mathematical texts which will produce a full semantic representation which might, for instance, be fed into a theorem prover. Work on distributional semantics concerns the development of models of meaning based on the context in which words and phrases are found in text; both Ann Copestake and Stephen Clark are interested in how such models can be combined with compositional semantics, as output by parsers. The group's links with other researchers in Cambridge working on language will be enhanced and expanded by the new Cambridge Language Sciences Strategic Initiative. This is expected to lead to more interdisciplinary collaboration, enhancing both applications and fundamental research into human language.

The Artificial Intelligence Group's future research will continue to be multi-disciplinary, but its strongest links will be with biology and medicine. One newly funded project involves collaboration with the Cambridge Centre for Proteomics to use machine learning techniques for studying the interaction of proteins and genes in cellular organelles. Another future focus will be the development of predictive methods to study metabolic network behaviour in the presence of perturbative events such as

Cambridge Computing: The First 75 Years

158

Chapter Ten: The Computer Laboratory on its 75th Birthday: A Centre of Research Excellence

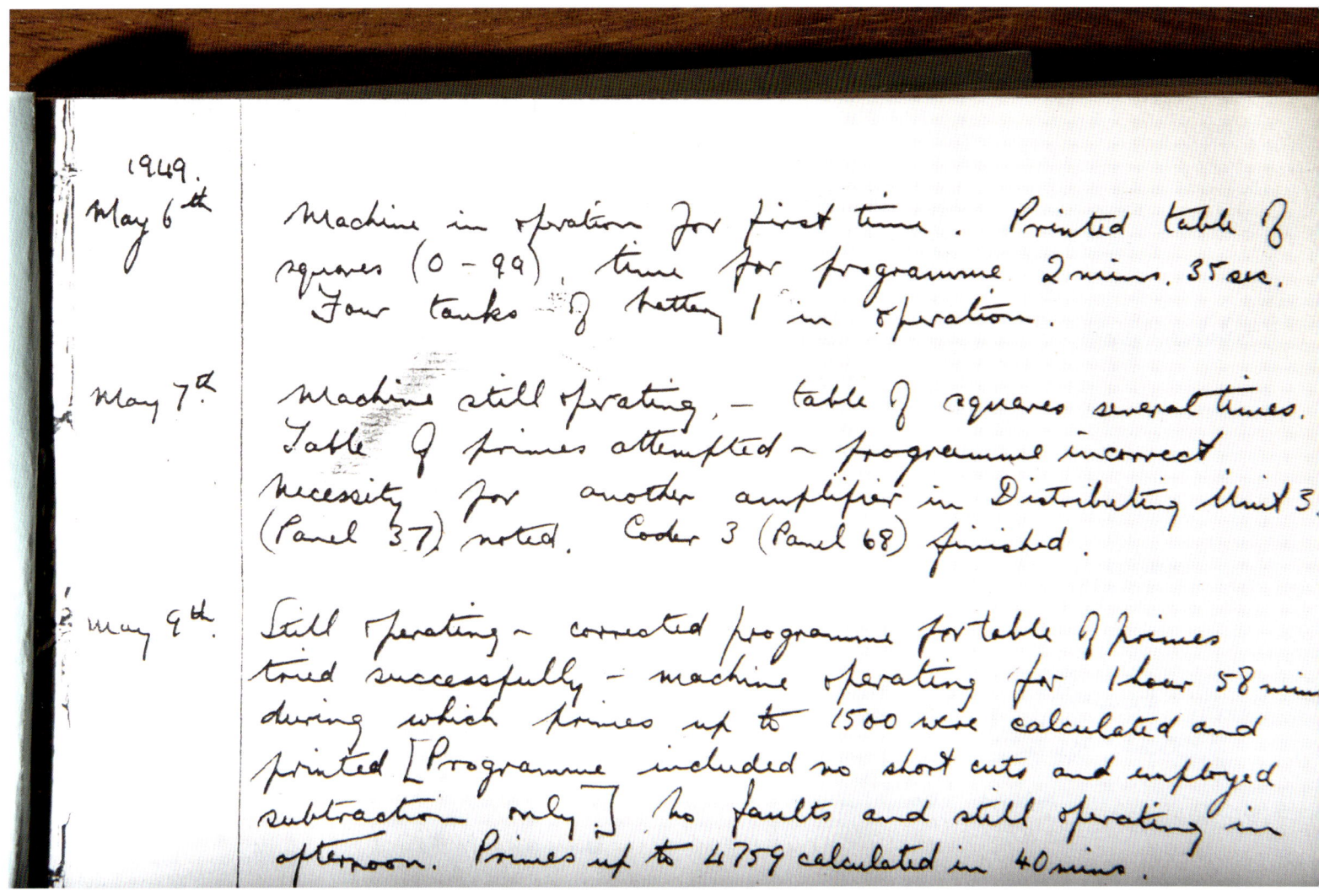

Above: First three entries in the EDSAC log book written by Wilkes.

Opposite: Celebrating the 75th anniversary of the Computer Laboratory on 14 May 2012. In the foreground on the right are Paul Hewett, Chairman of the Faculty Board of Computer Science and Technology, and Andy Hopper, Head of the Computer Laboratory.

infections, inflammation, comorbidities and multi-drug therapies, with the goal of tissue models that link basic research to clinical practice. Finally, as one-fifth of the world's population will have been biometrically enrolled by the iris recognition algorithms developed at Cambridge by 2014, long-term scientific support is committed for those national-scale programmes.

The Graphics and Interaction Group will continue to explore technologies that make it possible for the computer to infer human mental states, and anticipates that these technologies will come into the mainstream in the next decade. The challenge will be to determine how to use the information effectively. Historically, the Rainbow integrated CAD system of the 1960s combined the modelling of large bodies of data, computer displays and graphical interaction

technology. These topics are equally important today. They will remain relevant into the foreseeable future and will continue to present the group's academic staff and research students with challenging new problems.

The overall aim of the Programming, Logic and Semantics Group is to capture – through formal models, languages, specifications and proofs – precisely how computer systems behave, down to the lowest level. These precise models and specifications are a prerequisite for designing complex systems that run both efficiently and correctly. The group is continuing to refine approaches to designing and modelling the semantics of programming languages and systems, to specify the architecture and behaviour of hardware and software, and to prove that implementations meet those specifications.

EDUCATION AND TEACHING

Education at all levels is the Computer Laboratory's key priority, and it is pioneering work aimed at modernising computer science education at school level. Together with influential national organisations such as the Royal Society, the Laboratory shares the view that current teaching of computing in schools is inappropriate, and it is urging the government to encourage schools to teach computing more rigorously. Training in the use of word processors and spreadsheets should be replaced by the description of the structure of computers and their programming. The Raspberry Pi project, based in the Laboratory, will provide schools with a spectacularly low-cost means for effective and appropriate teaching. In the teaching of undergraduate courses the Laboratory will explore online teaching, interactive teaching and peer-to-peer learning schemes, and will try to encourage closer interaction between college and department teaching.

LOOKING BACK – MILESTONES IN THE HISTORY OF THE COMPUTER LABORATORY

Lennard-Jones must have read the *University Reporter* of 14 May 1937 with much gratification. The General Board had, at long last, approved his proposal to found a Computer Laboratory, albeit renamed the 'Mathematical Laboratory'. The Laboratory was there to stay, and its 75th anniversary was marked on 14 May 2012.

Twelve years following the approval of the proposal, on 6 May 1949, there must have been great excitement in the Mathematical Laboratory. After three years' gestation EDSAC had come to life. The computer had been stuttering into action for some time but on this momentous day it printed out exactly the results it had been programmed to produce, the squares of numbers from 0 to 99. Wilkes immediately started a logbook to record EDSAC's progress. The first entry in his own hand states 'Machine in operation for the first time'. He and his team had no inkling then that EDSAC would become famous, and the 50th anniversary of that day would be marked in 1999 with a commemorative event, EDSAC 99. By then Wilkes, Wheeler and Needham would be Fellows of the Royal Society, and Wilkes would have been awarded the Turing Prize in 1967, followed in 2000 by a knighthood for his services to computing.

Wilkes and Renwick with EDSAC in the final stages of construction.

Thirty years after foundation the Computer Laboratory marked another milestone, when it became an independent Department within the School of Physical Sciences, and its computing service was separated from research and teaching. The era of research based on designing and building mainframe computers ended in the mid-1960s, and Wilkes started to give the Laboratory new research directions. He started projects on Computer-Aided Design, on memory protection with the CAP computer, and on distributed computing with the Cambridge Digital Ring and the Cambridge Distributed System. These projects established the Computer Laboratory as a centre of world-class research in computing science and technology.

In 1980, after a reign of 35 years, Wilkes retired and Roger Needham, Wilkes's successor, expanded the Laboratory and increased its international presence. He supported an enterprise culture by collaborating closely with the Olivetti Research Laboratory, which in turn led to the beginning of a large number of entrepreneurial activities by graduates in Computer Science.

The Computer Laboratory was transformed in 1999 when Needham made the 'Microsoft Deal'. A benefaction from the William Gates Foundation enabled the Laboratory to escape from its cramped conditions in the New Museums Site to be re-housed in the striking, purpose-built William Gates Building, giving a fresh impetus to research and teaching.

Chapter Ten: The Computer Laboratory on its 75th Birthday: A Centre of Research Excellence

'Did all this happen because of my journey through the small green door almost 75 years ago?' Professor Sir Maurice Wilkes has a well-deserved cup of coffee in the courtyard of the new William Gates Building, the modern home of his Mathematical Laboratory.

161

Bibliography

1. Swade, D (1998), *Charles Babbage and his Calculating Engines*, Science Museum, London.

2. Swade, D (2000), *The Cogwheel Brain*, Abacus, London.

3. Swade, D (2001), *The Difference Engine*, Viking, London.

4. Brewster, D (1832, reprinted 2011), *Letters on Natural Magic*, Coachwhip Publications, Pennsylvania, USA.

5. *The Mechanics Magazine* (1833), Vol. XVII.

6. Toole, B A (1992), *Ada, the Enchantress of Numbers*, Strawberry Press, California, USA.

7. Hodges, A (2012, Centenary Edition), *Alan Turing the Enigma*, Vintage Books, London.

8. Copeland, J, ed. (2010), *The Essential Turing*, Clarendon Press, Oxford.

9. Turing, S (2012, Centenary Edition), *Alan M Turing*, Cambridge University Press, Cambridge.

10. Archives of Corpus Christi College, Cambridge, Lennard Jones's papers.

11. Cambridge University Reporters: 2 February 1937, 21 April 1937, 22 October 1946, 27 November 1946, 19 July 1949, 26 May 1965, 22 October 1969.

12. Leedham-Green, E (1996), *A Concise History of the University of Cambridge*, Cambridge University Press, Cambridge.

13. Archives of Churchill College, Cambridge, Lennard-Jones's papers.

14. Wilkes, M V (1985), *Memoirs of a Computer Pioneer*, The MIT Press, Cambridge, Massachusetts.

15. Spärck Jones, K (1999), *A Brief Informal History of the Computer Laboratory*, University of Cambridge Computer Laboratory, Cambridge.

16. Wilkes, M V (1956), *Automatic Digital Computers*, John Wiley & Sons, New York, USA.

17. Archives of the University of Cambridge, University Library, Manuscript Room.

18. Boden, M A (2006), *Mind as a Machine* (Vol.1 Preface ii The Background), Clarendon Press, Oxford.

19. Croarken, M (1990), *Early Scientific Computing in Britain*, Clarendon Press, Oxford.

20. Campbell-Kelly, M, ed. (1992), *IEEE Annals of the History of Computing*, Vol. 14, No. 4.

21. Papers and reports published by M V Wilkes, D J Wheeler and R M Needham.

22. Campbell-Kelly, M (2006), 'David John Wheeler' *Biogr. Mems Fell. R Soc.*, 2006 52, 437–453.

23. Robinson, P and Spärck Jones, K (1999), *EDSAC 99*, University of Cambridge Computer Laboratory, Cambridge.

24. Hartley, D (1999), *EDSAC 1 and after – a compilation of personal reminiscences*, University of Cambridge Computer Laboratory, Cambridge.

25. Archives of St John's College, Cambridge, Maurice Wilkes's papers.

26. Hoare, A and Wilkes, M V (2004), 'Roger Michael Needham', *Biogr. Mems Fell. R Soc.* 2004 50, 183–199

List of Subscribers

Philip A Abbey	1994–95	Sandro Bauer		Ted Briscoe	
Billal N Ahmed		Alison and Roy Bayley	1962–70, 1961–73	Chris S Brookes	1975–76
Rehana Ahmed		Philip Bearcroft	1984–85	David Brooks	1970–71
Suhael Ahmed		Mike Beasley	1977–78	Chris Barrington Brown	1979
Linda D Aitken (née Taylor)	1962–63	Gwennan Beasley	2000–03	Dr D J Brown	1982–84
William Aitken	1962–63	Simon J Beaumont	2009–12	Patrick J Brown	1963–64
Paul Alexander		David Bell	2004–07	Peter Bullman	
David Allsopp	2001–04	Jason R Bell	2008–11	James Bulpin	1996–2005
Agustin Almansi	2007–10	Sam Bell	1983	Oliver Burns	1998–99
Dr O Andersen	2005–	Stephen D Bell	1991	Ian Burton-Palmer	
John W Anderson	1972–75	Giampaolo Bella	1996–2003	Anthony Butler	1964–65
Richard Ansorge		Frank Bellosa	2012–13		
Kumar Arasu		Ben Benfold and		Colin Campbell	
Andrew Armit	1966–70	Kathryn Benfold (née Hill)	2001–04	Tim Cartledge	1992–95
Tim Arnold	1979–81	Ayesha Bennett		Dr Michael Farinton Challis	1967–70
Malcolm P Atkinson		Frazer Bennett		Mary Champion	1981–84
	1966–67, 1970–74, 1975–78	Dr Jeremy Bennett	1979–82, 1983–86	T H Philip Chang	1963
Louise Auger	1995–98	Dr I A Benson	1987–92	Mark Chapman	1982–84
Dr Paul Austin	1985–88	Jonathan Benwell	2008–11	Charles Chen	1988
Jonathan Ayres	1989–92	Alastair Beresford	1996–99, 2004–	Nicola Chessher (née Watson)	1988
		Andrew Besford	1995–98	Oliver Chick	2008–
Professor Jean Bacon	1985–	David Bethell	1984–87	Robert Chipperfield	2003–06
Zhen Bai	2010	Iain Betson	1991–94	Chih Hui Alan Chu	1996–97
David Ball		Chris Birchall	2002–05	Phung Hee Chye	1989
Jeremy Ball	1985–91	Gerard M Blair	1982–83	Paul Clark	1986–88
Professor Vasile Baltac	1966–67	Julian Blake	1962–66	Robin Clark	1976–77
Tadas Baltrusaitis	2006–13	Joseph Bonneau	2008–12	Stephen Clark	2009–
R G Barber	1965–68	Roland Boorman	1977–80	David J Clarke	1985–86
Dave Barker	1977–80	Youssef Bouguerra	1997	Richard Clayton	2000–
Robin N Barrett	1970–73	Philip Bowman	1971	Dr John R A Cleaver	
A M Barringer	1972	Dr J C Bradfield	1986–87	Brian Collings	1980–83
Neil Barton	1972	Ian C Braid	1968–80	Tristram Colville-Foley	
Nick Batterham	1988–	Nick Brasier	1985–86	Revd Andrew Connick	2001–04
Nick Battle	1981–84	Dr James P Bridge	2005–	Nick Connolly	1981–83

163

Paul Conyers		Dr Jeff Fenton	1969–75	Stuart Grace	1983–85
Prof Miriam Leeser and		Dr Innes A Ferguson	1988–92	David J L Gradwell FBCS	1968–71
Dr Robert Cooper	1983–88	John Ferguson	1966–67	Al Grant	
Tim Coote	1979–80	Sarah Ferris (née Hanley)	1979–81	Dr John Grant	1959–63
Ann Copestake		Susan Pancho-Festin	1998–2001	James Green	1993–96
Charles Cotton		Michael Field	1972–75	Laurie Griffiths	2008–11
Robert Coull	1984–86	Dr Martin Fieldhouse	1957–61	Andrew Grigg	1986–89
Giles Courtice	1987–88	James Fissler	2002–05	Dr Matthew J Grounds	1997–2000
Peter Cowley	1976–77	Raoul Fleming	1993–96	Francisco J Guerra-y-Rullan	1971–75
Daniel James Craig	2002–05	Benjamin Flynn	1994–97		
Nick Crossley	1973–75	Robert Folkes	1980–82	Chris Hadley	1989–
Jonathan Crowcroft		Helen Foord		Daniel Hagon	2005–08
Colin Cryer	1958–62	David Forbes	1988	Rob Hague	1996–99, 2000–04
Jonathan Custance	1992–95	Jodie Forbes	1987–90	Professor Stephen Hailes	1985–91
		C V D (Vic) Forrington	1958–59	Alistair Hancock	1988–90
S J Dann	1989	Paul James Fox	2003–	Michael Hardy	1981–83
Jeremy C R Davey	1986–89	Peter Fox	1984–87	Ian Hargrave	1991–92
Andrew S Davidson	1972–74	John Francis	1971	David Hart	1970–71
Paul K Davies	1987–90	Keir Fraser	1996 2007	Dr Andy Harter FREng	1980–90
Aubrey de Grey	1983–85	Bernard Fromson	1979–80	Dr David Hartley	1958–94
Lindsey E Deaves (née Turner)	1970–71	Dave Fuggle	1982–85	Jan Haseler	1972–73
Dr Carl N R Dellar	1977–81	Ian Furlonger	1993–96	Demis Hassabis	1994–97
Michael Dickenson	1971–72	Nicholas Furness		Phil Hassall	1997
Dr Peter Dickman	1983–84, 1987–91			Paul Hatton	1972–76
Stephan Diestelhorst	2004–05	Christopher Galley	1984–87	Dr Hermann Hauser	
Matthew B Doar	1986–2003	Julian Gallop	1969–70	Dr Stuart P Hawkins	1985–89
Dr Simon R Dodds	1979–82	Nigel R Gamble	1978–79	Annette Haworth	1968–69
Professor Neil Dodgson	1989–	John Garbutt	2003–06	Guy Haworth	1968–69
Dr Austin Donnelly	1993–2002	Dr Nick Garnett	1979–83	Jiang He	2001
Neil Dunlop		Dr Donald A Gaubatz	1984–86	Peter Headland	1978–79
Herve P Duteil	1989–90	Donnla Nic Gearailt	1997–2001	John Helliwell	1978–80
		Martin Gee	1994–95	Dr Andrew J Herbert FREng OBE	1975–85
Warren East		Jason Gibbs	1993–96	Steven Herbert	2010–
Nicholas Edwards	1999–2002	Sergio Gigli	1989–90	Philip Herlihy	1985–86
Philip A Ekstrom	1963–64	Dr C Gray Girling	1978–83	Thomas Heron	1991–92
Michael and Tania Elliott		Professor John Glauert	1978–81	Kevin Herrmann	1979–81
1963–69 and 1971–72		Artem Glebov	2011–	Philip Hewinson	2001–04
Gary Ernest	1980–82	Li Gong	1987–90	Simon S Higginson	1983–85
Vaughan Eveleigh	2006–10	James Gooding	2003–06	Roger Hill	
Alan Every	1995	Henry Philip Goodman	1955–56	Professor Mike Hinchey	1992–95
		David Goodwin	1960–61	Richard Hinchliffe	1979–81
Luana Teodora Fagarasan	2012–	Professor Andrew D Gordon	1987–97	Richard Cheuk Fung Ho	2006–09
Robin Fairbairns	1968–	Richard Goto	1982–83	Tony Hoare	2010–
Ian W Farminer	1968–72	Lise Gough	1999–	Mark William Hogan	2008–11

Matt Holgate	1995–98	Chee Yoong Lai	1998–2001	Ursula Martin	1972–75
Andy Hopper		Fabre Lambeau	2000–05	Richard Mason	1982–84
Jan Hruska	1977	Barry Landy	1961–2002	Peter McBrien	1985–86
Paul Hurtley	1975	David L Landy	1982–85	Jeremy McCarthy	
Khursheed Hussain		Charles Lang	1965–75	Andrew McDonald	1996–99
		Jack Lang	1969–	Bruce McLaren	1984–87
Chris Ip	1990–93	Stewart Lang	1970–75	Peter Mead	1994
		Dr Paul A Langley	1979–82	Professor T F Melham FRSE	1983–92
Alan Jacobs	1975–76	Bridget Langridge (née Bryant, Scutt)		Julian T J Midgley	1995–99
Laura James			1974–75	Professor Richard J Millar	1984–86
Mateja Jamnik	1994–95, 2002–	Ho Yin Lau	1992–95	David Milway	1982–86
Dr Karl Jeacle	2002–05	Dominic Lawn	1982–85	Shan Ming Woo	1994–97
Richard Jebb	1987–88	James Lean	1994–97	Alan Mitchell	1997–2001
Neil Jenkins	2006–10	Dr Henry Jong-Hyeon Lee	1996–2000	Duncan Mitchell	2000–03
Paul Jessop	1981–83	Dr Jochen L Leidner	2001–02	Dr Jagdish J Modi	1978–79
Xiaofeng Jiang	1988–92	Martin Mariusz Lester	2003–06	Carsten Moenning	2001–05
Adam Jollans	1979–80	Dr John Levine	1986–92	Francisco A T B N Monteiro	2005–09
Dr Alan Jones	1981–86	Dr I J Lewis	1995–98	Sue Bok Moon	
Andrew M Jones	2006–09	Guang X Li	1989–93	Dr Simon Moore	1991–
Ian M L Jones	1980–83	Hao Li	2012–13	Dr Terry A Moore	1985–86
J M O Jones	1976–77	Jin C Lim	1996–99	Tyler Moore	2004–08
Professor Matt Jones	1990–91	John Lindley	1958–59	Charles W T Morgan	1981–84
Dr Mervyn E Jones		Mimie Liotsiou	2009–12	Professor Gareth G Morgan	1976–77
Mathai Joseph	1965–68	Dr Ruoshui Liu	2007–11	Fr John Moriarty	2000–03
Achala Joshi	1985	Anton Lokhmotov	2004–07	Alistair Mortimer	1985
Vinay Joshi	1985	Lio Lopez-Welsch	1992–93	Nigel Morton	1977
		Professor Gillian Lovegrove	1964–65	Dr John R L Moxon	1982–83
Songphol Kanjanachuchai	1995–99	Isabel Luckett	1998–2001	Steve Muir	1992–96
Jerry Keates	1969–72			Mike Muller	1977–80
A J Keeping	1956–57	Chaoying Ma	1988	Dr Robert Mullins	2000–
Stan Kelly-Bootle	1953–54	Colin K Mackinnon	1956–57	Dr Wes Munsil	1972–73
Mike Kemp	1973–75	T J Macura	2004–08	Simon Munton	1981–82
Peter Kenny	1971–72	Anil Madhavapeddy	2002–	General Pervez Musharraf	
Peter T Kindersley	1974–77	Jackie Major	1985–89	Alan Mycroft	1977–78, 1984–
Dr Tim King	1975–79	Charalampos Manifavas	1995–2000		
John Kleeman	1979–81	Tony Mann		D J Nancekievill	1998–2001
Martin Kleppmann	2003–06	David Mansell	1996–99	Graham Nash	1972
Brian Knight	1972–84	Bill and Katherine Manville	1969–73	John Benedict Philbin Naylon	1991–98
Jonathan Knight	1985–87	Roger Marlow	1989–92	Peter Newman	1985–89
Andreas Koltes	2010–	Pierre-Arnoul de Marneffe	1974–77, 1979–81	David Ng	1978–79
Professor Sailesh Kotecha	1978–81	Margaret Marrs (née Lewin, Mutch)	1952–69	Dr Viet Anh Nguyen	2007–
Dr Markus G Kuhn	1997–	Scott Marshall	1986–89	Ben Nicholson	2002–03
Olivia O Y Kwong	1995–2000	Gerard Martin	2007–10	Cosmos Nicolaou	1987–91
Dr Lycourgos Kyprianou	1977–80	Professor Peter Martin		Christine Northeast	1988–2011

Rory M O'Brien	1982–83	Dr Andrew J Redman	1967–70	Mufid Shawwa	1996–97
James O'Connell	2003–06	Andrew Rice	1998–	Christopher Shore	1985–86
Terry Oddy	1961–62	Dr Martin Richards	1962–	Andrew Simms	1971–74
David Oliver	1977–82	Tristan Richardson	1987–91	Professor Daniel Simonovich	1991–92
Angela Maria Opladen	1994–95	Philip Le Riche	1969–70	Dr David Singer	1977–81
Dominic Orchard	2008–	Martin Rix	1993	Dhruv Singh	
Andrew Owen	2001–04	Ben Roberts	2005–13	Dr Kulwant Ajay Singh	1995
		Clifford Robinson	1951	Wai Jung Justin Siu	1997–2000
Valeria de Paiva and		Peter Robinson	1975–	Dr Sergei Skorobogatov	2000–
Richard Crouch	1987–95	Andrew Robson	1988–91	Olga Skripnikova	2005–07
Leon G Palm	2006–09	Val Robson	1979–82	Chris Slinn	1972–76
Colin Palombo	1987–90	Kerry Rodden	1995–01	Andrew Smith	1984
Marco Palomino	2000–05	Mads Rosendahl	1987–90	Derek Smith	
Sonia Panchen	1984–87	Michael Rosner	1974–75	John Smith	1983–84
Ioannis Papaefstathiou	1997–2000	Chris Royle	1993–96	Julian M Smith	2003–09
Ulrich Paquet	2003–07	Philip Rushby		Owen S Smith	1984–87
Christopher Paradine	1962	Richard Russell	1993–96	Ripduman Sohan	
Clive Partridge	1978–81			Bernie Solomon	1977–81
Stephen Payne	1994–97	Zeynep Sagar	2009	Lorne Somerville	1983–86
Stephen Peel	1978–79	Dr Michael Salmony	1974–77	Ken Sonoda	1975–78
Andrew Pepperell	1993–96	Sanjay Samani	1992–95	Dr Donald Z Spicer	1983–84
Boma Claudius Pepple	1991–92	S S Samra	1991–94	Professor Cormac J Sreenan	1988–93
James Percival	1971	Norman Sanders	1956–57	James Srinivasan	1999–2011
Robert J D Perera	1990	Dr Robert Sansom FREng	1979–81	Quentin Stafford-Fraser	1987–96
Michael Perry	1971	Amit Sarna	2003–06	Frank Stajano	1998–
Dr Simon Pilgrim	2003	David S Saunders	1985–86	Jonathan Stankler	1990–92
Professor Andrew M Pitts	1988–	Richard Savage	1970–71	Andy Stevens	1996
Christis Christodoulos Plastiras	2004–07	Tony Sawford	1978–79	Dr Daryl Stewart	1992–2001
David Plummer	1974–75	Scarlet Schwiderski	1992–96	Hugh Stewart	
Simon W Plummer	1996–99	Chris Scoggins	1986–87	Dave Storey	1972–74
Calicrates Policroniades-Borraz	2002–06	James Scott	1995–2002	Neil Stratford	1993–99
Peter Polkinghorne	1976–79	Peter J Scott	1981–83	Roger Stratford	1963–2005
Stephen Poulson	1995–96	Kamiar Sehat	1986–92	Jeff Strauss	1957–58
Ian Pratt	1989–2007	Ginni Dhindsa Shah		Bjarne Stroustrup	1975–79
Geraint Price	1994–99	Safwan Shah		Gillian Elizabeth Stuart (née Cattell)	1982
Gerry Zdzislaw Przybyszewski	1992–95	Sanah Shah		Richard Ian Stuart	2008
Milos Puzovic	2008–	Sulaiman Shah		Jana Z Sukkarieh	1994–2001
		Zoyah Shah		Andrew G Swales	1971–73
Peter Radford	1964–68	Zubeida Shah		Tony T L Sze	1994–97
Gautham Radhakrishnan	1990–93	Muhammad Shahbaz			
David Raftis	1991–94	Nadeem Shaikh		Srinivas Tadigadapa	1988–95
Dr J E Raiswell	1964–65	Ravi Sharma	1967–68	John Tait	1978–83
Lawrence Rao	1984–87	Michael Shaw	1971–72	Patrik Talas	1986–89
Valluri R M Rao	1972–83	Philip Shaw	1967–69, 1972–73	Dr Audrey Tan Hayes	

List of Subscribers

Richard Tandoh	1997–98	Hugo Tyson	1979–82	Ron Wheelhouse	1978
Sonali Tandon	2000–03			Colin Whitby-Strevens	1965–69
Lawrence Tarlow	1977–78	Beverley Vara (née Fear)	1989–90	Norma White	1964–65
Martin Tasker	1982–85	Niel Viljoen	1990–92	Paul White	1968–69
Jane Tatchell	1981	John Viner	1963	Martin Whittaker	1979–82
David J Taylor	1992–96			Professor Geraint A Wiggins	1982–84
Mark Taylor	1995–98	Dr Jennifer Li Kam Wa	1993–97	Jeremy Wilde	1976–77
Anton Teodorescu	1980	Adam Wagner	2003–04	Paul Wilkinson	2006–09
Paul Theobald	1988–90	Daniel T Wagner		Professor Dr Ian Willers	1968–72
Ellis N Thomas	1969–70	Elizabeth Waldram	1960–	Adrian Williams	1959–60
Eric and Judy Thomas	1965–66 and 1961–67	John R Walliker	1977–78	Richard Williams	1985–88
James Thomas	1994–99	Simon Wallis	1989–92	Christopher Wilson	2007–10
Peter Thompson	1987–89	Jonathan Warbrick		Dr Ian D Wilson	1978–85
Philip Thompson	1981–2002	Tim Ward	1975–77	Jack Wilson	
Peter Thorne	1972–75	Tony Warren	1960–61	Sophie Wilson	1978–79
Stephen J S Thornhill	1995–98	Mike Warriner	1988–91	Dr Tim Wilson	1986–92
Graham Tigg	1973–76	Dr Panit Watcharawitch	1999	M F Winiberg	
David Titterington	1969–70	Mark Watkins	1996–99	Matthew Wiseman	1994–97, 2001–02
Adrian Tollet	1974–75	Andrew Watson	1983–85	Lorenzo Wood	1989–93
Yan Tordoff	1991–94	Bob Watson	1974–77	Stuart Wray	1979–81, 1982–86, 1996–98
Alexandros Toumazis	2006–10	Des Watson	1973–77	Karen Wrench	1987–90
Dr Christopher Town	1997–	Mike Watson	1965–68	Andy Wright	1972–73
Dr Jason Trenouth	1985–86	Dr Robert N M Watson	2005–	Zhixue Wu	1989
Celement Chiu Sing Tse	1981	James M Watt	1954–55	Gareth Wynn-Williams	
Iain Tuddenham	1993–94	Gareth Webber	1993–96		
Dr D C Turner	2004–09	Dr Paul Webster		David Young	1987–90
Dr Martin J Turner	1987–94	Richard C Wenzel	1972–73		
Michael Turnill	1962	Dr Brian Westwood	1970–2003	Dr Mark Yudkim	1980–83
Tom Tweddell	1993–96	Joyce Wheeler	1954–57	Enzhe Zhang	2006–09

167

Index

Principal locations are denoted in **bold**.
Illustrations are denoted in *italics*.

3D TV 151

Abadi, Martin 107
ACE computers 32, 96
ACM Special Interest Group in Information Retrieval 118
ACM Turing Prize 33, 142 *see also* Turing, Alan
Acorn Computers **125–7**; BBC Micro *125*, 132; Olivetti Research Lab 111; start-up 122; Unison 106
Acting Directors 34, 42
Active Badge Project *112*, 113, 115, 121
Ada, Countess Lovelace 10, 11, **14**
Ada Lovelace Medals *117*, 118
Addenbrookes Hospital 90, 111
Addison-Wesley 63
Adie's Museum 115, *116*
Adobe Photoshop 76
Advanced Computer Science 101, 117
Advanced Computer Technology Initiative 79
Advanced Research Laboratory (Japan) 107
Albasiny, Ernest 97, 98
Algarve 128
ALGOL 60 73
ALGOL 68C 75
algorithms 31, 149
Allott, Stephen 136, *136*
Allterton, David 144
AltaVista search engine 107, 117
Alvey, John 104
Alvey committee 104

Alvey Programme 105, 117
Amazon 129, 142
America *see* United States of America
American National Academy of Engineering 76
Ampex 62
Analytical Engine 10, 14, 15–17, *17*
Analytical Society 12
Anatomy Laboratory 27
Anatomy School 29, 45
Anderson, Ray 128–9, *128*
Anderson, Ross 145, 146, 147, *147*
Apax Partners 130
Apple Macintosh 93, 127
Application Programming Interfaces (APIs) 146, 148
Applied Mathematics 27
ARM Holdings *126*, **127**, 133
Armament Research 29
Armaments Experimental Station 22
Artificial Intelligence (AI) Group **151–2**, 157
Arup Building *69*, 71, 79
Assembly Language Programming 55
Associate Professors 118
Association for Computational Linguistics 118
AT&T Bell Laboratories 76, 111
Atari 131
Atlas computers 66–7, 70, 85
Auckland 26
Auckland University College 36
Autocode 70, 73, 84
Automated Reasoning Group 147
Automatic Computing with the EDSAC (David Wheeler) 54
Autonomy 131
Azure Cloud Service 143

Babbage, Charles: Ada Countess Lovelace and 11, 14; Analytical Engine 15–17; biography 12; Difference Engine No 2 17–18; engraving *12*; family deaths 15; importance of 6; inventions 10; Joseph Clement 15; Maurice Wilkes 16, 19; numbers tables 11–13, *11*
Backs, The 31
Bacon, Jean 107, **110**, *110, 142*, 143
Bailey, Judy *88*
Baker, Sir John 21
ballistics 29
BAN logic 107
Bango 122, **128–9**
Bangor University 48
Barron, David 67, 69, 73
Barton, D 73
Barton, S A *52*, 56, *57, 61*, 65
Basic Combined Programming Language (BCPL) 73
Bastin, Ted 116
batch processing systems 68
BBC Micros 125–6, *125*, 132
Bennett, Jem *133*
Bennett, John 45, *52, 57, 61*, 62
Bennett, Max *24*
Bennet, Peter *85*
Beresford, Alastair *139*, 148, *149*
Berkeley (University of California) 127
Bernoulli numbers 14
'Best Way to Design an Automatic Calculating Machine, The' (Maurice Wilkes) 58
Bézier, Pierre 72
Bézier curves *150*
Bill and Melinda Gates Foundation 137

Bio-informatics 153
Birrell, Andrew 74, *100*
Black Cloud, The (Fred Hoyle) 53
Blackler, Joyce *see* Wheeler, Joyce
Blackwell, Alan 151
Bletchley Park 31, 33
Boden, Margaret 116
Bodleys 31
Bollée, Leon 26
Bootle, Stanley 97, 98
Boulton Paul 22
Bourne, Steve 69
Bowden, B V 95
Boys, Frank (S F) *22*, 63
Bragg, Sir William 21, 34
Braid, Ian 72, 74, 124, *124*
Braithwaite, Margaret *see* Masterman, Margaret
Braithwaite, Professor Richard 115
Bratt, J B 26, 28, 37, 43
Breakwell, Eileen 84
Brenner, Sheila 97
Brewster, Sir David 10
Briscoe, Ted 154
Bristol University 21, 22
British Academy 118, 142
British Association for the Advancement of Science 12
British Computer Society 35, 79, 85, 107, 142
British Empire 11
Broers, Sir Alec 105, 137
Brooker, R A 57, 97
Brookes, Alexis 52, 71
Brooks, Piete *157*
Brown, Andrew 144
Brown, Gordon 33
Brown, Jerry 97
Brown University, Rhode Island 98
Brunel, Isambard Kingdom 15, 16
Brunsviga machines 23, *24, 25*
BUILD 72
'Bun Shop' 50, *51*, 95
Burrows, Mike 54, 55, 107, *107*, 117
Burrows-Wheeler Transform (BWT) 54, 107
Bush, Vannevar 25

Bush Differential Analysers 84
Bush machines 26, 27, 37, 39 *see also* differential analysers
Business Studies 139
Byron, Augusta Ada 10, 11, **14**

C++ **76**, 77, 148
C++ Programming Language (Bjarne Stroustrup) 76
CAD (Computer Aided Design): centre 74, 85, 125; Charles Lang 72, *74*, 122; DEC-Titan 114; Maurice Wilkes 70; Rainbow system 159; Robin Forrest's design *72*; subdivision surfaces 151
'Calculating Laboratory' 28
California 117, 134, 137
Cam, River 31
Cambridge Angels 133
Cambridge Centre for Computational Chemistry 23
Cambridge Centre for Proteomics 157
Cambridge Computer Lab Ring 136–7
Cambridge Consultants 115
Cambridge Crystallographic Data Centre 85
Cambridge Differential Analyser- *see* differential analysers
Cambridge Digital Ring **77–9**; Andy Hopper 121; Maurice Wilkes 160; Lab Ring and 136; Project Universe *106*; *Ring* magazine 136; separate sites 105–6; server access 75
Cambridge Distributed System **79–80**; Cambridge Digital Ring 105; CAP and 77; diagram *79*; expansion 80; Maurice Wilkes 160; research 142; Roger Needham 106
Cambridge Enterprise 138
Cambridge ESOL 154
Cambridge Fast Ring 106
Cambridge Instrument Company 24
Cambridge Language Research Unit (CLRU) 108, 115, *116*
Cambridge Language Sciences Strategic Initiative 157
'Cambridge Phenomenon' 124
Cambridge Philosophical Society 20, 25, 35

Cambridge Programming Language (CPL) 73
Cambridge Programming Research Group 147
Cambridge University Press (CUP) 114
Cambridge University Reporter 22, 27
Camrivox 132
CAP computers: Cambridge Distributed System 80; design automation 74; drawbacks 77; internal construction *75*; original computer *147*; pioneer project 145; research 142; research students *75*
capability systems **74–7**; 147
Capsicum 147
Cavendish Laboratory: expertise 48; Laser-Scan Ltd 72; Maurice Wilkes 34, 35, 46; Professor Ryle at 49; site 20; space for laboratory 27; tea at 97; x-ray crystallography 63
Central Unix Service (CUS) 91
CERN 76, 92
Chandratillake, Suranga 131, *131*
Charles Babbage Road 19 *see also* Babbage, Charles
Chemical Laboratory 20, 23, 25, 27, *29*
Chemistry Department (Keele University) 23
Cheney, Chris *91*
CHERI CPU 147
Chicago, University of 75
China 145
chip and pin 146
Church, Alonzo 31
Churchill, Winston 41
Citrix 134
Clark, Stephen 154, 157
Claydon, Vic 74, *85*
Clayton, Richard 145, *147*
Clement, Joseph 10, 15, **16**
Clerk Maxwell, James 19
cloud computing 133, 142, 145
clumps theory 108
Cold War 41
Combined Programming Language (CPL) 73
Committee of Science Professors 21
'Communication Locality in Computation: Software Chip Multiprocessors and Brains' (Daniel Greenfield) 144

169

Communications and Controls in Distributed Computer Systems (Bjarne Stroustrup) 76
Compaq 107
Compatible Time-Sharing System (CTSS) 68
Computer-Aided Design *see* CAD
Computer Architecture Group 144, 156
Computer Automation LSI 4 minicomputers 80
Computer History Museum, California 55
Computer Laboratory Supporters Club 139
computer languages **73**, 76, 84
Computer Science 96, **98–101**
Computer Speech and Language Processing 101, 117
Computer Syndicates 82, 86, 89
Computer Systems: Papers for Roger Needham 108
Computing Service 93, 102
Comrie, L J 35, **36**, 41
Conexant Systems 132
Cook, Douglas 77
Copestake, Ann *110*, 154, *154*, 157
Corn Exchange Street 95, 105
Corpus Christi College 21, *21*, 23, 30, 121
Cotton, Charles 132
Coulouris, George *176*
Cox, Professor E G 95
Cox, Ken 74, *85*
CRAB project 153
Crackle system 143
Creed teleprinters 47
Crick, Francis 97
Crofts, Peter *64*, *91*
Crowcroft, Jon 143
CRT memory 51
Crucible 151
Cruickshank, Durward 95
CTSRD 145, 147
Curry, Christopher 125
Custance, Jonathan 132, *132*
Customer Relationship Management (CRM) systems 132

DARPA 147
Darwin, Charles 33
Darwin, Horace 24

Data Encryption Standard (DES) 130
'Database State' (Ross Anderson) 145
Daugman, John 107, 109, 152, *152*
Davy Medals 23
Dawar, Anuj 148
DEC PDP 7 computers 70, 114
DEC-Titan computing system 114
Decca Radar 56, 61
delay line memories 45–7, *45*, *47*, 49, 57, 59
DELPH-IN 154
Dennis J B 75
Department of Defense (US) 41
Department of Education and Science 126
Department of Scientific and Industrial Research 23, 56
Department of Trade and Industry 104, 105
DEUCE 96
'Development of New Computing Machines' (Maurice Wilkes) 38
Device Analyser 148
Difference Engine No 1 10, *10*, 11–15, 17, 18
Difference Engine No 2 10, 17–19, *18*
Differential Analysers *see also* Bush machines **24–6**; describing 28; Maurice Wilkes 35; Metropolitan Vickers *29*; photograph *43*; Second World War 34; space needed for 37
Digital Desk 150
Digital Equipment Corporation: Maurice Wilkes 35; Michael Burrows 107, 117; ORL 111; Roger Needham 105, 106
Digital Technology Group 148, *149*, 157
Dirac, Paul 97
DNA 86
Dodgson, Neil 98, 109, 151, *151*
Domain Name System 80
Dynamic Alternative Routing 143
Dynamic Convolution 128

East, Warren *126*, 127
Eckert, J Presper 38, 41
EDSAC **44–65**; computer languages 73; David Hartley 85; delay line memories 45–7, *45*, *47*, 49; Douglas Hartree 42; EDSAC 2 57–65, 66; Eric Mutch 71; 50th anniversary celebrations 70; final stages of construction *160*; gestation 160; lectures 109; LEO computers 55–6; Mallock Machine 24; Maurice Wilkes 19, 41, 42, 84, 94, 109, 160; naming 41; night time difficulties 51; operational 49–53; S F Boys 22; shut down 62; Sir Martin Ryle 49; switched off 69; transition period 66; uniqueness 84; user service 68; von Neumann 38; women users 109
'EDSAC 99' 57
EDVAC *43*, 44, 45
Elizabeth II, Queen *81*
Elliot W S (Bill) 66
Elliot machines *60*
emotional intelligence 150
Endace 143
Engineering Department: Alexis Brookes 52; CAD 74; Computer Speech and Language Processing 101, 117; Douglas Hartree 25; heads of 21; Mallock Machine *24*; mercury delay line 46
English Electric Company 56, 96
ENIAC 41, *41*, 42, 44, 49
Enigma Machine 33
Epiphany Philosophers 116
Ept Computing 134
ESOL 154
Estate Management, Department of 111
Ethernet 143
EU 145
EU SPACEBOOK 154
European Space Agency 106
Evans & Sutherland Computer Corporation 125
Executive Computers Ltd 130
Experimental Machine (Manchester) 51

Fabry, Bob 75
Facebook 129
Facit mechanical calculators *37*
Fairbairns, Robin 74, *157*
Falcon 93
Faraday Society 23
Farmer P F 35, *52*, 56, *57*, *61*, *65*
Fendragon 115

Index

Ferranti Ltd 66, 95, 109
ferrite cores *58*, 71
Field Programmable Gate Arrays (FPGAs) 144
'Fifth Generation Computer Project, The' 104
Financial Board 27 *see also* General Board
Fiore, Marcelo *147*, 148
'First Draft of a Report on the EDVAC' (John von Neumann) 38
First World War 22
Fischer, Charlotte 109
Fisher, Sir Ronald 62
Fitch, J P 73
Fleming, Ambrose 48
Fock, Vladimir 25
Folkes, Robert 137
formalin 45
Forrest, Robin 72
Forster, E M 31
Fortran 70, 73, 85, 102
France 11
Fraser, Sandy 69
Free School Lane 20, 21, 105
FreeBSD 147
Fujitsu 56, 86
funding 27, 44, 66, 70
Furber, Steve 126, 127, 144
FUSE project 153

Ganesalingam, Mohan 157
Gates, Bill *55*, 137, 138
Gates, Melinda 137
Gates scholarships 137
General Board: approval 160; computing service review 91; differential analysers 26; Mathematical Laboratory 39, 81–2; reports 22, 27, 28, 80, 94; Science Research Council pressures 81
genetics 62
Geodesy and Geophysics, Department of 81
Gerhard, Mark 131
Gibbens, Richard 143
Gill, Stanley 62, 63, 71, 96
Girton College 90
Globespan 113

Gödels Theorem 33
Gold, Tommy 46, 56
Goldstine, Herman 53
Google: Capsicum 147; Chrome 147; Gmail 134, 136; licensing software for 130; MapReduce 143; search engine 76
Gordon, Mike 105, *147*, 148
Göttingen, University of 22
Gower, Andrew 131
Gower, Paul 131
Granta Backbone Network 85, **90**, 91, 92, 93
Grants Committee 66, 105
Graphics and Interaction Group 149–50, 159
Grayer, Alan 72, 124
Greaves, David 144
Green, James 132, *132*
Green Custard 132
Greenfield, Daniel 144
Griffin, Tim 143, 147
Guy, Mike 69

Hadley, Chris *59*, *157*, 176
Hadley, Ivo *133*
Hall of Fame companies *123*
Halliday, Michael 116
Hand, Steven 143, 145, 147
Harle, Robert *139*, 148, 149, *149*
Harter, Andy *129*
Hartley, David **85**; computer languages 73, 84; contribution of 7; first director 82; IBM computer *87*; national role 86; Titan 69; videotaped lectures 102
Hartree, Professor Douglas **25, 42**; advanced lectures 94; Babbage 19; Charlotte Fischer 109; differential analysers *29*; EDSAC 56, 57; EDVAC report *43*; important role 21; Lennard-Jones 25, 26; Lyons corner houses 53; Maurice Wilkes 35, 45; moves from Manchester 39; Peter Wegner 97
Hartree-Fock equations 25
Harvard University 145
Hauser, Hermann 111, 125, 126, *126*
He, Jiang *155*, *157*
HELIX 145

Henry VI, King 30
Herbert, Andrew: appointments 82, 138; CAP computers *75*, 77; photo *137*; UNIVERSE 106
Hermes 92, 143
Hewett, Paul *158*
Higgs boson 76
High-Speed Automatic Calculating Machines 52, 94
Hill, Rosemary 84
Hillmore, Jeff 62
Hitachi SR2201 parallel processing machine 107
Hodge, Professor 43
Holden, Sean *152*, 153
Hopper, Professor Andy **120–1**; Acorn Computers 125; Cambridge Rings 78, 79, 106, 136; CAP 75; chip design 127; commercial exploitation of research 112; Digital Technology Group *149*; Head of Department 121, 155, *158*; lecturing appointment 82, 105; maintaining projects 149; Maurice Wilkes 65; Olivetti Research Laboratory 111, 113, 124; research student *75*, 76
Hoyle, Professor Fred 53, 60
Hruska, Jan 130, *130*
Humber Bridge 149
Hunter, Don 48

IBM: compatibility issues 80–1, 86; computer purchased 82; Deep Blue 152; early days 84; equipment issues 89; high cost of 66; learns from Maurice Wilkes 62; mainframes 86, 87, 89, 90–1; preferred choice 74; research facilities 81; Stanley Bootle 98
ICL (International Computers Ltd) 56, 82, 86
ICT (International Computers and Tabulators) 66–9
ILexIR 154
Illinois, University of 54, 114
In the Beginning-Recollections of Software Pioneers (Robert L Glass) 45
India 152
Industry Legend Prizes 131
Information Flow Control 110
Information Retrieval (IR) 117, 118

171

Inglis, Sir Charles 21
Intel 78, 127, 130, **138**, 145
Internet: beginnings 9; Domain Name System 80; government censorship 145; Marconi 138; mobile phones and 129; Network Address Translation 79; Suranga Chandratillake 131; video content 132; vital protocol 106–7
Inverse Document Frequency (IDF) 117
iPads 127
iPhones 127
Iran 145
Irwin, Conrad 134, *135*
Isabelle 107, 148
IXI 129

J J Thomson Avenue *19*, 155
J Lyons 53, 55–6, 124
Jagex Ltd 122, **131**
Jamnik, Mateja 109, *110*, 152, *152*
JANET network 85, 92
Japan 104, 107, 117, 127, 129
Java 131
JCL interfaces 87
JNT PAD 91
John Humphrey Chair of Theoretical Chemistry 21
Jones, Alan 112
Jones, Brian *157*
Jones, Karen Spärck: **115–18**; AltaVista 107; British Academy 142; promotion 110; wedding *108*
Jones, Timothy 145

Kalumpit *112*
Kasparov, Gary 152
Kearsey, Steve *91*
Keele University 23
Kelvin, Lord 24
Kemp, Mike 127–8, *128*
Kendrew, Sir John 63
Keynes, John Maynard 31, 33
Kilburn, Tom 95
Kindersley, David *114*, 115
King, Frank 82, *102*

King, William Earl of Lovelace 14
King's College *30*, 31, 32, 33, *33*
Klepmann, Martin 134, *135*
Korhonen, Anna 153, *154*
Kuhn, Markus 145, *146*

Laboratory of Molecular Biology 86
Lammer, Peter 130
Lanaerts, Ernest 55
Landy, Barry 69, *87*
Lang, Charles: CAD *74*, 114, 122; Maurice Wilkes 70, 72, 125; Shape Data Ltd 122, 124, *124*
Lang, Jack 133, 139, *139*
LANs (Local Area Networks) 77, 105, 106
Lapwing 93
Large Hadron Collider 92
Large-Scale Programming Research Department 76
Larmouth, John *88*
Laser-Scan Ltd 72
Leech, Jennifer 64
Leeds University Laboratory 95
Leibniz, Gottfried 97
Lennard, Kathleen 22
Lennard-Jones, Professor Sir John Edward **22–3, 28**; appointment 27; background 84; Brunsviga machines *24*; Douglas Hartree 25, 42; foresight of 6, 42; importance of 43; Maurice Wilkes 34, 35; Metropolitan Vickers machine 26, 29; Ministry of Supply lease 29, 34; proposal approved 160; research projects 21; silver salver *23*; Vannevar Bush 25
Lennard-Jones Centre for Computational Materials Science 23
LEO (Lyons Electronic Office) computers *53*, 55–6, 124
Leslie, Professor Ian **119**; bridge design 78; energy information systems 143; graduate association 136; head of department 138; Project Unison 107; Systems Group *142*; UNIVERSE 106
letter spacing *114*
Levitt, Margaret *154*

Lewis, Ian 86, *92*
Liberal Democrats 145
Lincoln Labs 70
Linkedin 135, 136
Lió, Pietro *152*, 153
'Local Area Computer Communication Networks' (Andy Hopper) 121
Logica 79, 105, 106
London Underground 149
Loughborough University 105, 106
Lovelace, Countess *see* Byron, Augusta Ada
Lovelace medals *117*, 118
LSI 4 machines 79
Lucas, Gary 128
Luff, Meredydd *100*
Lyons Corner Houses 53

Macintosh 91, 93
Madhavapeddy, Anil *142*, 143
Madison, James 33
magnetic core memories 59
mainframe computers 6, 80, 104 *see also* IBM
Mallabone, Lee 134, *135*
Mallock, RRM **24**
Mallock machine **24**, 27, 37, 39, 56
Managed Cluster Services (MCSs) 91–2
Manchester University: Alan Turing 32, 33; ATLAS computers 66; Autocode 73, 84; development centre 42, 45; differential analyser *29*; Douglas Hartree 25; Lennard-Jones 22; progress being made 8
MapReduce 143
Marconi 138
Marrs, Margaret *51*
Mars Rovers 76
Kay, Martin *116*
Martin, Ursula 109
Mascolo, Cecilia *110*, *142*, 143
Masterman, Margaret 108, 115, 116
Mathematical Tables & Other Aids to Computation conference *94*
Mathematical Tripos 30–1, *31*, 94
Mathematics Faculty: laboratory operational 39; Lennard-Jones approaches 21–2; Mallock

machine 24; modern computation 27; postgraduate needs 96; resources required 43; Wilkes interviewed 34
Matlab 102
Mauchly, John 38, 41
McAuley, Derek 138
Meccano: differential analyser *29*, 37, 39, *43*; importance in computer development 26; location *22*; use of parts 25–6, *26*
Media Dynamics Ltd 122
Medical Research Council (MRC) 86
Menabrea, Luigi 14
MEng degrees 100
Mercury Delay Line memory **46–7**, *48*; 49, 57, 59
MetiTarski 148
Metropolitan Vickers 26, 29, *29*, 37, 39, *43*
Micromuse 136
microprogramming 19, 33, **59–60**, 62
Microsoft 77, 105, 127, 129, **137–8**, 160
Microsoft Research Cambridge 137–8
middleware 110, 143
Millington Road 115, *116*
Millionaire Machine *26*
Milner, Robin **118**; ACM Turing Prize 142; EDSAC 50th anniversary 65; Head of Department 113 *119*; resignation 138; successor 119; William Gates Building opens *119*
Ministry of Defence 49
Ministry of Supply 23, 29, 34, 35
Mirage 143
MIT (Massachusetts Institute of Technology): capability work 75; Eric Mutch 71; magnificent facilities 81; Martin Richards 73; time sharing work 68, 97; Vannevar Bush 25
mobile phones 129, 146
Molecular Biology Laboratory 86
Monroe, Elizabeth 29
Monroe machines 23, *36*
Moody, Ken 107, 110
Moore, Andrew *101*, 143, *144*, 145, 147
Moore, Gordon 78
Moore, Simon *99*, 144, *144*, 145, 147, *147*
Moore School of Engineering, Pennsylvania 38, 41, 42, 44, *44*

Motorola 80
Mullard Ltd 59
Mullins, Robert 133, *139*, 144, *144*
Multiple Virtual Tasks (MVTs) 87
Murdoch, Steven 145, 146
Mutch, Eric (E N) **71**; appointed 56; EDSAC film direction 52; EDSAC 2 84; group photo *52, 61, 65*; key person 55; multiple access system users 70; Priorities Committee 63; successor to 88
Mutch, Margaret *59*
Mycroft, Alan 133, 144, 147
Myhrvold, Nathan 137

NASA 76
NASDAQ 127, 136
National machines 23, 27
National Physical Laboratory (NPL) 32, 42, 45, 96, 97, 98
National Research and Development Corporation (NRDC) 73
Natural Language and Information Processing Group (NLIP) 117, 118, 153, 157
Naur, Peter 62
Nautical Almanac Office, Greenwich 36
NC Graphics 125
Needham, Professor Roger **104–8**, *108*; appointments, various 105; Bjarne Stroustrup 76; CAP 74; criticises bureaucracy 70; death 138; gifted student 55; Head of Department 86, 104, 118, *119*; Maurice Wilkes 74, 82–3; meets wife 115; Microsoft 137–8, 160; Neil Wiseman 115; nonces 107; ORL 113, *113*, 160; paid consultancies 124; programming language adopted 75; relaxing *107*; responsibilities 67; scrambling passwords 69–70; team leader 69; thesaurus construction 116; UNISON and other projects 106; United States 105; UNIVERSE 105, 106; William Gates Foundation 7; Xerox PARC 80
Needham-Schroeder authentication protocol 106
NetFPGA 143
Network Address Translation 79
Network Time Service 80

New Museums Site 20, *22*, 105, 137, 160
New Zealand 26, 36
Newman, Max 33
Newman, William 70
Newton, Isaac 12, 33
Nobel Prizes: Cavendish Laboratory 48; computing equivalent 33; differential analyser 35; J Pople *22*; Sir George Thomson 23; Sir Martin Ryle 49, 63; two physicists 21
Noble, Ben *52*; 56
nonces 107
Norris, Herbert 47
'Note on the Application of Machinery to the Computation of Astronomical and Mathematical Tables' (Charles Babbage) 13
Nuffield Foundation 57, 62
'Numerical Analysis' (Douglas Hartree) 94
Numerical Analysis and Automatic Computing 96, 108
NURBS 151

Oatley, Professor Sir Charles 49
Ocaml 143
Olivetti 79, 111, 113, 127
Olivetti Research Laboratory (ORL) **111–15**, *112, 113*; Andy Hopper 121, 124; collaborative project 79; Maurice Wilkes 35; Roger Needham 160; spin offs 132
Olivetti Research Ltd 122
'On Computable Numbers with an application to the Entscheidungsproblem' (Alan Turing) 31
On the Economy of Machinery and Manufactures (Charles Babbage) 12
Open Days *103*
OpenFlow controllers 143
Opera Research Group 110
opthalmoscopes 12
Orbis 125
Orbital Test Satellite 106
Orford Ness 22
Output Tanks *86*
outreach activities 156
Oxford University 23, 73, 130

173

Packet Assembler/Dissemblers (PADs) 90
parsing 154
Paulson, Larry 99, 107, 148
PCBs 78
Peierls, Rudolf 97
Pennsylvania, University of 41 see also Moore School of Engineering
Personal Workstation Facilities (PWFs) 91
Peterhouse College 13
Phoenix 88, 89, 90, 91–2
Physics Department 34
Pilkington Teaching Prizes 98
Pinkerton, John 55
Pitts, Andrew 148
placets 27, 28
Plessey 77
Plummer Chair of Theoretical Physics 39, 42, 53
Pople, J 22
Portugal 128
PPDP awards 148
Pratt, Ian 133, *133*, 134
Preparation of Programs for an Electronic Digital Computer, The (Wilkes, Wheeler and Gill) 63
Princeton University 31, 33, 38, 53
Priorities Committee 63, 71
Programmic, Logic and Semantics Group 159
provenance chains 149
Psymetrics Ltd 137

quantum mechanics 21, 22, 23
Queen, The *81*
Queen's Awards 113, 121, 130, 131

Radford, Peter 69
radio waves 35
Rainbow projects 79, 114, 115, 159
Rapportive 134–6
Rashid, Rick 137
RASP 154
Raspberry Pi **132–3**, 160
RealVNC 129–30
Redmond, California 137
Regent House 27
Remote Procedure Calls (RPCs) 143

Renwick, Bill: appointment 53, 56; course run with Wilkes 94; designing commences 58; EDSAC pictures *56, 57, 160*; group photos *52, 61*; key person 50
Research Assessment Exercises 121
Rice, Andrew 148, *149*
Richards, Martin 73, 82
Richardson, Owen 48
Richens, Richard (Dick) 116
Ring, The 136
RISC computers 127
Robert Sansom Chair of Computer Science 119
Robertson, Stephen 117
Robinson, Clifford *96*
Robinson, Peter 96, *99*, 105, 109, 150, *150*
Role-Based Access Control 110
Romulus 125
Royal Academy of Engineering 121, 142
Royal Astronomical Society 12, 13
Royal Greenwich Observatory 36
Royal Society: Alan Turing 32; Andy Hopper 121; Charles Babbage 12, 13, 15, 18; David Wheeler 55; Lennard-Jones 23; Maurice Wilkes 64; Roger Needham 107; sharing views 160; various Fellowships 142, 160
RSA encryption 130
Runescape 131
Runge-Kutta-Gill method 62, 97
Running the Gauntlet 132
Rutherford, Lord 21, 27, 48
Ryle, Professor Sir Martin 49, 54, 63

Sabin, Malcolm 151
Samols, Jan *136*
Saxby, Sir Robin 126, 127
Sayers, Mike 86, *92*
School of Physical Sciences 20, 21–2, 24, 27, 82, 160
Schroeder, Michael 106, *107*
Science Museum 12, 18, 19
Science Research Council 70, 81, 105, 124
Scientific Computing Services Ltd 35, 36
Second World War: Alan Turing 31, 33; Cavendish Laboratory 48; Charles Babbage 10, 15; computer circuits 48; computers, meaning of the word 20; Differential Analyser 26; Douglas Hartree 25; EDSAC 84; Maurice Wilkes 35; Scientific Computing Services Ltd 36; state of computing 23
Secretary-General of the Faculties 34
security 145–6, *147*
'Semantic Analysis of Normalisation by Evaluation for Typed Lambda Calculus' (Marcelo Fiore) 148
Sen, Amartya 97
Senate House 27, 43, 93
sensor networks 143
Sewell, Peter 147
Shape Data Ltd 122, **124–5**
'shares' 89
Sheppard, John 31
Silicon Valley 80
SIM cards 146
Simple Proven Approaches to Text Retrieval (Karen Spärck Jones and Stephen Robertson) 117
Sintefex 127–8
Sketchpad 70
Skinner, Professor Quentin *117*
Skorobogatov, Sergei 145–6, *146*
Smith's Prize 31
social networks 143, 146
Sohan, Ripduman 149
Sophos plc 130
Space War 70
Spaceward 128
Spärck Jones, Karen see Jones, Karen Spärck
St John's College *40*, 83
Stajano, Frank 146, *146*, 149
Stanford University 81, 117, 143
start-ups 122
Staton, Sam 147
Steiger, Otto 26
Stevens G S 56, *57*, *61*
Stibbs, Richard 89
Stokes, Sam 134, *135*
Stone, Professor Sir Richard 63
Strachey, Christopher 73
Stratford, Roger *91*

Streaming Media Service 92
Stroustrup, Bjarne 55, *75*, **76**, 77
Studio Audio and Video Ltd 128
summer schools 95
Sunday Times Rich List 131
Support Staff *155*
Sutherland, Ivan 70
Swade, Doron 18, 19
Swinnerton-Dyer, Sir Peter 55, 69, *69*, 81, 91
'Synonymy and Semantic Classification' (Karen Spärck Jones) 116
Systems Research Groups 79, 105, 107, **142**, 155
tables of numbers 11–13, *11*
Tait, John 118
Tennenhouse, David 138
Teufel, Simone 153
Texas A&M University 76
Theory and Semantics Group 147
'Theory and Techniques for the Design of Electronic Digital Computers' (course of lectures) 41
Thomson, Sir George 23
Thomson J J 48
Thomson, James 24
Time Sharing Option (TSO) 87
Tiny Encryption Algorithm (TEA) 54
Titan **66–70, 84–5**; airlifted 71; compatibility 87; computer language 73; David Wheeler 54; Neil Wiseman 114; reminiscences 57; Roger Needham 108; Titan Room *83*; unsuitability 80–1; user numbers 89; writing the software 72
Titmus, Graham *157*
Tor 145
Torch Computers 129
torque amplifiers 25
Training Booking System 93
Turing, Alan **30–3**; blue plaque *33*; most famous computer scientist 6; returns to Cambridge 95; statue *32*; Turing Machine 31

UIDAI 152
undergraduate teaching 7
UNISON **106**, 107

United Kingdom Education and Research Networking Association (UKERNA) 85
United States 8, 41, 51, 52, 105
UNIVERSE 105–6, *106*
University Demonstrators 28
University Library 92
Unix 91, 92, 129
Upton, Eben 133

van Rijsbergen, Keith 71
VAX 80
Veenman, Peter 124
Vigilante 143
VIPER chips 107
Virata 113, 132
Virtual Network Computers 129
VNC 113
Vohra, Rahul 134, *135*
Voice over Internet Protocol (VoIP) 93, 132
von Neumann, John 32, 36, **38**, 41, 45

Waldram, Elizabeth 63
Walkmans 114
Wass syndicate 105
Wassell, Ian *149*
Watson, Robert 145, 147, *147*
Watts, Richard 109
Webber, Valerie 84
WebCams 109, *109*
Wegner, Peter **97**, *97*, 98
Westwood, Brian *93*
Wheeler, David **54–5**; Andy Hopper 121; Bill Gates *55*; Bjarne Stroustrup 76; Cambridge Digital Ring 77–9; CAP 77; EDSAC 2 60, 61, 62; first book on computer science 96; group photos *52*, *61*, *65*; joins project 56; microprogramming 59; Mike Burrows 107; ORL 111; responsibilities 58; table of square numbers 50; Titan 67; wedding *54*
Wheeler, Joyce (neé Blackler) *54*, 60, 63, 109
Widdowson, Simon 128
Wilks, Yorick 116
Wilkes, Professor Sir Maurice **34–43, 44–65, 66–83**; ACM Turing Prize 142; Acting Director 34, 42; Alan Turing 31, 32, 33; analogue drawbacks perceived 39; anniversaries 6, 7, 64; ATLAS 66; Barry Landy *87*; biography **35**; Cambridge Digital Ring 77; CAP 77; Charles Babbage studied 16, 19; Charles Lang 70, 72, 125; death 65, 83; differential analyser 28, *29*, 35, 37; Douglas Hartree 42; EDSAC 19, 41, 42, **44–65**, 84, 94, 109, 160; Eric Mutch 71, 84; far reaching proposals 81–2; first book on computer science 96; full time work 37; group photos *52, 57, 61, 65*; Head of Department 53; High Speed Automatics conference 94; knighthood *81*; Lennard-Jones 34, 35; mainframes 104; Mallock machine 24; name changes 28; recruiting girl 'computers' 20; research funding 70; research philosophy 82–3; retirement 83, *83*, 86; Roger Needham 104; summary of the person 82–3; terms of employment 39; Titan 66–70, 80–1; William Gates Building *119*, 161
William Gates Building: annual fair *101*; Cambridge Enterprise 138; cost of 138; Hall of Fame 123; Margaret Levitt *154*; Maurice Wilkes *119*, *161*; opens 119, *119*, 155; Robin Milner 118; WebCam 109
William Gates Foundation 7, 55, 160
William Proctor Prize 76
Williams, F C (Freddie) 51, 95
Willis, Donald (D W) 56, 61, *61*
Wilson, Sophie 125, 126, 127
Windows 8 127
Winskel, Glynn 148
Wireless Sensor Networks 149
Wiseman, Neil **114–15**; appointed 82; designs data link 70; Mike Kemp 128; ORL 111;
project title 67;
women students 20, 109
women@CL 109, 111
Worsley, Beatrice Helen *61*, 109
Wynn-Williams, C E 48, *48*

XenSource 133–4
Xerox PARC 79, 80, 105, 106, 124, 150

Yoneki, Eiko 143

175

Acknowledgements and Picture Credits

Acknowledgements

It is a pleasure to acknowledge the help I have received from a number of individuals. Andy Hopper is thanked for his encouragement and support throughout the course of this project. The efficient and cheerful support of Caroline Matthews on all administrative matters is also gratefully acknowledged.

Margaret Levitt provided me with much valuable information from the Department records. Chris Hadley introduced me to the relics held in the Computer Laboratory. George Coulouris read the whole of the manuscript and helped me to avoid mistakes in technical matters. Jan Samols helped me to write about the 'Ring' and the entrepreneurs who have links with the Computer Laboratory. Bjarne Stroustrup, David Hartley, Rob Harle, Robert Watson, Andrew Herbert, Joyce Wheeler, Margaret Marrs, David Greaves, Charles Lang, Jack Lang, Ayesha Ahmed, Rehana Ahmed, Simon Moore, Doron Swade and Benedikt Leowe read parts of the work and made valuable suggestions and I am grateful for their support.

I benefited from conversations with a number of individuals and I would like to thank Andy Hopper, Peter Swinnerton-Dyer, Joyce Wheeler, Ken Moody, Keith Van Rijsbergen, David Hartley, Margaret Marrs, Andrew Herbert, Bjarne Stroustrup, Ian Leslie, Don Hunter, Elizabeth Waldram, William Newman and Martin Richards for the information they provided in the course of the discussions.

The imaginative and high-quality photography by Alan Davidson of Stills Photography is a feature of this book and his contribution is acknowledged. My editors, Susan Millership, Neil Burkey and Matthew Wilson of Third Millennium Information Ltd are thanked for helping me to improve the manuscript.

Margaret Smart, Lida Kindersley, Charles Lang, Joyce Wheeler, John Lennard-Jones, Margaret Marrs and Simon Moore are thanked for letting me use pictures from their private collections.

Picture Credits

The majority of images found within the book are from the Cambridge Computer Laboratory Archives. The Laboratory would also like to thank Alan Davidson of Stills Photography for taking photographs specifically for this publication, as well as the individuals and organisations below for granting permission to publish material on the following pages:

©Science Museum/Science & Society Picture Library – all rights reserved: 10, 11, 14, 16, 17, 18, 42; From the collection of Mr T Midwinter (www.swindon.gov.uk/swindoncollection): 20; The Walsh Memorial Library, Museum of Transport and Technology, Auckland, New Zealand: 26; By permission of the Master and Fellows of St John's College, Cambridge: 35, 81; ©Royal Astronomical Society/Science Photo Library: 36 (left); Alan Richards photographer, from the Shelby White and Leon Levy Archives Center, Institute for Advanced Study, Princeton, NJ, USA: 38; ©Bettmann/CORBIS: 41; Courtesy MIT Museum: 43; LEO Computers Society (www.leo-computers.org.uk): 53; ©University of Pennsylvania: 44; Richard Stibbs: 89; By permission of the Master and Fellows of Churchill College, Cambridge: 107; Arthur Chang (artchang.com): 134.